T0314271

RESEARCH IN MARITIME HISTORY
NO. 33

MARITIME TRANSPORT AND MIGRATION: THE CONNECTIONS BETWEEN MARITIME AND MIGRATION NETWORKS

Edited by
Torsten Feys, Lewis R. Fischer, Stéphane Hoste and Stephan Vanfraechem

International Maritime Economic History Association

St. John's, Newfoundland
2007

ISSN 1188-3928
ISBN 978-0-9738934-3-4

Research in Maritime History is available free of charge to members of the International Maritime Economic History Association. The price to others is US$25 per copy, plus US$5 postage and handling.

Back issues of *Research in Maritime History* are available:

No. 1 (1991)   David M. Williams and Andrew P. White (comps.), *A Select Bibliography of British and Irish University Theses about Maritime History, 1792-1990*

No. 2 (1992)   Lewis R. Fischer (ed.), *From Wheel House to Counting House: Essays in Maritime Business History in Honour of Professor Peter Neville Davies*

No. 3 (1992)   Lewis R. Fischer and Walter Minchinton (eds.), *People of the Northern Seas*

No. 4 (1993)   Simon Ville (ed.), *Shipbuilding in the United Kingdom in the Nineteenth Century: A Regional Approach*

No. 5 (1993)   Peter N. Davies (ed.), *The Diary of John Holt*

No. 6 (1994)   Simon P. Ville and David M. Williams (eds.), *Management, Finance and Industrial Relations in Maritime Industries: Essays in International Maritime and Business History*

No. 7 (1994)   Lewis R. Fischer (ed.), *The Market for Seamen in the Age of Sail*

No. 8 (1995)   Gordon Read and Michael Stammers (comps.), *Guide to the Records of Merseyside Maritime Museum, Volume 1*

No. 9 (1995)   Frank Broeze (ed.), *Maritime History at the Crossroads: A Critical Review of Recent Historiography*

No. 10 (1996)   Nancy Redmayne Ross (ed.), *The Diary of a Maritimer, 1816-1901: The Life and Times of Joseph Salter*

No. 11 (1997)   Faye Margaret Kert, *Prize and Prejudice: Privateering and Naval Prize in Atlantic Canada in the War of 1812*

No. 12 (1997)   Malcolm Tull, *A Community Enterprise: The History of the Port of Fremantle, 1897 to 1997*

No. 13 (1997)   Paul C. van Royen, Jaap R. Bruijn and Jan Lucassen, *"Those Emblems of Hell"? European Sailors and the Maritime Labour Market, 1570-1870*

No. 14 (1998)   David J. Starkey and Gelina Harlaftis (eds.), *Global Markets: The Internationalization of The Sea Transport Industries Since 1850*

No. 15 (1998)   Olaf Uwe Janzen (ed.), *Merchant Organization and Maritime Trade in the North Atlantic, 1660-1815*

No. 16 (1999)   Lewis R. Fischer and Adrian Jarvis (eds.), *Harbours and Havens: Essays in Port History in Honour of Gordon Jackson*

No. 17 (1999)   Dawn Littler, *Guide to the Records of Merseyside Maritime Museum, Volume 2*

No. 18 (2000)   Lars U. Scholl (comp.), *Merchants and Mariners: Selected Maritime Writings of David M. Williams*

No. 19 (2000)   Peter N. Davies, *The Trade Makers: Elder Dempster in West Africa, 1852-1972, 1973-1989*

No. 20 (2001)   Anthony B. Dickinson and Chesley W. Sanger, *Norwegian Whaling in Newfoundland: The Aquaforte Station and the Ellefsen Family, 1902-1908*

No. 21 (2001)   Poul Holm, Tim D. Smith and David J. Starkey (eds.), *The Exploited Seas: New Directions for Marine Environmental History*

No. 22 (2002)   Gordon Boyce and Richard Gorski (eds.), *Resources and Infrastructures in the Maritime Economy, 1500-2000*

No. 23 (2002)   Frank Broeze, *The Globalisation of the Oceans: Containerisation from the 1950s to the Present*

No. 24 (2003)   Robin Craig, *British Tramp Shipping, 1750-1914*

No. 25 (2003)   James Reveley, *Registering Interest: Waterfront Labour Relations in New Zealand, 1953 to 2000*

No. 26 (2003)   Adrian Jarvis, *In Troubled Times: The Port of Liverpool, 1905-1938*

No. 27 (2004)   Lars U. Scholl and Merja-Liisa Hinkkanen (comps.), *Sail and Steam: Selected Maritime Writings of Yrjö Kaukiainen*

No. 28 (2004)   Gelina Harlaftis and Carmel Vassallo (eds.), *New Directions in Mediterranean Maritime History*

No. 29 (2005)   Gordon Jackson, *The British Whaling Trade*

No. 30 (2005)   Lewis Johnman and Hugh Murphy, *Scott Lithgow: Déjà vu All Over Again! The Rise and Fall of a Shipbuilding Company*

No. 31 (2006)   David Gleicher, *The Rescue of the Third Class on the Titanic: A Revisionist History*

No. 32 (2006)   Stig Tenold, *Tankers in Trouble: Norwegian Shipping and the Crisis of the 1970s and 1980s*

Research in Maritime History would like to thank Memorial University of Newfoundland for its generous financial assistance in support of this volume.

Education and Culture DG

Lifelong Learning Programme

European University Institute

This book has been published with financial subsidy from the European University Institute.

Table of Contents

Contributors' Notes / iii

Contributions

Stéphane Hoste and Lewis R. Fischer, "Migration and Maritime Networks in the Atlantic Economy: An Introduction" / 1

Jelle van Lottum, "The First Waves of Internationalization: A Comparison of Early Modern North Sea and Nineteenth-Century Transatlantic Labour Migrations" / 9

Torsten Feys, "The Battle for the Migrants: The Evolution from Port to Company Competition, 1840-1914" / 27

Nicholas J. Evans, "The Role of Foreign-born Agents in the Development of Mass Migrant Travel through Britain, 1851-1924" / 49

Nicolas Manitakis, "Transatlantic Emigration and Maritime Transport from Greece to the US, 1890-1912: A Major Area of European Steamship Company Competition for Migrant Traffic" / 63

Annemarie Steidl, "The 'Relatives and Friends Effect:' Migration Networks of Transatlantic Migrants from the Late Habsburg Monarchy" / 75

G. Balachandran, "Crossing the Last Frontier: Transatlantic Movements of Asian Maritime Workers, c. 1900-1945" / 97

Drew Keeling, "Costs, Risks and Migration Networks between Europe and the United States, 1900-1914" / 113

Michael B. Miller, "Conclusion" / 175

i

ABOUT THE EDITORS

TORSTEN FEYS < Torsten.Feys@EUI.eu > is currently working on a PhD thesis at the European University Institute in Florence entitled "The Battle for the Migrants: The Competition between Various Emigration Ports for the Migrant Trade from the European Mainland to New York, 1840-1914." He is a specialist in nineteenth- and early twentieth-century migration from Europe to North America.

LEWIS R. FISCHER < lfischer@mun.ca > is Professor of History and Graduate Coordinator of History at Memorial University of Newfoundland, where he serves as Editor-in-Chief of the *International Journal of Maritime History* and Series Editor of *Research in Maritime History*. He specializes in the international economic and social aspects of maritime history.

STÉPHANE HOSTE < Stephane.Hoste@UGent.be > is a doctoral student at the University of Ghent, where he is writing a PhD thesis on "The European 'Bunge Group:' Aspects on the Primacy of Port-related Entrepreneurship, 1870-1970." His research has focused on comparative handling costs in the ports of Antwerp and Rotterdam, and he has contributed two articles (with Reginald Loyen and Hugo van Driel) to Ferry de Goey (ed.) *Comparative Port History of Rotterdam and Antwerp (1880-2000). Competition, Cargo and Costs* (Amsterdam, 2004). Other recent publications include a chapter on the history of the Dutch Shipping Inspectorate ("De Nederlandse scheepvaartinspectie (1906-2001)," in *150 jaar toezicht Verkeer en Waterstaat. Rampen, wetten en inspectiediensten* (Den Haag, 2004), 117-179); and *Bunge in the Low Countries. Two Centuries of Maritime Trade from Amsterdam, Antwerp and Rotterdam* (Tielt, forthcoming).

STEPHAN VANFRAECHEM < Stephan.vanfraechem@alfaportantwerpen. be > is a policy advisor for Alfaport Antwerp, the federation of port companies and logistic service providers in the port of Antwerp. A specialist on labour relations in the port of Antwerp, 1880-1972, he is currently working on the impact of labour conditions and wages on the inter-port competition in the Hamburg-LeHavre range.

CONTRIBUTORS

G. BALACHANDRAN <bala@hei.unige.ch> is Professor of International History and Politics at the Graduate Institute of International Studies in Geneva. He has published widely on financial and imperial history, and is currently completing a monograph on Indian seafarers in international merchant shipping in the nineteenth and twentieth centuries. His maritime publications include "Conflicts in the International Maritime Labour Market: British and Indian Seamen, Employers, and the State, 1890-1939," *Indian Economic And Social History Review*, XXXIX, No. 1 (2002), 71-100; and "Recruitment and Control of Indian Seamen: Calcutta, 1880-1935," *International Journal of Maritime History*, IX, No. 1 (1997), 1-18.

NICHOLAS J. EVANS <n.evans@abdn.ac.uk> is Lecturer in History at the University of Hull, from where he received his PhD in 2006 for a thesis entitled "Aliens *en route*: European Transmigration via the UK, 1836-1914." His recent publications include "The Emigration of Skilled Male Workers from Clydeside during the Interwar Period," *International Journal of Maritime History*, XVIII, No. 1 (2006); "Socio-economic Dislocation and Inter-war Emigration to Canada and the United States: A Scottish Snapshot," *Journal of Imperial and Commonwealth History*, XXXIV, No. 4 (2006), 529-552 (with Marjory Harper); and *Jewish Migration to South Africa: The Records of the Poor Jews' Temporary Shelter, 1885-1914* (Cape Town, 2006, with Aubrey Newman, Saul Issroff and Graham Smith).

DREW KEELING <drewkeeling@yahoo.com> is a repeat transatlantic migrant, currently teaching part time in the History Department of the University of Zurich. He first moved to Europe to work there in banking and finance before returning to the United States to pursue a doctorate in History at the University of California, Berkeley. His PhD thesis, "The Business of Transatlantic Migration between Europe and the USA, 1900-1914," won the 2005 Alexander Gerschenkron Prize of the Economic History Association, and he is working now to revise the dissertation for publication.

NICOLAS MANITAKIS <nicolas.manitakis@wanadoo.fr> has studied in Greece, Spain and France, and currently teaches European and Greek history at the University of Cyprus. His research interests include the history of student migration and labour migration, as well as the history of tourism.

MICHAEL MILLER <mbmiller@mail.as.miami.edu> is Professor of History at the University of Miami. He is the author of several books and articles and has held a number of major fellowships, including Guggenheim, NEH, ACLS and German Marshall grants. He is currently writing the final chapters for a book on Europe and the maritime world in the twentieth century. His most recent publication is "Pilgrims' Progress: The Business of the Hajj," *Past and Present*, No. 191 (2006), 189-228.

ANNEMARIE STEIDL <annemarie.steidl@univie.ac.at> is a research assistant in the Department of Economic and Social History at the University of Vienna, where she is currently working on transnational migration in Central Europe, 1860-1914. Her research interests include European migration history from the eighteenth to the twentieth centuries, gender history and the history of artisans. She has published several articles on regional mobility of artisans and on aspects of European transatlantic migration, including "Young, Unwed, Mobile, and Female: Women on their Way from the Habsburg Monarchy to the United States of America," *Przegląd Polonijny*, IV (2005), 55-76; "Relations among Internal, Continental, and Transatlantic Migration in Late Imperial Austria," *Social Science History*, XXXI, No. 1 (2007, with Engelbert Stockhammer and Hermann Zeitlhofer); and *Auf nach Wien! Die Mobilität des mitteleuropäischen Handwerks im 18. und 19. Jahrhundert am Beispiel der Haupt- und Residenzstadt* (Vienna, 2003).

JELLE VAN LOTTUM <jellevanlottum@hetnet.nl> is currently writing a PhD thesis at the International Institute for Social History in Amsterdam on labour migration in the North Sea region as part of a project on "Close Encounters with the Dutch. The North Sea as a Near-core Region in a Nascent Modern World (1550-1750)." He has published on migration and labour markets in the early modern period and the nineteenth century.

Migration and Maritime Networks in the Atlantic Economy: An Introduction[1]

Stéphane Hoste and Lewis R. Fischer

European migration rose from an average of just over 110,000 people per year in the period 1821-1850, to 270,000 between 1851 and 1880 and to more than 900,000 in the years 1881-1915. In total, some eleven or twelve million Europeans migrated before the 1880s compared with thirty-two million after that date. The Americas, led by the United States (sixty-two percent), Argentina (nine percent), Canada (eight percent) and Brazil (seven percent), received more than eighty-five percent of recorded immigration.[2] In the heyday of this transatlantic passenger shipping between 1900 and 1914, the four largest US ports alone welcomed eleven million European migrants. Italy, the largest exporter of labour across the Atlantic, accounted for twenty-three percent of total European migration, while Britain and Germany, the two largest transmigration countries, handled about one-fifth of the total flow. Added to the tens of thousands of migrants who departed each year from the ports of Bremen, Hamburg, Liverpool and Southampton were similar numbers who travelled to Antwerp, Genoa, Le Havre, Marseille, Naples, Rotterdam and Trieste to commence the transatlantic crossing.

The acceleration in the migration rate from the 1880s coincided with a remarkable shift in the labour outflow from northern and western Europe to southern and eastern Europe. The incidence of migration was, however, not spread evenly across countries but was higher from some than from others.

[1]Drafts of the chapters in this volume were presented during an international conference held in Florence, Italy, 18-19 November 2005, with funding from the Research Foundation Flanders (FWO), Research Group Labour, Labour Relations and Labour Markets in Western Europe, 1500-2000 (headed by Professor Hugo Soly), the European University Institute and Ghent University (Department of Modern and Contemporary History). The organizers, Professors Heinz-Gerhard Haupt and Eric Vanhaute, Dr. Stephan Vanfraechem, Torsten Feys and Stéphane Hoste would like to thank all the participants, including Dr. Adam McKeown, whose contribution is not included here. This book has been published with a financial subsidy from the Department of Modern and Contemporary History and the Faculty of Arts at the University of Ghent.

[2]A.G. Kenwood and A.L. Lougheed, *The Growth of the International Economy, 1820-2000: An Introductory Text* (London, 1971; 4th ed., London, 1999), 45-47.

For this reason, the nation-state may not be the appropriate unit of analysis, although state and nation should not be excluded from any study of the networks that facilitated transatlantic migration.[3] On the other hand, the history of the major European port cities suggests that the Atlantic labour market was segmented.[4] If the development of the Atlantic economy was a significant cause of emigration, we would expect that the earliest migrants came from areas near ports.[5] But emigration rates from the vicinity of port cities were particularly low, although some pioneers, often merchants, emigrated. First and foremost, these cities became important migration ports for people from other countries.

Migration and shipping are both as old as human history, but this has not hindered migration historians from neglecting, to a certain extent, the impact of maritime networks on migration, while it is also true that few maritime historians have considered migration patterns and their networks. What connects both disciplines, however, is the desire to formulate coherent explanations to the question why relatively few emigrants left Europe compared with the large number of people who were at the time affected by the socio-economic forces of change.[6] Nonetheless, there are numerous explanations why emigration was not greater than it was: for example, because some people knew too little about the advantages of emigration or were too poor to undertake the journey.

This volume presents a scholarly overview of the state of the art in the study of the migration and maritime networks that carried out the physical relocation of transatlantic mass-migration, particularly between Europe and the United States. In addition to the personal networks of migrants and the government regulators of migration, two other networks come into play: the transatlantic shipping companies and the agents who represented them. Migration on the one hand was the largest contributor to the earnings of passenger shipping, while on the other hand there could be no transatlantic migration without

---

[3]Dirk Hoerder, "Transcultural States, Nations and People," in Hoerder, with Christiane Harzig and Adrian Shubert (eds.), *The Historical Practice of Diversity: Transcultural Interactions from the Early Modern Mediterranean to the Postcolonial World* (New York, 2003), 13-32.

[4]Robert Lee, "Configuring the City: In-migration, Labour Supply and Port Development in Nineteenth-century Europe," *International Journal of Maritime History*, XVII, No. 1 (2005), 91-122.

[5]Dudley Baines, *Emigration from Europe 1815-1930* (Basingstoke, 1991; reprint, Cambridge, 1995), 23-24.

[6]*Ibid.*, 22.

first boarding a ship.[7] How these migration and maritime networks influenced the motives behind mass migration offers the framework for historical reflection. Transatlantic migration grew during the first quarter of the nineteenth century, and half a century later rising volumes transformed passenger transport into an important westbound trade carrying out one of the most diverse mass migrations of all time.

A first important aid to this rising migration was the maritime transition from canvas to coal, making cheaper, more accessible and integrated transport available for transatlantic migration. The shift to steam allowed shipping to develop more reliable, scheduled services and freed it from its traditional subservience to winds and tides. As steam came to dominate passenger transport, sailing ships were increasingly forced out of the migrant trade in the 1870s; this speeded up travel significantly and placed the passenger trade in the hands of steamship companies. And it was the large passenger liners of established transatlantic steamship companies such as Anchor, American Compagnie Générale Transatlantique, Cunard, Hamburg-America, Hamburg South America, Holland-America, Navigazione Gerale Italiana, Norddeutscher Lloyd, Red Star, Union Castle and White Star, that at the dawn of the twentieth century became the key players in a new shipping milieu. Thanks to the invention of more efficient turbines, these transatlantic steamships were five or six times as fast and twelve times as voluminous as their sailing predecessors. Thirty million migrants reached America on steamships compared with less than eight million by sail. On the other hand, it was especially due to competitive maritime location and infrastructure, accumulated expertise and international contacts that the major European ports dominated the migrant trade.

The price of a transatlantic ticket fell at first in large part due to the widespread adoption of steam at sea and railroads on land, although after the 1880s ticket prices hardly changed. Nonetheless, it is clear that competition between steamship companies resulted in continuous improvements in accommodations for migrants, and cut-rate fares sometimes affected the routing and timing of those whose initial decision to leave Europe had already been made. International networks were vital to the transatlantic steamship firms as they co-ordinated their core business with railroad companies and national governments. Each major shipping line was at least to some degree protected by regulatory authorities in its home port and country. The networking among transport firms and co-ordination with governments led to some very effective market cartels in the migrant trade.

A second important support to the rising flow of migration was the nodal function of agencies within the maritime networks formed by the steamship companies. Emigrant agents carried out widespread campaigns for the

---

[7]It was only in 1958 that the first commercial jet aircraft crossed the Atlantic.

steamship companies in their efforts to guarantee full passenger lists. Competing networks of these agents, based in the major European ports, spread over the continent. Besides the emigrant agents, other occupations were essential in the evolving system. For starters, there were the recruiting agents who worked for industrialists and landowners in the Americas and the trade consuls who established contacts to promote overseas commerce. A special characteristic of the former were the foreign-born agents, who in some ways were analogous to the international crews of the transatlantic shipping companies. The services offered by steamship agencies were essential to the competitive position of the different steamship companies, especially because of the importance of the foreign migrant market. Emigrants, leaving for higher wages, greater opportunities or the better availability of land, were channelled by these networks into distinct routes.

A third network that influenced the rate of migration was the set of governmental actors in Europe and the Americas. Because of the importance of America to this mass migration, the most decisive set of legislative actors were the public authorities in the US. Indeed, changes in European policy towards the unrestricted nature of transatlantic migration resulted mostly from American rules designed to regulate the flow. The slow progress in Europe of national migration laws contrasted with the more rapid development of migrant transport sea legislation after 1870, although the enforcement of more safety measures and better passenger transport accommodation for transatlantic migrants suffered from a lack of government funds, at least in some European ports. This growing government interference coincided with attempts by the various European nations to attract part of the flow to their ports, hence facilitating migrations out of other countries. Policies in the United States essentially were designed to curtail the limited risks of a growing, but still quite small, minority of unwelcome migrants from the 1890s onwards. The increase in migration led to the establishment of an informal network of foreign governments, immigration officers, port authorities, railroad executives and shipping lines, in part to reduce the risks of congestion and overcrowding.

A fourth and final migration network was characterized by the interlinkages among groups of migrants themselves.[8] Chain migration, in which pioneers were followed by families and friends as if they were links in a chain, shaped the decisions of millions of European migrants regarding how, when and where to move. These networks managed the risks and reduced the costs

---

[8]Walter D. Kamphoefner, "German Emigration Research, North, South and East: Findings, Methods and Open Questions," in Dirk Hoerder and Jörg Nagler (eds.), *People in Transit: German Migrations in Comparative Perspective* (Washington, DC, 1995), 19-33; and A. Walazak, "Labour Diasporas in Comparative Perspective: Polish and Italian Migrant Workers in the Atlantic World between the 1870s and the 1920s, in Hoerder with Harzig and Shubert (eds.), *Historical Practice of Diversity*, 152-176.

of the crossing by providing information about overseas economic conditions, and were therefore arguably the most important of the networks in motivating the decision of whether to migrate in the first place. These migrant networks can be understood as the set of interpersonal ties that connected migrants and non-migrants through ties of kinship, friendship and shared community origin. These networks lowered both the financial and psychological costs and risks associated with transatlantic migration.

The bulk of the migrants depended on their own resources or those of their families and friends to make the crossing. An important manifestation of the networks was the flow of remittances sent home by successful settlers. Indeed, after 1900 between one-quarter and half of all immigrants to the US travelled on tickets prepaid by relatives in America. In most cases these migrants joined kin, fellow workers or villagers in the US, and the evidence suggests that most migrants bound for the US had relatives or friends awaiting them. While agricultural labourers depended upon close kin during the first years after their arrival in the US, friends functioned as a more important first contact group for those bound for the cities. Transatlantic migrants during the great boom of the late nineteenth and early twentieth centuries were certainly not helpless people moving in a disorganized fashion into unknown territory.

The interaction of these migration and maritime networks is a central theme in this collection, which brings together a sample of the diverse approaches adopted by scholars interested in the topic. The variety of historical problems, questions and methodologies in migration and maritime history, however, is too broad to fit within the pages of a single volume, and the editors make no pretext of being either exhaustive or comprehensive. Nor has it been our intent to ask the contributors to construct a general synthesis. What we have tried to do is to bring together a group of scholars to suggest some lines of research, to tackle some specific empirical problems and to provide some insights into the operation of migration and maritime networks within the Atlantic economy. Throughout the book three important approaches are especially noticeable.

The first is to look at the rate of development of the continental and transatlantic transport networks that were accessible to migrants from the various European countries. A distinction can be made between the rise of an "Atlantic migrant market" through Belgian, British, Dutch, French and German ports after 1850 to handle the massive movement of people from northern and central Europe and a "Mediterranean migrant market" through Austro-Hungarian, Greek and Italian ports, especially after 1880, to handle the increasing traffic from southern Europe. The appearance of more integrated transport options for the transatlantic crossing shortened travel times and reduced the risks and costs for ever-larger parts of the European population.

A second approach is to look at how competition between shipping companies and ports influenced transatlantic migration.[9] Competition between ports within a certain spatial range suggests that lower costs removed an important barrier to mass migration. Nonetheless, it is clear that analyzing the trade in migrants in much the same way as the trade in commodities has significant limitations. First of all, the trade in emigrants required different business tactics than the trade in goods.[10] Second, the shipping companies involved in the migrant trade enjoyed a great range of benefits due to their often monopolistic relations with major European ports and, especially after 1900, from the impact of transatlantic passenger conferences. Third, the total cost of travel was for most migrants not as important as the role of networks in limiting the risks of overseas settlement, a consideration that was not as relevant to the consignors and consignees of commodities.

Finally, a third approach is to look at the integration of labour markets in Europe and those in the Americas.[11] Economies in the latter were marked by a larger supply of natural resources relative to the supply of capital and labour than in Europe. This encouraged, for example, the shipping of less expensive food and raw materials in large quantities from the Americas to Europe, particularly from the 1870s. In turn, this made some European agriculture unprofitable and, combined with the difficulties of industrial adjustment, enabled transatlantic mass migration to redistribute some of Europe's agricultural population to new primary-producing regions overseas where more per unit of labour could be produced.[12] Although cheap imports were not responsible for increasing pressure on rural communities in every European country, the most common denominator of European migrants was that most were rural workers, either peasants or artisans. As newcomers and parents, these growing numbers provided both the labour force and the expanding market in the US essential to industrialization and large-scale production. On the other hand, the loss of human capital had some less positive effects in many European countries.

---

[9]Reginald Loyen, Erik Buyst and Greta Devos (eds.), *Struggling for Leadership: Antwerp-Rotterdam Port Competition between 1870-2000* (Heidelberg, 2003); and Ferry De Goey (ed.), *Comparative Port History of Rotterdam and Antwerp (1880-2000). Competition, Cargo and Costs* (Amsterdam, 2004).

[10]L. Dunn, "Passenger Vessels," in Robert Gardiner and Ambrose Greenway (eds.), *The Golden Age of Shipping. The Classic Merchant Ship 1900-1960* (London, 1994), 14-37.

[11]Baines, *Emigration*, 181-189.

[12]Kenwood and Lougheed, *Growth*, 48-50 and 54-56.

The essays that follow highlight these and a number of other issues. If taken together the authors raise more questions than answers, we believe this not only reflects the state of the field but also is a positive harbinger of future scholarship. It is our hope that this collection will spur a dialogue among those interested in migration and maritime history, and in the process stimulate a greater degree of interest – and even more useful studies – on this important topic.

The First Waves of Internationalization: A Comparison of Early Modern North Sea and Nineteenth-Century Transatlantic Labour Migrations[1]

Jelle van Lottum

The nineteenth century is commonly regarded as the period in which Europe experienced the first wave of globalization. Kevin O'Rourke and Jeffrey Williamson's seminal *Globalization and History* argues plausibly that between 1840 and 1914 the world underwent a radical change.[2] One of the most striking elements of what they call a "wave of globalization" was treated more thoroughly in another of Williamson's books, this time co-authored with Timothy Hatton, entitled *The Age of Mass Migration*.[3] In this latter work the authors deal with the economic causes and consequences of the mass migration from Europe when about fifty-five million Europeans relocated to the New World between 1850 and 1914.

Despite its important contribution to the historiography of migration in general and nineteenth-century migration in particular – not least because of its econometric approach – it is possible to criticize Hatton and Williamson's book for its narrow limits in time and space. Spatially, the authors' focus is almost solely on the migration of Europeans to North America, thereby neglecting the movements of people from Europe to South America, the Caribbean and Asia. It would be useful to know whether the inclusion, for instance,

[1]This research is part of the project "Close Encounters with the Dutch: The North Sea as Near-core Region for a Nascent Modern World (1550-1750)," funded by the Netherlands Organisation for Scientific Research (NWO). I want to thank Drew Keeling, Lex Heerma van Voss, Ulbe Bosma, Christiaan van Bochove and Harm Kaal for valuable comments on earlier drafts of this paper. A previous version of this essay was presented at the Social Science History Conference in Portland, Oregon, in November 2005.

[2]Kevin H. O'Rourke and Jeffrey G. Williamson, *Globalization and History: The Evolution of a Nineteenth-century Atlantic Economy* (Cambridge, MA, 1999). See also O'Rourke and Williamson, "When Did Globalization Begin?" *European Review of Economic History*, VI (2002), 23-50.

[3]Timothy J. Hatton and Jeffrey G. Williamson, *The Age of Mass Migration: Causes and Economic Impact* (New York, 1998).

of the forced deportation of Englishmen to Australia, or the emergence of new colonial regimes through the migration of civil servants from Europe to the new colonies, would fit the model that is now based solely upon the migration of free labour across the North Atlantic.[4] In this essay, however, I will deal not with the book's narrow spatial focus but rather with Hatton and Williamson's claim that the nineteenth century was unique in terms of mass migration.

In *The Age of Mass Migration* – as in much of the pre-1980 historiography on European migration – European population before the onset of the nineteenth-century transatlantic migrations is treated as fairly immobile. This may be true compared with the explosion of European emigration beginning in the mid-nineteenth century, but to analyze pre-industrial European mobility this way is wrong because not only were America and Europe less integrated in this era but pre-industrial Europe itself was far less integrated than in the second half of the nineteenth century.[5] As we will see below, in certain parts of the continent the differences in international mobility levels between the early modern period and the nineteenth century were not always as large as this general argument might suggest.

In this essay the focus will be on the North Sea region, which includes all the countries bordering that body of water.[6] I will argue that for these countries the wave of globalization in the "Age of Mass Migration" was preceded by an earlier era of large-scale, international, long-distance migration. Since the flow of people in the North Sea region between 1600 and 1800 was mainly, though not exclusively, intra-regional, we cannot refer to it as globalization. Instead, I will use the more appropriate term "internationalization wave," which can be defined as a period in which nations had increased contacts with each other. Although migration is the focus here, factor markets and cultures also became more integrated.

---

[4]For a broader spatial approach, see Adam McKeown, "Global Migration 1846-1940," *Journal of World History*, XV, No. 2 (2004), 155-189.

[5]Cf. Christiaan van Bochove, "Market Integration and the North Sea System (1600-1800)," in Hanno Brand, Poul Holm and Leos Muller (eds.), *The Dynamics of Economic Culture in the North Sea- and Baltic Region (ca. 1250-1700)* (2 vols., Hilversum, 2006, forthcoming); O'Rourke and Williamson, *Globalization and History*; and David S. Jacks, "Market Integration in the North and Baltic Seas, 1500-1800," *Journal of European Economic History*, XXXIII (2004), 285-329.

[6]The countries that comprise the North Sea region in modern terms are Norway, Sweden, Denmark, Germany, the Netherlands, Belgium and the United Kingdom (Scotland and England for much of the early modern period).

The bulk of this paper is dedicated to a quantitative analysis of Northwest Europe's first waves of internationalization.[7] By constructing emigrant stock rates (ESR: the number of expatriates per 1000 in the home population) for a number of years between 1550 and 1950 the impact of migration will become apparent. Finally, some preliminary comparisons and contrasts about the causes of the two waves will be advanced. First, however, I will take a closer look at the least known of the two waves of internationalization: the North Sea migrations of the seventeenth and eighteenth centuries.

Migration within the North Sea Region, 1550-1800

During the early modern period, the North Sea countries were linked by the sea, which facilitated close commercial relations between the coastal regions of Scotland, England, the Austrian Netherlands, Germany, Denmark, Sweden and Norway. Because of the strong maritime contacts, these countries shared a number of characteristics, including broad linguistic, demographic and cultural similarities.[8] Whereas before the second half of the sixteenth century trade was almost the sole driving force behind this development, by about 1580 labour migration tied the region together even more closely.

From the start of the seventeenth century the booming economy of the Dutch Republic badly needed foreign labour. Due mainly to demographic developments, the expanding Dutch economy was unable to rely solely on a domestic labour force. Sailors, maidservants, carpenters, bricklayers and mowers came in large numbers to the coastal provinces of the Republic in search of work.[9] High wages and abundant employment possibilities in the Netherlands, combined with local demographic pressures in the donor countries, were the main factors behind these moves.

There were also migrations to destinations other than the Netherlands. Scotland, the Austrian Netherlands and the coastal regions of Germany, for example, had migratory contacts with other countries in the region, and in the

---

[7]I acknowledge that other waves of internationalization likely preceded these two. One might, for instance, think of the invasion by the Vikings of continental Europe and the British Isles.

[8]Lex Heerma van Voss, "The North Sea and Culture, 1500-1800," in Juliette Roding and Lex Heerma van Voss (eds.), *The North Sea and Culture (1550-1800)* (Hilversum, 1996), 21-41.

[9]Cf. Jan Lucassen, "The North Sea. A Crossroad for Migrants?" in *ibid.*, 168-184; Jelle van Lottum, "Migration in the North Sea Region. An Assessment" (IISH research paper, forthcoming); and van Lottum, "Some Aspects of the North Sea Labour Market, c. 1550-1800," in Brand, Holm and Muller (eds.), *Dynamics of Economic Culture* (forthcoming).

seventeenth century in particular, the Americas and Ireland attracted large numbers of migrants, the latter mainly from England and Scotland. In the eighteenth century, as was already the case for the majority of countries a century earlier, North Sea migrations were dominated by the trek to the Netherlands. Figures 1 and 2 depict the migratory relationships for the individual countries: the first shows the destination and size of migration in 1650, while the second shows the situation a century later.

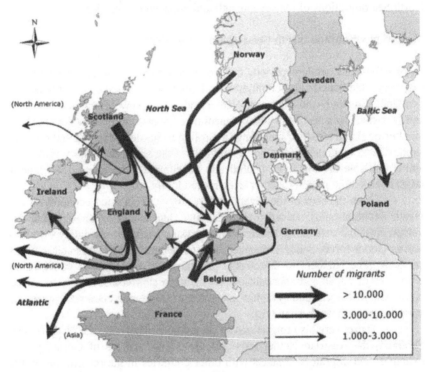

Figure 1: Destinations of North Sea Migrants around 1650

Source: Jelle van Lottum, "Migration in the North Sea Region. An Assessment" (IISH research paper, forthcoming).

Apart from the dominant position of the Dutch Republic, figures 1 and 2 show that England was far more oriented toward the Atlantic than toward Europe. In 1650 there were a considerable number of English migrants in the Netherlands and Scotland. The lion's share, however, went to Ireland and North America. In the eighteenth century, England lost most of its migratory relations with the continent and sent almost all its migrants across the Atlantic. The Dutch migrated to both North and South America, and their overseas possessions in Asia also absorbed a relatively large number of migrants.

If we ignore England, since it relied mostly on domestic labour, it is clear that in Northwest Europe the migratory system was dominated and structured by the Dutch Republic, which was a magnet for large numbers of Scandinavians, Germans, Flemings and Walloons. Even when the volumes decreased, the Netherlands remained the most important destination for migrants from most of the North Sea countries. The contrast between the more diffuse picture of the migration flows in figure 1 and their concentration toward the Dutch Republic in figure 2 illustrates this trend.

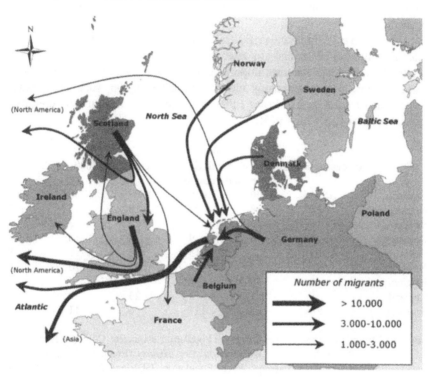

Figure 2: Destinations of North Sea Migrants around 1750

Source: See figure 1.

Emigrant Stock Rates, 1550-1950

Now that we have given some attention to the early modern period, we can focus on comparing the migrations from the North Sea region for the periods 1550-1800 and 1850-1950. The best starting point is the size of the two waves. What was the impact of mass migrations in the two eras? This question cannot be answered properly just by plotting the size of migration over time because

Jelle van Lottum

population growth over the three centuries would render the figures meaning-less. Instead, a comparison of the impact of migration on the donor country can best be made by constructing ESRs. Unfortunately, we have few migration statistics for the early modern period; in most countries the enumeration of foreigners began only in the first half of the nineteenth century. But I have made a crude assessment which can be used to construct ESRs for 1550, 1600, 1650, 1700, 1750 and 1800 (see tables 1 and 2).[10] In table 1 the estimates for six survey years have been used, while in table 2 the size of migration is based upon US censuses and Imre Ferenczi's estimates of migration to countries other than the US.

In table 1, the Scottish ESR stands out, mainly because of the large-scale migration to Ulster and at a later stage to North America. The North Sea region, however, was the most important and stable destination. Still, countries whose inhabitants predominantly moved within the region, such as Norway, Sweden and Denmark, had lower ESRs than Scotland. Germany, on the other hand, had a relatively high ESR.[11]

Table 1
Emigrant Stock Rates of North Sea Countries, 1550-1800
(per '000 Population)

Country	1550	1600	1650	1700	1750	1800
Norway	3	8	26	18	13	7
Sweden	1	1	3	11	3	1
Denmark	1	4	9	8	10	4
Germany	10	11	15	11	13	9
Netherlands	2	1	12	11	10	9
Belgium	6	45	35	9	3	2
England	1	1	12	23	2	3
Scotland	28	89	111	96	11	12

Sources: Migration estimates: see figure 1. Population estimates: Colin McEvedy and Richard Jones, *Atlas of World Population History* (London, 1978), database A; and Angus Maddison, "World Population, GDP and Per Capita GDP, 1-2001 AD" (http://www.eco.rug.nl/~Maddison/).

Table 2 shows that in the nineteenth century Sweden, Denmark and Norway had the highest ESRs in the region. Belgium, a country with one of the highest rates in the seventeenth century, never again exceeded that level.

---

[10]Van Lottum, "Migration."

[11]It is important, however, to note that in the construction of the ESRs – in contrast to figures 1 and 2 – data on the entire German Empire rather than just on the coastal regions were used because the available evidence did not permit a distinction between coastal and inland regions.

Scotland had only one survey year (1930) in which the highest early modern ESR was surpassed. In figure 3 below, where the ESR for four countries between 1550 and 1950 is plotted, the differences between the early modern and industrial periods become more visible.

Table 2
Emigrant Stock Rates of North Sea Countries, 1850-1940
(per '000 Population)

Country	1850	1860	1870	1880	1890	1900	1910	1920	1930	1940
Norway	9	28	68	97	163	157	185	155	139	99
Sweden	1	5	24	43	101	116	127	120	103	74
Denmark	1	7	19	36	62	66	74	70	61	43
Germany	19	38	47	51	63	50	42	38	34	2
Netherlands	3	9	13	15	20	22	23	21	18	13
Belgium	0	2	3	3	5	6	9	13	12	10
England	19	27	31	35	41	37	40	38	36	26
Scotland	30	44	52	63	79	75	91	91	130	96

Source: Immigration numbers: *Historical Statistics of the United States from Colonial Times to 1957* (Washington DC, 1975), series C 218-283; and I. Ferenczi, *International Migrations* (2 vols., New York, 1929; reprint, New York, 1969), I, 255-260. Population estimates: Maddison, "World Population."

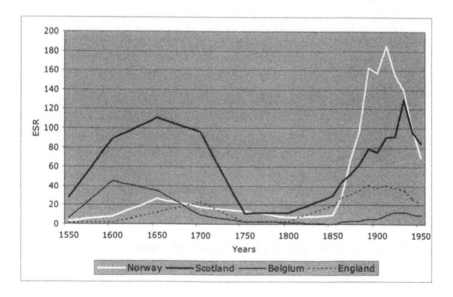

Figure 3:   ESRs for Norway, Belgium, England and Scotland, 1550-1950 (per '000 Population)

Source: See table 1.

Figure 3 shows that the impact of early modern Scottish migration to mainland Europe, Ulster and, to a lesser extent, North America was comparable to that of the nineteenth-century migrations; the highest ESR in the early modern period reached almost similar levels 300 years later. Mass migrations to Ireland and North America around 1700 also had a significant impact on England, though not as great as the migrations to North America, Australia and Asia would have two centuries later. The differences between the English early modern and industrial ESRs are relatively small, however, compared to the other countries. The Belgian ESR peaked around 1600 – caused by the exodus of Protestants to the Dutch Republic and to a lesser extent Germany – and had more impact than emigration in the industrial era.[12] The emigration level of 1600 (forty-five expatriates per 1000 population) was much higher than in modern times. The Norwegian experience was the opposite: early modern migration – twenty-six per 1000 – although among the highest in the early modern period was relatively small compared to the second wave when the ESR boomed, as in Denmark and Sweden. In sum, all variants existed: high ESRs in both periods (Scotland); low ESRs in both (England); first high, then low (Belgium); and first low, then high (Norway).

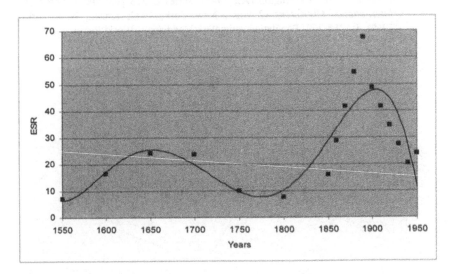

Figure 4:   Average ESR for the North Sea Region, 1550-1950

Source: See table 1.

---

[12]Due to the emerging industrial and agricultural centres, in the nineteenth century countries like Belgium, Germany and France had become immigration countries themselves. See Jan Lucassen, "In Search of Work" (IISH research paper 39, Amsterdam, 2000), 32.

Despite the fact that the peaks and overall levels of ESR differed among countries, tables 1 and 2 – but especially figure 3 – demonstrate that the ESR for all North Sea countries followed a more or less similar course. The ESR between 1550 and 1950 had a dual, wave-like shape: starting low in the sixteenth century, peaking halfway through the seventeenth, and declining (or stagnating at relatively low levels) until the 1850s when the rate started to rise again through the early twentieth century. The two waves of internationalization that characterized the North Sea countries from 1550 until 1950 are depicted in figure 4, which demonstrates that the wave of internationalization of the nineteenth century, when millions of people from Northwest Europe sought a better life in the New World, was preceded by an earlier and smaller wave of internationalization. The relatively sudden rise in migration levels in the nineteenth century was not preceded by a constant increase of mobility levels but by an identically-shaped curve, peaking around 1670 and then declining until the end of the eighteenth century.

That the mobility transition pattern – as the evolution of the ESR over time has been labelled – had a parabolic shape has been found in other migration flows around the world.[13] This fact, which has emerged from various national studies in the industrial period, has also been used to predict future migrations.[14] That the same pattern was apparent in pre-industrial Northwest Europe as well allows us to compare the early modern migration wave to its nineteenth-century counterpart more closely.

Comparisons and Differences: Four Phases in Mobility Patterns

Although more research on the causes and consequences of both waves remains to be done, I will briefly comment on the backgrounds of the two. But I will limit myself to what I regard as the two most elementary questions. First, what was the main initiator of the rise of migration during both periods? Second, what caused the end of both waves?

In answering these questions the earlier mentioned migration pattern can serve as an explanatory framework. This pattern, depicted in figure 5, is based on Sune Åkerman's study of Swedish transatlantic migration, and was demonstrated by Hatton and Williamson, among others, to apply to a number of other European countries in the nineteenth century.[15] Within the pattern four

---

[13]Wilbur Zelinsky, "The Hypothesis of the Mobility Transition," *Geographical Review*, LXI (1971), 219-249.

[14]Hatton and Williamson, *Age of Mass Migration*, 13.

[15]*Ibid.*, and Sune Åkerman, "Theories and Methods of Migration Research," in Harald Rundblom and Hans Norman (eds.) *From Sweden to America: A History of the Migration* (Minneapolis, 1996).

different periods can be distinguished: the introductory, growth, saturation and regression phases.

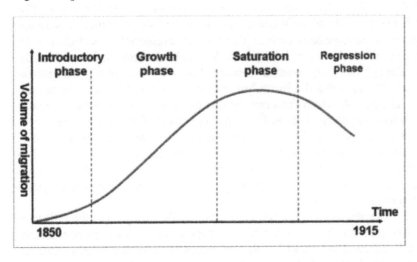

Figure 5:   Pattern of European Late Nineteenth-Century Emigration

Source: Timothy J. Hatton and Jeffrey G. Williamson, *The Age of Mass Migration: Causes and Economic Impact* (New York, 1998).

Since early modern migration from the North Sea region had a similar shape as the nineteenth- and early twentieth-century wave, we can ask if Hatton and Williamson's explanations for each of the phases can also be applied to the first wave of internationalization. With regard to the introductory and growth phases, Hatton and Williamson note that three factors were especially important in increasing the number of migrants: the demographic transition, industrialization and the cumulative impact of previous emigrants abroad. Were these also the main forces behind the first wave in the North Sea region?

Let me summarize briefly how these processes explain the first two phases in figure 5. The so-called "demographic transition" started about half-way through the eighteenth century. By escaping the "Malthusian trap," population volumes and growth rates increased rapidly in all the North Sea countries. At the same time, industrialization grew, which in combination with the first development led to a "rural exodus," in which the people moved from the countryside into urban areas, where work was easier to find. The latter development and the increase in emigration during the first two phases of the mobility transition were linked because a large share of the urban labour force was relatively young and more likely to migrate because they were usually unattached to family or possessions. Moreover, the first group – which was still in the process of establishing households – was more responsive to wage differentials, the most important pull-factor favouring the New World. An additional factor, which mainly applies to the growth phase, was the cumulative impact of previous emigrants abroad. "Chain migration," or the "friends-and-families-effect," played a huge role in nineteenth-century transatlantic migration, not only because previous emigrants often financed the cost of passage of new migrants but also because they were valuable sources of information.[16]

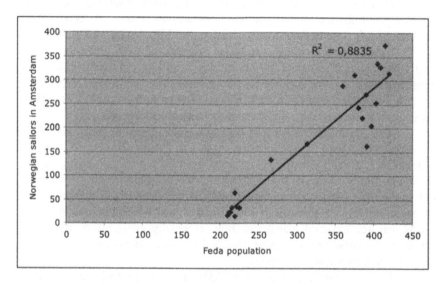

Figure 6: Population of Feda versus Norwegian sailors in Amsterdam, 1595-1700

Note: R^2 and F-value were both significant at the one-percent level.

Source: Margit Loyland, *Fjordfolk. Fedas historie fra de eldste tider og fram til 1963* (Kvinesdal, 1999); and Municipal Archives, Amsterdam (GA), 883, collection of Dr. Simon Hart.

How do these three processes compare to the early modern wave? First, let us deal with the demographic transition. It is obvious that this particular transition was a late eighteenth- and early nineteenth-century phenomenon. Nevertheless, in different parts of the region demographic pressure was one of the most important reasons for early modern migration in specific locales. This was the case, for example, for Scottish migration to Ulster in the seventeenth century when Scotland had a bigger labour force than the largely

---

[16]*Ibid.*, 14.

rural economy could absorb.[17] In southern Norway, a similar development occurred in the first half of the seventeenth century, as the experience of the small town of Feda shows. Between 1630 and 1670 the population almost doubled, which was typical of other Norwegian towns.[18] When we compare this with the rise in migration during the same period we find a strong relationship. Figure 6 uses the number of Norwegian sailors – the most popular profession for Norwegian migrants from this region – in the Amsterdam marriage registers as a proxy for the total migration of Norwegian seamen. A regression of this and Feda's population between 1595 and 1700, which yields an R^2 of 0.8835, demonstrates a strong correlation between the two. When the mainly rural labour market in southern Norway was unable to absorb the sudden increase in population, the superfluous labour force migrated in large numbers to Holland. Since the Norwegian population continued to increase in this period, it appears that the migration did not unduly harm the local economy.

The next factor Hatton and Williamson mentioned in their explanation of the first two phases in the migration curve was industrialization. Although it is clear that this is a modern phenomenon (and I do not want to claim that the North Sea region was already industrial in the seventeenth century), when we look at the most important recipient labour market – the Dutch Republic – we can see many features that can be called modern and which resemble the main effects that accompanied industrialization, especially urbanization and proletarianization. These two processes also had positive effects on emigration in the early modern North Sea region.

In the Netherlands after about 1580 a large share of the population had already been converted into proletarians. As a result of extensive drainage projects in Holland, the number of large commercial farms increased, leaving less land for small landholders and depriving them of the possibility of earning a living from farming. Simultaneously, new capital-intensive industries emerged in de Zaanstreek and Amsterdam. While industrial windmills, refineries and wharves provided some employment opportunities for those who had once worked in the rural proto-industrial textile industry, they also helped to transform the former rural workers into an urban proletariat.[19] As more people became fully dependent upon wages, the once large elastic labour force slowly disappeared. At the same time, the urban population began to have difficulties

---

[17]Michael Perceval-Maxwell, *The Scottish Migration to Ulster in the Reign of James I* (London, 1973), 310.

[18]Margit Loyland, *Fjordfolk. Fedas historie fra de eldste tider og fram til 1963* (Kvinesdal, 1999).

[19]J.L. van Zanden, *The Rise and Decline of Holland's Economy. Merchant Capitalism and the Labour Market* (Manchester, 1993), 35.

reproducing itself, although the Dutch economy kept growing. As natural population growth became insufficient to supply the booming industries with sufficient labour, additional workers had to be recruited.[20] In short, proletarianized and urbanized Holland became a magnet for a rural foreign labour force; the booming Dutch economy, with its continuing dependence on foreign labour, functioned more or less as an international labour market.[21]

Chain migration also played a role in maintaining migration flows in the early modern period. It is known, for instance, that seamen abroad often wrote to their families at home.[22] Although Erika Kuijpers has demonstrated that migrants were often well informed about conditions at their potential destination, there is no evidence in the early modern North Sea region of the popular nineteenth-century system of prepaid boat tickets supplied by earlier migrants.[23]

Finally, we should admit that here were additional "push factors" which did not receive much attention from Hatton and Williamson, such as natural disasters, wars and persecution. During short periods, such factors also influenced demographic behaviour and affected mobility in general.[24]

We may now examine the saturation and regression phases. At the end of the nineteenth century the surge in transatlantic migration ended as the forces of the demographic transition diminished and the effects of industrialization became less significant. In their explanation of these phases, Hatton and Williamson emphasize that real wage convergence was the most important

---

[20]Jan de Vries and Ad van der Woude, *The First Modern Economy. Success, Failure, and Perseverance of the Dutch Economy, 1500–1815* (Cambridge, 1997), 632-636.

[21]Cf. van Lottum, "North Sea Labour Market."

[22]See Jelle van Lottum and Sølvi Sogner, "Magnus og Barbara. Mikrohistorie I Nordsjøregionen på 1600-tallet," *Historisk Tidsskrift* (Norway), forthcoming.

[23]Cf. Erika Kuijpers, *Migrantenstad. Immigratie en sociale verhoudingen in 17e-eeuws Amsterdam* (Hilversum, 2005), especially chapter 1.

[24]See *ibid.* for the influence of the large floods in 1634 on migration from Nord-Friesland (Germany). For the exodus of Protestants from the Southern Netherlands in the second half of the sixteenth century, see Leo Lucassen and Boudien de Vries, "The Rise and Fall of a Western European Textile-worker Migration System: Leiden, 1586-1700," in Gérard Gayot and Philippe Minard (ed.), *Les ouvriers qualifiés de l'industrie (XVIe-XXe siècle) formation, emploi, migrations: actes du colloque de Roubaix, 20-22 novembre 1997* (Lille, 2001), 281-305.

factor in the decline of migration at the end of the century.[25] As European wages approached US levels, this "pull factor" lost much of its importance.

Did wage convergence play a major role in the decline of migration in the early modern North Sea region? Although more research clearly needs to be done, early evidence suggests that it was not important in the decline of the ESR simply because there does not appear to have been a diminution of wage differentials.[26] Real wages in the Netherlands remained high, and there does not appear to have been any significant catch-up in the main donor countries as far as we can tell from the limited time series that have been constructed.

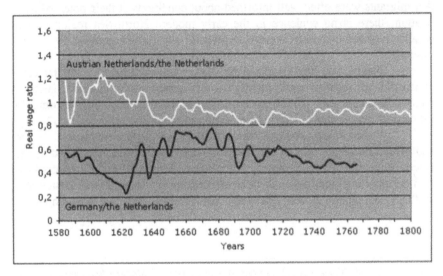

Figure 7: Real Wage Ratio for Labourers between the Austrian Netherlands, Germany and the Netherlands, 1580-1800 (five-year moving averages).

Note: German real wages are based upon Augsburg; Austrian Netherlands' real wages are based upon Antwerp.

Source: Robert C. Allen, "Database on European Prices and Wages" (http://www.economics.ox.ac.uk/Members/robert.allen/WagesPrices.htm).

Figure 7 shows the ratio of real wages between the Austrian Netherlands and Germany, on one hand, and the Netherlands on the other. It demon-

---

[25]Hatton and Williamson, *Age of Mass Migration*, 52.

[26]See also Christiaan van Bochove, "Inequality in Europe: Wages around the North Sea during the Seventeenth and Eighteenth Centuries" (Unpublished paper presented at the Second Conference on Economic History of the Low Countries, April 2006).

strates that there was no wage convergence between the Belgian and German towns and Amsterdam over the entire period. During the exodus of Protestants from the Southern Netherlands at the start of the seventeenth century, migration even flowed "uphill:" the suppression of Protestants by the Habsburg rulers clearly was the main incentive to leave home, and Holland provided a reasonable alternative.[27] But even when "normal" labour market forces prevailed, real wages remained relatively stable, and migration between the two countries and the Netherlands did not cease. In the Austrian Netherlands between 1640 and 1800, real wages averaged between eighty and ninety percent of Amsterdam wages. In Germany after 1650 there was even a divergence rather than a convergence; that is, the wage gap became larger over time.[28]

What then could have caused the declining ESRs? Unlike nineteenth-century transatlantic migration, there cannot be a single answer or set of answers. Apart from the Netherlands, Ireland was also a popular destination. When the decline in migration from Scotland and England to Ulster and Munster (Ireland) set in, the overall level of migration in the region naturally dropped. The end of the Ulster and Munster plantations, which were organized operations, had an effect on the decline of migration.

With regard to the intra-regional migration directed mainly at the Dutch Republic, labour market forces did play a role.[29] From research by de Vries, van der Woude and others we know that after the economy peaked midway through the seventeenth century, the Dutch labour market underwent a process of segmentation caused mainly by decreasing price levels, stagnation of population growth and a sudden fall in infrastructure investment.[30] The post-1670 labour market came to be comprised of three distinct segments: a core dominated by large public and semi-public organizations, guilds and capital-intensive enterprises; a casual, seasonal and labour-intensive segment focused on construction, agriculture, peat, whaling, fisheries and manufactures; and finally, what de Vries and van der Woude described as the "employer of last

---

[27]Kevin O'Rourke, "Did Labour Flow Uphill? International Migration and Wage Rates in Twentieth Century Ireland," in George Grantham and Mary MacKinnon (eds.) *Labour Market Evolution. The Economic History of Market Integration, Wage Flexibility, and the Employment Relation* (London, 1994), 139-160.

[28]See Van Bochove, "Inequality in Europe."

[29]Even if we exclude the extra-regional migration – to Ireland and the Americas, for instance – the parabolic shape of the wave remains. Therefore, the division into phases depicted in figure 5 also applies to this migration flow.

[30]De Vries and van der Woude, *First Modern Economy*, 636-637.

resort," the Dutch East India Company (VOC).[31] Although all three provided opportunities for foreigners, it was the second and third sectors that absorbed the largest number of immigrants.

Because of the economic upheaval after the 1670s, especially within the first segment "security measures" were taken to protect it from outsiders, thereby decreasing opportunities for migrants. Although there was still a demand for foreign labour, forms of protection such as guild regulations ensured that the best jobs were reserved for natives, which meant that wage differentials between donor and recipient nations had no effect whatsoever. Foreigners were increasingly forced to take temporary jobs in the second sector or more dangerous employment with the VOC.[32] The relatively open labour market of the Dutch Republic – which like the US in the nineteenth century was perceived as a "land of opportunity" – was transformed into a market in which risks were shifted to foreigners and the best jobs were reserved for natives. As in the US, increasing barriers to entry were eventually introduced to staunch the influx of foreign labour. Hatton and Williamson, however, argue that real wage convergence would have stemmed the wave of mass migration from Northwest Europe to the US even in absence of quotas, which were imposed to limit emigrants from southern and eastern Europe and hence had little influence on migration from the North Sea region.[33]

Conclusion

The ESRs for North Sea countries between 1550 and 1950 demonstrate that migration in the region followed a path similar to the second wave that began midway through the nineteenth century. Although the amplitude of the first wave did not reach nineteenth-century levels, the average early modern ESR demonstrated that the populace in the pre-industrial North Sea region was fairly mobile. Indeed, there are even countries that had higher, or at least comparable, ESRs during the early modern period than during the so-called "age of mass migration."

Although an analysis of the structural factors behind the rise and fall of the two waves of internationalization has not been the main focus here, it is still possible to use this study to draw some preliminary conclusions. Apart from the impact of wars and persecution, demographic changes appear to have

---

[31]*Ibid.*, 646.

[32]Jelle van Lottum and Jan Lucassen, "A Quantitative Reconstruction of the Dutch Maritime Labour Market: Some Cross-sections 1607-1850," in Richard Gorski (ed.), *Maritime Labour in the Northern Hemisphere c. 1600-1950* (Amsterdam, 2007, forthcoming).

[33]Hatton and Williamson, *Age of Mass Migration*, 52.

been important in creating a potential supply of labour during both waves. In both periods, urbanization and proletarianization led to the migration of a young age cohort. Moreover, chain migration maintained the flows for long periods, and networks were important throughout.

When we look at the decline of the two waves, however, there are fewer similarities. In the nineteenth-century wave, real wage convergence has been advanced as the main cause for the slowing of emigration. Although more research needs to be done, in the early modern North Sea region there is no evidence of convergence between the Dutch Republic and the donor countries. But the decline in demand for foreign labour does appear to have played a major role. Labour market segmentation caused by economic stagnation, resulting in diminishing opportunities for foreigners, had a direct effect on the ESRs for most of the North Sea countries.

In this paper, one major issue has been omitted. The existence of the early modern wave of internationalization in the North Sea region implies that a framework existed to stimulate the free movement of labour. For the nineteenth-century wave Hatton and O'Rourke have argued that the "transport revolution," the shift from mercantilism to free trade and national market integration created an Atlantic economy in which the international labour market played an important role. Given that in the North Sea region this wave was preceded by an earlier one, it needs to be determined whether such a framework existed in the early modern period. The answer will be the subject of future research.[34]

---

[34]This will be the subject of a forthcoming paper by Christiaan van Bochove, Lex Heerma van Voss and myself.

The Battle for the Migrants:
The Evolution from Port to Company Competition, 1840-1914

Torsten Feys

Introduction

The importance of information flows for migration and shipping has been discussed by both maritime and migration historians. Among the former, John Gould's theories about the impact of "diffusion" and "feedback" on patterns of European inter-continental migration have been particularly important. Successful pioneers in the nineteenth century stimulated migration through letters and remittances, establishing "chain migration" patterns involving both kin and others from local areas. The spread of information and technological evolutions in transport and communication lowered the psychological fear of migration.[1] Gould's work inspired migration historians to shift their focus from the nation to more localized regions, in the process uncovering the fact that the "path dependency" of migrants in their quest to reduce uncertainty was often based upon choices made by previous emigrants. But Dudley Baines has argued that the emphasis on chain migration may overestimate the importance of such networks, especially since migrants who moved outside these structures are much harder to trace and hence more difficult to understand.[2] Moreover, these studies have too often simplified the concept of chain migration by failing to consider the dynamics of networks and by ignoring recruiting and government agents. As well, the impact of newspapers, governments and transport

---

[1]J.D. Gould, "European Inter-Continental Emigration: The Role of 'Diffusion' and 'Feedback,'" *Journal of European Economic History*, IX, No. 2 (1980), 267-314; Gould, "European Inter-Continental Migration 1815-1914: Patterns and Causes," *Journal of European Economic History*, VIII, No. 3 (1979), 593-679; and Gould, "European Inter-Continental Migration, The Road Home: Return Migration from the USA," *Journal of European Economic History*, IX, No. 1 (1980), 41-112.

[2]Dudley Baines, *Emigration from Europe 1815-1930* (London, 1991); and Baines, "Labour Markets, Emigration and Internal Migration in Europe 1850-1913," in Jeffrey G. Williamson and Timothy J. Hatton (eds.), *International Labour Market Integration and the Impact of Migration on the National Labour Markets since 1870* (Milan, 1994), 51-62.

companies on providing information about opportunities to relocate has received little attention from migration historians.

To make a bad situation worse, migration scholars have failed to inte-
grate their work with the studies of maritime historians. While this has hindered our understanding of the impact of maritime networks on migration, it is
also the case that few maritime scholars have considered migration patterns
and their networks. For example, research on passenger liners has failed to
link the companies to chain-migration patterns because it has tended to ignore
the strategies that shipping companies adopted to attract migrants. Such tactics
were strongly influenced by intense competition among shipping companies
that led eventually to the introduction of conference agreements between major
passenger lines. Among other things, these conferences supported inter-firm
learning and sustained growth.[3] Moreover, most studies with a maritime focus
have examined only a single company; on a broader scale, only the Anglo-
German-American rivalry has received much attention.[4] The most important
conference in North Atlantic passenger transport, the Nord-Atlantischer
Dampfer-Linien Verband, was first analyzed as early as 1922, but its history
still awaits reassessment more than eight decades later.[5] Indeed, Robert Greenhill has underlined the lacunae that exist in research on conference agreements,
particularly about how members gained and exchanged information.[6] Until

---

[3]Gordon Boyce, *Information, Mediation and Institutional Development: The
Rise of Large Scale Enterprise in British Shipping 1870-1919* (Manchester, 1995); and
Frank Broeze, "Connecting the Netherlands and the Americas: Ocean Transport and
Port Rivalry," in Rosemarijn Hoefte and Johanna C. Kardux (eds.), *Connecting Cul-
tures: The Netherlands in Five Centuries of Transatlantic Exchange* (Amsterdam,
1994), 77-99.

[4]Frank Broeze, "Albert Ballin, The Hamburg-Bremen Rivalry and the Dynamics of the Conference System," *International Journal of Maritime History*, III, No.
1 (1991) 1-32; Boyce, *Information, Mediation and Institutional Development*; Drew
Keeling, "Transatlantic Shipping Cartels and Migration between Europe and America
1880-1914," *Essays in Economic and Business History*, XVII (1999), 195-213; Keeling, "The Transport Revolution in the Transatlantic Migration 1850-1914," *Research in
Economic History*, XIX (1999), 39-74; and Simon Ville, *Transport and the Development of the European Economy 1750-1918* (London, 1990).

[5]Erich Murken, *Die grossen transatlantischen Linienreederei-Verbande, Pools
und Interessengemeinschaften bis zum Ausbruch des Weltkrieges: Ihre Entstehung,
Organitsation und Wirksamkeit* (Jena, 1922).

[6]Robert G. Greenhill, "Competition or Cooperation the Global Shipping Industry: The Origins and Impact of the Conference System for British Shipowners before 1914," in David J. Starkey and Gelina Harlaftis (eds.), *Global Markets: The Internationalization of the Sea Transport Industries since 1850* (St. John's, 1998), 53-79.

recently, maritime historians have failed to examine the international information networks upon which shipowners and merchants relied to connect the foreland with the hinterland, despite the fact that Gordon Boyce has shown their importance to discovering business opportunities. The focus of Boyce's studies has been on the impact of intangible resources, such as information, knowledge and reputation. He argues that shipping enterprises depended to a great degree upon the ability to create and use channels of information.

Shipping agents played a crucial role in information gathering and decision-making.[7] The organization of shipping agencies and their role as nodal points in maritime networks was further elaborated by Michael Miller, while Leos Müller and Jari Ojala have stressed the importance of consuls in establishing initial contacts for the development of new markets.[8] This article will discuss the role of the Dutch and Belgian consular agencies in the opening of transatlantic steamship lines from Rotterdam and Antwerp to the United States; their role in defending the reputation of these European ports as gateways for migrants bound for the New World; and the importance of the agencies in gathering information on migrant opportunities in the US. In the second section of the essay we will use the experience of the Holland America Line to analyze how shipping agents assumed most of these responsibilities once a steamship line was established. Finally, based upon the correspondence of the Line's New York shipping agents with the Board of Directors, we will examine briefly its inter-firm relationships and business strategies.

The Role of Consuls in Gathering Information and Promoting Migration

The importance of consuls as a source of information on legal, commercial and political developments abroad has only recently been stressed in maritime history. Consuls established contacts with local authorities and merchant communities to promote trade relations with shipping enterprises based in their homelands. Especially in new markets, where uncertainties and hence transaction

---

[7]Gordon Boyce, *Co-operative Structures in Global Business: Communicating, Transferring Knowledge and Learning across the Corporate Frontier* (London, 2001); Boyce, *Information, Mediation and Institutional Development*; and Boyce and Richard Gorski (eds.), *Resources and Infrastructures in the Maritime Economy, 1500-2000* (St. John's, 2002). See also "Forum: Information and Maritime History," *International Journal of Maritime History*, XIII, No. 1 (2002), 153-246.

[8]Leos Müller, "Swedish-American Trade and the Swedish Consuls, 1780-1840," *International Journal of Maritime History*, XIV, No. 1 (June 2002) 173-188; Müller and Jari Ojala, "Consular Services of the Nordic Countries during the Eighteenth and Nineteenth Century: Did They Really Work?" in Boyce and Gorski (eds.), *Resources and Infrastructures*, 23-41; and Müller, *Consuls, Corsairs and Commerce: The Swedish Consular Service and Long-distance Shipping 1720-1815* (Uppsala, 2004).

costs were considerable, consuls played a vital role.[9] In the nineteenth century two systems were adopted to organize the rapidly-expanding consular corps. On the one hand, there was the system of honorary consuls, often merchants who received no remuneration other than the fees derived from certain specified activities. Such consuls lived off the profits from trade, while the title of "consul" conferred a certain prestige within the business community. The Netherlands, Belgium and the cities of the German Hanse employed this system, albeit with some salaried consuls in key locales. On the other hand, countries such as France and the UK used a system of salaried officials, career consuls who were forbidden to engage in trade.[10] A study of the correspondence between the Belgian consul in New York and the Dutch envoy in Washington with their respective Ministries of Foreign Affairs reveals that these diplomatic representatives played an important role in gathering information on opportunities to open new steamship connections for migrants.[11]

In 1840 the Belgian government passed a special navigation law to subsidize the opening of a transatlantic steamship line.[12] This decision was stimulated by the subsidies granted by the British government to Cunard and the plans of neighbouring ports, such as Rotterdam and Le Havre, to open new transatlantic lines. The Belgian consul in New York was asked to shepherd the Belgian project and to publicize it on the other side of the Atlantic. Two proposals were made to operate the service: one by an American businessman named David Cadwallader Colden, who proposed to operate under the banner of the Belgian and American Transatlantic Steamship Company, and one by a group of Antwerp businessmen led by Jean-François Catteaux-Wattel, Jules Lejeune and George Jullie. Since it wanted to keep the ships under the Belgian flag, the government chose the latter.

---

[9]Müller, "Swedish-American Trade;" and Müller, *Consuls, Corsairs and Commerce.*

[10]Charles Stuart Kennedy, *The American Consul: A History of the United States Consular Service, 1776-1914* (New York, 1990); Ginette Kurgan van Hentenryk, "Belgian Consular Reports," *Business History*, XXIII, No. 3 (1981), 268-270; and C.A. Tamse, "The Netherlands Consular Service and the Dutch Consular Reports of the Nineteenth and Twentieth Centuries," *Business History*, XXIII, No. 3 (1981), 271-276.

[11]The correspondence of the Dutch consul in New York has only been preserved from 1874 onwards and has been completed with an analysis of the correspondence of the Dutch envoy in Washington after 1840.

[12]On 19 June parliament passed a law awarding a yearly subsidy of 400,000 *francs* for the opening of a transatlantic steamship line; see Karel Veraghtert, "De havenbewegingen te Antwerpen tijdens de 19e eeuw: een kwantitatieve benadering" (Unpublished PhD thesis, Leuven University, 1977).

There were three reasons why the government wanted such a line. First, by promoting Antwerp as a commercial node and attracting the transit trade from neighbouring countries, it wanted to strengthen its international political relations. Nations that enjoyed the benefits of Antwerp could later be lobbied to push for the free navigation of the Scheldt.[13] Second, it wanted to stimulate American and Belgian merchants to examine the opportunities for increased trade between the two nations. Third, it wanted to improve the competitive position of the port of Antwerp. To this end, it stipulated that tariffs for cabin passengers and valuable goods had to be ten percent lower than those of Cunard and could not exceed the prices of the projected French line. As well, unlike Cunard, which offered only first-class passage, a second class had to be available to make transatlantic passages accessible to travellers from all social classes.[14] The authorities were later contacted by Georges Schuyler, a civil engineer in New York who had studied the emigrant question and believed that the traffic could easily be diverted from Le Havre to Antwerp. He proposed to construct a steamship in New York to complement the service of *British Queen*. This ship was bought by the Belgian government under the authority of the navy and entrusted to Catteaux-Wattel, Lejeune and Jullie, who managed the line.[15] He also applied, without success, for the position of agent

---

[13]*Ibid.* To enhance the trade through Antwerp the Belgian government decided to refund the tolls levied by the Dutch authorities on all ships except those sailing under the Dutch flag. With the increasing commerce, however, this started to weigh heavily on the government's funds. Moreover, with the liberalization of trade there was a tendency to eliminate such tolls. The Sont and Stade toll had been bought out by the maritime nations, leaving the Scheldt with the only remaining toll, which the Belgian authorities continued to lobby against. These efforts materialized in 1863 when the Belgian government and the maritime nations agreed to pay 36,278,560 Belgian *francs* to make the navigation of the Scheldt free.

[14]Belgium, Algemeen Rijks Archief (ARA), I 215, no. 4052, Vaart der *British Queen*, eerste stoomvaart verbinding Antwerpen, 1840-1847, "Report on the Opening of a Steamship Line between Antwerp and New York," 25 April 1840.

[15]Despite the subsidy from the government, Catteaux-Wattel, Lejeune and Jullie found it difficult to raise sufficient capital. Moreover, the construction of the ships took much longer than anticipated. The government therefore intervened by purchasing two ships, *President* and *British Queen*, from the Anglo-American Steamship Company. *President* sank while being delivered, which seriously damaged the reputation of its sister ship. See *ibid.*, Minister of the Interior to Minister of Foreign Affairs, 8 April 1842; Veraghtert, "De havenbewegingen te Antwerpen;" G.J. De Boer, *125 jaar Holland-Amerika Lijn* (Rotterdam, 1998); and P-H. Laurent, "Antwerp versus Bremen: Transatlantic Steamship Diplomacy and European Port Rivalry 1839-1846," *Journal of World History*, IX (1965), 938-952.

in New York for the projected company.[16] The losses made by *British Queen* were considerable, pushing the company to halt operations after the third voyage. The lack of publicity in England, Europe and the US, the damage to its reputation caused by the loss of *President* and the lack of solid support in America for the enterprises were the main causes of its failure.[17]

These efforts did not go unnoticed by US authorities when evaluating ports of call for the opening of an American service to compete with Cunard. In 1845 a bill to subsidize a steamship line triggered rigorous efforts by European consuls to promote their own ports as the destination. A preliminary list was assembled, including Liverpool, Southampton, Bristol, Lisbon, Brest, Hamburg, Bremen, Le Havre and Antwerp. The last three were at the top of the list.[18]

The absence of Amsterdam and Rotterdam alarmed Dutch merchants and their government and alerted them to the need to do something about their deteriorating non-colonial trade routes. Rotterdam had pioneered networks for migrant transport in the eighteenth century but lost its edge to other ports in the nineteenth.[19] While in 1839 a project was presented to the Dutch government to open a steamship line between Rotterdam and New York, with the principal revenue to be derived from migrant transport, it was never seriously considered by the authorities.[20] When it appeared that Antwerp would be chosen as a port of call by US officials, the issue was revived. The government urged its envoy in Washington to promote the advantages of Rotterdam and Amsterdam in the press and among members of Congress.[21] The envoy was also instructed to publish the laws regarding migrant passage through the Netherlands in order to refute claims that Dutch ports were poor gateways for

---

[16]ARA, I 215, Zeewezen 4052, Vaart der British Queen, eerste stoomvaart verbinding Antwerpen, 1840-1847, Georges Schuyler, civil engeneer, New York, to Jean-Baptiste Nothomb, Belgian Minister of the Interior, 31 January 1842.

[17]Laurent, "Antwerp versus Bremen."

[18]*Ibid.*; and Broeze, "Connecting the Netherlands and the Americas."

[19]Marianne Sophia Wokeck, *Trade in Strangers: The Beginnings of Mass Migration to North America* (University Park, PA, 1999).

[20]Rotterdam Community Archives (GAR), Holland America Line Archive (HAL), W.A., No. 6, Stoomvaart Amerika 1839, F.H. Nollen to the Dutch Ministry of Foreign Affairs, 3 April 1839.

[21]Netherlands, National Archives (NA), 2.05.13, Gezantschap in de Verenigde Staten van Amerika, 1814-1940, Dutch Ministry of Foreign Affairs to J.C. Gevers, envoy in Washington, DC, 11 January 1845.

migrants bound for the New World.[22] When information was provided by the Dutch consuls at Antwerp and Bremen that the German port was likely to be chosen by the Americans, a new lobbying campaign was started to promote Rotterdam.[23] In the end, the US subsidies went to a line connecting New York with Bremen partly because German merchants had more experience in dealing with officials in Washington and partly because the Germans understood the value of public relations.[24] Despite this setback, the Dutch envoy in Washington was ordered to continue lobbying in favour of Rotterdam. His superiors stressed the importance of preventing the opening of another line to Le Havre or Antwerp, since such a development would seriously limit the prospects of opening one to Rotterdam.[25]

In the interim, the Belgian envoy in Washington tried to convince the American authorities to let the Bremen line alternate its ships between Bremen and Antwerp. Shortly thereafter, the US approved subsidies to open additional lines to Le Havre and Liverpool. Nonetheless, both Rotterdam and Antwerp persevered in their efforts to open a direct steamship service. A group of Rotterdam merchants founded the Rotterdam-American Steamship Company in 1850. The Minister of Foreign Affairs then asked the envoy in Washington to do everything possible to assist the project.[26] When the unsubsidized company failed to raise the required capital at home, its backers turned to New York. Unfortunately, the lack of subsidies from the Dutch government was used as the main argument by Americans to refuse to invest.[27] After a second refusal by the Dutch authorities to grant subsidies, the company even turned to the Prussian government, which refused because it would conflict with the signifi-

---

[22]*Ibid.*, Dutch Ministry of Foreign Affairs to Gevers, 3 October 1844.

[23]*Ibid.*, Dutch Ministry of Foreign Affairs to Testa, envoy in Washington, DC, 21 February 1846.

[24]Broeze, "Connecting the Netherlands and the Americas."

[25]NA, 2.05.13, Gezantschap in de Verenigde Staten van Amerika, 1814-1940, Dutch Ministry of Foreign Affairs to Testa, 22 October 1846.

[26]*Ibid.*, Dutch Minister of Foreign Affairs to Testa, 22 January 1851.

[27]One of the merchant houses contacted in New York was Boonen and Graves. The spelling of the name "Boonen" was partly erased. It might just as well have been "Rooran." The merchant house mentioned that it had connections with Cunard; to underline its expertise, it noted that it had collaborated with the Havre Line. GAR, HAL, 3.04.16, W.A., 7 Stoomvaart Amerika 1850, Boonen and Graves to Jan Willem Louis van Oord, 14 May 1851.

cant support it had given to Bremen.[28] In the meantime, another attempt to open a line from Antwerp was made by the Société belge de bateaux à vapeur transatlantiques. The Belgian government subsidized the project and provided a ten-year guarantee of four percent on the capital raised in 1853. The honorary Belgian consul in New York, Henri Mali, actively worked to establish the necessary contacts in the US.[29]

This discussion also illustrates the general maritime policies of the governments of the two countries. After obtaining its political sovereignty, Belgium tried to consolidate it by becoming economically independent. The loss of commercial ties with the Dutch colonies pushed Antwerp merchants to redirect their long-distance trade routes to the Americas. The Belgian government actively supported the expansion of commerce and the national fleet. Yet the reluctance of many conservative Antwerp merchants to invest would push the government to change its methods after the 1860s. Instead of supporting new initiatives that relied on the ability of the Antwerp merchants to raise funds, the government decided to subsidize companies started with foreign capital.[30] On the other hand, Dutch maritime interests were strongly dominated by trade with the colonies in the East Indies. Between 1815 and 1850 these colonies came to dominate Dutch shipping, while the US became relatively insignificant. Government intervention in colonial trade through the Nederlandse Handels Maatschappij offered high freight rates and guaranteed a return

---

[28]M. Mees, *Geschiedenis der stoomvaart van Nederland op Amerika* (Rotterdam, 1883); and De Boer, *125 jaar Holland-Amerika Lijn*.

[29]Belgium, Archives of the Ministry of Foriegn Affairs (AMBZ), Consuls et Consulats, New York, pers. 623; Belgian Ministry of Foreign Affairs to Henri Mali, consul, New York, n.d.; Greta Devos, "Belgische Overheidssteun aan scheepvaartlijnen 1867-1914," in *Bijdragen tot de internationale maritime geschiedenis* (Brussels, 1988), 81-96; Karel Veraghtert, "The Slow Growth of Steam Navigation: The Case of Antwerp 1816-1865," in Christian Koninckx (ed.), *Proceedings of the International Colloquium "Industrial Revolutions and the Sea"* (Brussels, 1991), 207-215; and de Boer, *125 jaar Holland-Amerika Lijn*. Again, the construction of the five vessels took much longer than planned. The company only began operations on 29 December 1855, but the first crossing of *Belgique* turned into a fiasco. Due to serious leaks the vessel had to call three times at English ports for repairs; after its last call on 24 January 1856, the crossing to New York was cancelled, and it took eight months before the ship could be put back into service. Although *Belgique* was joined by *Constitution* and *Leopold J*, the costs has been seriously underestimated, and the company soon was making significant losses. After the Crimean War, many vessels returned to transatlantic service, depressing the demand for shipping capacity. As a result, the company folded in 1857 before the next two vessels could be launched.

[30]Veraghtert, "De havenbewegingen te Antwerpen;" Devos, "Belgische Overheidssteun;" and Veraghtert, "Slow Growth."

cargo. The colonial trade was organized in such a way that there was no need for rapid transport. As a result, merchants continued to use less expensive sailing ships rather than invest in more costly steamers. The Dutch institutional structure therefore slowed the transition from sail to steam and the evolution to large-scale shipowning companies. Sailing ships for the colonial trade thus attracted capital flows which were crucial for the transport of passengers. Moreover, this colonial trade policy caused the Dutch business community to have an aversion to the German transit trade. During this period the German states forced the Dutch government to make concessions that liberalized transport on the Rhine. This facilitated the transit of goods, the volume of which started to rise as early as the 1830s. The colonial trade brought tropical goods to the Dutch ports which were trade further up the Rhine and with other European ports. The focus on these staple trades delayed the transition to the transit traffic, i.e., from an emphasis on trade to a concern with transport. As well, the Nederlandse Handels Maatschappij favoured the port of Amsterdam over Rotterdam, despite the fact that connections from the former port to the German hinterland were far inferior to those emanating from Rotterdam and therefore less suitable for transit traffic. For these reasons, commercial relations between Rotterdam and the US deteriorated. Only when the protected Dutch colonial system collapsed did the government alter its maritime policy.[31]

During the 1850s the transport of migrants on steamships became profitable due to an innovation introduced by the Inman Line, which convinced migrants to pay a little bit more in exchange for a faster crossing, more comfort and better food.[32] The prospects discussed above anticipated this breakthrough. The growth of migrant traffic through Bremen, which enabled its merchants to gain control of its cotton and tobacco trades in the 1830s, did not go unnoticed in other ports, as a report to the Belgian government made clear:

> We know that Germany sends out thousands of emigrants to America every year. The city of Bremen has passed such perfect regulations for the transport of emigrants, that only this port organizes these transports. Once arrived in Bremen

---

[31]Edwin Horlings, *The Economic Development of the Dutch Service Sector 1800-1850: Trade and Transportation in a Premodern Economy* (Amsterdam, 1995); Thimo De Nijs, *In veilige Haven: Het familieleven van het Rotterdamse gegoede burgerij 1815-1890* (Nijmegen, 2001); and Jochen Blasing and Ton Langenhuyzen, "Dutch Sea Transport in Transition: The German Hinterland as Catalyst, 1850-1914," in Starkey and Harlaftis (eds.), *Global Markets*, 103-126.

[32]Keeling, "Transport Revolution;" and Francis E. Hyde, *Cunard and the North Atlantic 1840-1973: A History of Shipping and Financial Management* (London, 1975).

this cargo moves itself without extra costs and it allows the
Bremen merchants on their way back to ship a variety of
goods such as tobacco and cotton at half the regular price. As
most of the German emigrants come from Westphalia, Tur-
ing and Switzerland it is very likely that they would prefer to
travel through Antwerp if they would find the same conditions as in Bremen.[33]

Merchants pressured their governments to take action to attract these
migration flows. Apart from supporting attempts to open steamship lines and
lobbying to increase the accessibility of the ports to regions of out-migration,
the mercantile communities lobbied for laws to regulate the trade and protect
migrants from abuse. Once passed, these acts also defended the reputation of
the ports, which proved crucial to attracting migrants.[34] Belgian and Dutch
consuls in regions of out-migration were asked to publish these laws in newspapers to promote their ports. Moreover, Belgian officials helped shipping
companies to find adequate representation, especially in Germany. Information
on the ports of embarkation was spread through emigration agents, migrant
letters and newspaper articles. Belgian and Dutch consuls in the German states
were asked to report on stories that discussed abuses in Antwerp or Rotterdam,
which were viewed as attempts by the German authorities to direct their nationals to Bremen and Hamburg. Consuls refuted these stories to defend their
national port's reputation.[35] The same was done in the US, especially in New

---

[33]AMBZ, 2020, Emigration I: 1834-1848, D. Behr, "Report on the Migrant
Transport through Bremen," 5 April 1838: "On sait que chaque année l'Allemagne
envoye des millers d'émigrants vers l'Amérique. La ville de Brême a établi des régle-
ments pour le transport des émigrants, tellement parfait, que seule elle fait ce transport.
Arrivée sur les lieux cette cargaison se disperse sans frais et les Brémois en retour se
chargent de plusiers marchandises telle que du tabac et du cotton qu'ils transportent
chez eux pour la moitié du frais. Comme les émigrants Allemands sont pour la plupart
d'origine de la Westphalie, de Thuringe et de la Suisse il est probable qu'ils viendraient
de préférence par Anvers s'ils y trouvaient les mêmes conditions que à Brême."

[34]Loes van der Valk, "Landverhuizers via Rotterdam in de negentiende
eeuw," *Economisch en Sociaal Historisch jaarboek*, XXXIX (1976), 148-171; Dirk
Hoerder, "The Traffic of Emigration via Bremen/Bremerhaven: Merchants' Interests,
Protective Legislation, and Migrants' Experience," *Journal of American Ethnic History*, XIII, No. 3 (1993), 68-101; Rolf Engelsing, *Bremen als Auswandererhafen 1683-
1880* (Bremen, 1961) and Mack Walker, *Germany and the Emigration 1816-1885*
(Cambridge, MA, 1964).

[35]Torsten Feys, "The Emigration Policy of the Belgian Government from
Belgium to the U.S. through the Port of Antwerp 1842-1914" (Unpublished MA thesis,
Ghent University, 2003); E. Spelkens "Belgian Migration to the United States and

York, where a port's reputation was equally important. As the migration flow increased, the chain-migration ties through letters and remittances grew tighter. A network of emigration agents selling pre-paid tickets developed in the US to meet this demand.

Apart from collecting information on business prospects, Belgian consuls were also asked to gather material on migration opportunities. From 1856 onwards circulars sent to the Belgian consuls specified what information about migration was to be included in their annual reports.[36] These reports were completed by special "exploration missions" set up by the envoy in Washington. The collected material was published in *Buletin Consulaire* and *Moniteur Belge*. Parts of the reports often also found their way into the press. To increase access to this information, the authorities decided to establish special information centres in the provincial capitals.[37] This was contrary to what happened in the Netherlands, where migration was barely mentioned in the Dutch consular reports, and no special information centres were established. Further, nothing indicates that special missions to investigate migration possibilities in the US occurred.[38] Indeed, information on opportunities in the US circulating in the Dutch press was often based upon the reports of Belgian officials. The influential report of Auguste-Gabriel Vandersteaten-Ponthoz, the Belgian envoy in Washington, was translated and published in the Netherlands.[39]

Other Overseas Countries at the Beginning of the 20th Century," in Ginette Kurgan van Hentenryk and Spelkens (eds.), *Two Studies on Emigration through Antwerp to the New World* (Brussels, 1976), 51-139; and van der Valk, "Landverhuizers."

[36]An 1884 circular specified that the report had to include the following sections: land, climate and population, legislation regarding foreigners, the best circumstances for emigration, how much capital an emigrant needed, depending on their professions, what emigrants should do on arrival, advice on where to live first, salaries and the cost of living, possibilities for erecting colonies and general observations. AMBZ, Catalogue par matières, Emigration, no. 2946, dl. III, Renseignements et documents fourni à la commission du travail 1886, Chimay to the consuls, 27 December 1884 and 11 August 1886.

[37]Feys, "Emigration Policy;" and Spelkens "Belgian Migration."

[38]The circular of 10 August 1864 specified the data on commerce, industry and shipping that the consular reports needed to include. Information on migrant opportunities was not mentioned. The annual reports of the consul of New York between 1902 and 1906 contain information on immigration through the city and migrant opportunities in general, but they do not seem to have been written to assist compatriots. NA, 2.05.13; Gezantschap in de Verenigde Staten van Amerika, 1814-1940; and 2.05.48.23, Consul, New York (1818), 1844-1954.

[39]Henri A. van Stekelenburg, *Landverhuizing als regionaal verschijnsel van Noord-Brabant naar Noord Amerika 1820-80* (Vught, 1991); Auguste-Gabriel

All of this then reflects migration policy during the nineteenth century: the Dutch tended to discourage migration, while the Belgians tended to encourage it. But the two governments did support attempts to found agricultural colonies in the early 1840s, the Dutch in Suriname and the Belgians in Santo Thomas de Guatemala. Both failed and were marked by high death rates which soured much of the public on migration. The economic crisis in the second half of the 1840s pushed the Belgians to undertake new attempts to encourage migration, while the Dutch continued to try to restrain it. With the help of the Belgian consuls in the US, new agricultural colonies were founded. Aware of the potential of successful migrants to encourage further relocations, the authorities hoped that success would stimulate further migration. Moreover, the government supported a network to send paupers, criminals and ex-prisoners to America. The consul-general in Bern was ordered to direct similar networks in Switzerland to Antwerp. In 1854 a diplomatic conflict erupted with the US when this practice was publicized in the New York press. While the Belgian consul denied the allegations, he urged his government to abolish the network because it not only compromised Antwerp's reputation as a migration port but also jeopardized the opening of the Société de Navigation Transatlantique, which expected migrant transport to provide its main revenues. This marked the end of direct support from the Belgian government to induce its nationals to migrate. But through the diffusion of information on migration opportunities and active support to some American recruiting agents, the Belgian authorities continued to encourage the migration of nationals.[40] The conviction that migration stimulated trade and helped to relieve the country of some of its poorer elements remained current throughout the nineteenth century in Belgium. In the Netherlands, on the contrary, the perspective that this type of migration deprived the country of important human capital prevailed.

Vanderstraeten-Ponthoz, *Rapport sur un voyage d'exploration dans les Etats-Unis d'Amérique du Nord* (Brussels, 1845); and Pieter Stokvis, *De Nederlandse trek naar Amerika 1846-1847* (Leiden, 1977).

[40]Feys, "Emigration Policy;" Feys, "Radeloosheid in crisistijd: pogingen van de Belgische regeringen om een deel van de arme bevolking naar de Verenigde Staten te sturen 1847-1857," *Belgisch Tijdschrift Voor Nieuwste Geschiedenis*, XXXIV, No. 2 (2004) 195-230; Spelkens "Belgian Migration;" Stokvis, *De Nederlandse trek naar Amerika*; van der Valk, "Landverhuizers;" and R. Boumans, "Een onbekend aspect van de Belgische emigratie naar Amerika: De gesubsidieerde emigratie van bedelaars en oud-gevangenen 1850-1856," in Jacques Willequet (ed.), *L'Expansion Belge sous Léopold Ier, 1831-1865* (Brussels, 1965), 476-515.

From Consuls to Shipping Agents and Port to Company Competition

In the early 1870s both Antwerp and Rotterdam opened their long-awaited steamship lines to New York. The Belgian government had abandoned its hopes to launch a national fleet with domestic capital. Instead, it contracted with foreign shipping companies willing to provide a regular postal service and to place their ships on the Belgian register in exchange for an annual subsidy. The authorities quickly reached an agreement with the representatives of the International Navigation Company (INC), a Philadelphia firm created by the Pennsylvania Railroad to found and operate a transatlantic steamship line.[41] In the meantime, the Dutch government invested heavily in its canal and railroad infrastructure to facilitate the transit trade with Germany. New trade agreements with the US were concluded to enhance commercial links. The 1837 laws regulating migrant passage, aimed mainly at preventing migrants from becoming a charge to the state and hampering their passage, were finally adopted in 1861. Indeed, the Dutch even considered subsidizing a steamship line from Flushing, but contemporary projects in Amsterdam and Rotterdam to open lines without state grants stopped the government from doing this.[42] With the foundation of the Red Star Line, as the branch of the INC in Antwerp became known, and the Holland America Line in Rotterdam, the activity of the consuls in defending the reputations of their respective ports shifted to the various companies' shipping and emigration agents. As these companies gained control of most of the migrant traffic through these ports to New York, migrants no longer were thought of solely as coming from Antwerp or Rotterdam but rather as travelling with the Red Star Line and the Holland America Line. In other words, the reputation of the port became linked with the reputation of the company.

A study of the correspondence of the Head Agent of the Holland America Line in New York with the Board of Directors back home reveals that the transition from consuls to shipping agents in producing reliable information on business opportunities, market fluctuations and competition, as well as defending the interests of the home port and company, was gradual.[43] In fact,

---

[41]William H. Flayhart III, *The American Line 1872-1901* (New York, 2000); Flayhart, "The Expansion of American Interests in Transatlantic Commerce and Trade, 1865-1893," in Starkey and Harlaftis (eds.), *Global Markets*, 127-147; Devos, "Belgische Overheidssteun;" and Veraghtert, "De havenbewegingen te Antwerpen."

[42]A.D. Wentholt, *Een brug over de Oceaan: een eeuw geschiedenis van de Holand-Amerika Lijn* (Rotterdam, 1973); Horlings, *Economic Development*; van der Valk, "Landverhuizers;" and Blasing and Langenhuyzen,"Dutch Sea Transport."

[43]Although little correspondence from the first decade survived, the entire general correspondence has been preserved from the appointment of W.H. van der

during the initial years the company was represented by the Dutch consul in New York, who also ran the shipping agency Burlange and Co., which traded predominantly with Dutch and Belgian ports.[44] The Directors were convinced that his function as consul would also serve the interests of the company.[45] But with the line's expansion in 1873, the shipping agency in New York was entrusted to Cazaux van Staphorst, while Funch Edye and Co. remained as shipbrokers. Cazaux's tasks, as described in the contract, focused on establishing contacts with export and import houses and supervising the ships arriving in New York. Priority was to be given to the appointment of a person "of confidence" at the immigration control station at Castle Garden who received a salary of 10,000 *guilders* and promised to abstain from other commercial activities.[46]

The economic crisis of the late 1870s sharply restricted the company's operations, and only at the beginning of the next decade did business pick up again. The assistance of state officials would henceforth concern mainly tariff and legal issues. In 1882 Congress enacted a new Passenger Act to regulate migrant traffic. All European countries with national passenger lines protested against the act as contravening their own laws. The Dutch envoy in Washington lobbied the American government for an international agreement with all the countries involved.[47] His efforts intensified when the authorities adapted

---

Toorn in 1884 and his successors, A. Wierdsma and J. Rypperda Gips. GAR, HAL, 318.02 Directie V, NR 112-118, Correspondentie brieven hoofdagentschap, New York, 1884-1914.

[44]R.C. Burlange was consul in New York from 1855 to 1881; see Hans Krabbendam, "Capital Diplomacy: Consular Activity in Amsterdam and New York, 1800-1940," in George Harinck and Krabbendam (eds.), *Amsterdam-New York: Transatlantic Relations and Urban Identities since 1653* (Amsterdam, 2005).

[45]GAR, HAL, W.A. 9-2, Plate Reuchlin en co, notullen, vennootschap, vergaderingen, Otto Reuchlin to the stockholders, 14 November 1871.

[46]*Ibid.*, W.A. 44, Correspondentie met hoofdagent in New York, H. Cazaux van Staphorst, 1874-1884, contract between Cazaux and NASM, 1874.

[47]The countries involved at the time were Great Britain, Germany, France, Belgium, the Netherlands, Italy and Denmark. These discussions were the result of a prior tentative decision by the American authorities at the end of the 1860s to unify all passenger legislation. In the end, disagreements over jurisdiction prevented an agreement; this led to numerous trials in the US through which the American authorities forced its legislation on ships flying foreign flags. See M. Jones, "Aspects of North Atlantic Migration: Steerage Condition and American Law, 1819-1909," in Klaus Friedland (ed.), *Maritime Aspects of Migration* (Köln, 1989), 321-331; and Jones, "Immigrants, Steamships and Governments: The Steerage Problem," in H.C. Allen and

the law to meet the criticisms of the German and English governments, but an international convention still failed to materialize.[48] Yet in times of need the envoy and consul still intervened to defend the reputation of the port and company. When in the early 1880s the Holland America Line suffered four shipwrecks within two years, its reputation was seriously blackened.[49] As a result, the Dutch government decided to support a campaign in the American press to defend the company's name.[50]

Events pushed the Board of Directors to undertake a drastic reorganization. They decided to send someone from Rotterdam to work under Cazaux van Staphorst in New York. A year later, W.A. van der Toorn replaced Cazaux to run the company's agency, and from then on an increasing number of staff in the US came directly from the Netherlands. Their training in the offices in Rotterdam or Amsterdam familiarized them with the company's philosophy. Moreover, the Directors preferred to appoint nationals to key positions. Coming from outside New York, van der Toorn had a great deal of difficulty establishing himself in the local business community, especially because Cazaux van Staphorst held a grudge for losing his position and did everything in his power to blacken the reputation of both van der Toorn and the Holland America Line. The Head Agent's gateway to credibility in the New York business community seems to have been his membership in the Holland Society of New York, an elitist group composed of Americans who could trace their Dutch roots back to the state's founding fathers. Through John R. Planten, the consul in New York, van der Toorn was introduced to the Society and began to make a name for himself.

Van der Toorn urged the Board to take more aspects of the business into its own hands. He proposed to take charge of the loading and unloading of the ships in New York, following the example set by the Red Star Line. Fur-

---

Roger Thompson (eds.), *Contrast and Connection: Bicentennial Essays in Anglo-American History* (London, 1976), 178-209.

[48]NA, 2.o5.13, Gezantschap te Washington. No. 210 Ingekomen brieven en uitgaande minuten over het vervoer van Landverhuizers; Correspondence between von Weckherlin, envoy, Washington, DC, and Minister of Foreign Affairs, 2 May 1882 until 18 June 1883.

[49]The directors stated in a circular to the captains that they were considering abandoning the passenger trade since the company's reputation had been damaged to such an extent that "freight may be the only thing left to transport." GAR, HAL, 318-02, Collectie Directie, No. 53 Correspondentie privaat kopieboek, November 1884-April 1887, circular to the captains, 2 November 1884.

[50]NA 2.o5.13, Gezantschap te Washington. No. 210 Ingekomen brieven en uitgaande minuten over het vervoer van Lv, Correspondence between von Weckherlin and Minister of Foreign Affairs, 24 April until 20 August 1883.

thermore, he suggested taking control of the freight business in Rotterdam, which was then entrusted to Wambersie and Son. By doing this, he argued, the company's interests would be much better served than by leaving it to ship-brokers. In New York, however, the freight business remained with Funch and Edye. The Holland America Line frequently received interesting propositions from other shipbrokers but feared that the expertise acquired on the Rotter-dam-New York route by Funch and Edye could result in the opening of a rival line on the same route. Unlike the Hamburg-America Line, which stipulated in its contract with Funch and Edye that it could not serve any other company shipping to Hamburg or Bremen, Holland America did not stop the brokers from working for other companies on competing routes. Indeed, Funch and Edye was allowed to act for the firm's Amsterdam rival, the Royal Dutch Steamship Company, on the condition that it share the profits. This meant that a rival profited from the expertise on Dutch-American trade that Funch and Edye had acquired. Moreover, it opened the possibility that an agent of the rival line would be appointed in the offices of Funch and Edye, thus enabling him to gain access to inside information about the Rotterdam-based company. This was already the case with the Antwerp-based White Cross Line for which Funch and Edye also acted as shipbrokers. The Head Agent stressed that the risk of conflicts of interests with the Royal Dutch Steamship Company was more important than the White Cross Line. As well, if business flourished on that route, the opportunistic behaviour of the shipbrokers could not be dis-counted. Despite these risks, management considered this the best way of get-ting informed about and controlling its rival.[51]

The Head Agent gathered vital information on all possible eastbound trade opportunities and on the different routes available. The intense competi-tion between major American railroad companies created interesting opportuni-ties to divert part of the freight and passenger traffic to other American ports. Indeed, this led to the opening of a line to Baltimore and Newport. The New York Central Railroad company even attempted to take over the Holland America Line to counter the competition.[52] Still, the challenges never resulted in diverting a significant share of the passenger traffic away from New York. Even the Red Star and American lines had to transfer most of their business to New York. With the increasing pre-paid market and return migration traffic, the agency in New York gained in importance. The volume of pre-paid tickets

---

[51]GAR, HAL, 318.14 Wentholt Archief, No. 18-3, Prive correspondentie tussen van der Toorn en President J. Wierdsma, van der Toorn to Board of Directors, 2 November 1883 until 22 October 1886; and No. 44, Correspondentie met hoofdagent in New York, H. Cazaux van Staphorst, 1874-1884, correspondence between Board of directors and Cazaux, 22 November 1880 until March 1882.

[52]*Ibid.*, Directie V, No. 114, Correspondentie brieven hoofdagentschap New York 1897-1914, van der Toorn to Board of Directors, 22 November 1898.

sold over the winter served as an indicator of the total migrant traffic, which peaked between May and September. By the early 1880s the Head Agent in New York had to supervise a network of 1400 sub-agents spread over the US. As the company grew, it opened other agencies to control this network. The heads of these new agencies sometimes acted as consuls in their area, as in Chicago and Newport. Given the importance of the passenger business in America, Van der Toorn pressured management to take control of it, too, instead of leaving it to the agency of Morris and Son. This policy would soon be followed by the Hamburg-America line.

Once the Holland America Line neutralized the competition from Amsterdam in 1882, it shifted most of its efforts to competing with the Red Star Line. This rivalry was partly responsible for the failure of the initial conference attempts among continental lines to end the constant rate wars in the North Atlantic passenger business. But even after the foundation of the Nord-Atlantischer Dampfer-Linien Verband, which divided the traffic into pools, tensions between the two companies remained. The German lines acted as mediators. The Holland America Line initially maintained good relations with its German rivals, especially with the Hamburg-America Line. The Dutch company rented docks in Hoboken next to the German berths and moved its offices to Broadway next to those of the Hamburg-America Line. They jointly conspired through lobbying campaigns in the American press and Congress against attempts by the president of the American Line, Clement Griscom, to secure subsidy laws favourable to the INC. Their lobbyist, G. Glavis, an attorney in Washington, followed by de Witt Warner and Claude Bennet, manager of the Congressional Information Bureau, approached Congressmen to prevent the passage of restrictive immigration laws.[53] They also established a Pro-Immigration League headed by Joseph H. Senner, the former Commissioner of

---

[53]The contacts between Glavis and the HAL can be traced back to 1888. He was introduced by van der Toorn to the Board of Directors to defend the Holland America Line over violations of the passenger laws. He was put forward as the lobbyist of the Continental Lines, members of the continental conference in New York which made agreements on eastbound and pre-paid tickets for continental traffic. Until his death he would provide the company with services in various law suits. He also influenced state officials inspecting emigration ports, for example by accompanying Spaulding, the Assistant Secretary of the Treasury, on his mission to Europe in 1892 to report on new laws that might be promulgated regarding passenger traffic. More important, he reported on the debates in Congress regarding the Ship Subsidy bill and immigration legislation. Van der Toorn often ascribed last-minute amendments to these laws in favour of the Dutch and German Steamship lines to the lobbying work of Glavis. He also functioned as an intermediate to channel funds into American presidential campaigns. His salary reached $9000 in 1897, not including extra commissions. After his death in 1898 he was followed by de Witt Warner for two years. In 1901 Claude Bennet took over these tasks as the lobbyist for the steamship lines.

Immigration at New York, which set up a lobbying campaign in the American press to influence public opinion in favour of immigration and to counter the campaigns of the Anti-Immigration League.[54] But the relations between the Dutch and German lines started to become bitter when after the cholera outbreak of 1892 the German companies used sanitary control stations at the eastern borders of Germany to divert the migrant traffic to Bremen and Hamburg.[55] Tensions grew when the *Reichstag* passed a law revoking the concession of emigration agents to contract passengers for the Holland America Line.[56] The Dutch envoy in Berlin lobbied unsuccessfully against the law until the First World War. As the first foreign passenger line, Holland America ordered two ships from German shipyards, naming the first one *Postdam* to regain the favour of German authorities. The company asked Albert Ballin, the head of the Hamburg America Line, to intervene on its behalf, but suspected at the same time that both German lines were behind the scheme. The tensions increased further when half of its stock came into the hands of the German lines during the formation of the International Mercantile Marine Co. (IMMC), Lord Pirrie of Harland and Wolf, which built many of Hamburg America's ships and was one of the main actors in the formation of the IMMC, became a mediator between the Dutch and German lines.[57] He pushed the

---

[54]Two journalists in Washington who worked as correspondents for various prominent American newspapers were paid eighty dollars per week by the German and Dutch lines to agitate against the Ant-Immigration League from 1895 onwards. In 1897, the pro-immigration lobby was established. Prior to his involvement with the shipping lobby, as Immigration commissioner of New York Senner often was described by van der Toorn as a person who worked out compromises and assisted charity institutions protecting migrants, shipping companies and European governments. Senner therefore was the ideal person to counter suspicions that the League was founded by the steamship lines. He travelled around the country to recruit members and established offices all over the US. His salary was $500 dollars a month plus costs.

[55]Hoerder, "Traffic;" and K. Wüstenbecker, "Hamburg and the Transit of East Europeans," in Andreas Fahrmeir, Olivier Faron and Patrick Weil (eds.), *Migration Control in the North Atlantic World: The Evolution of State Practices in Europe and the United States from the French Revolution to the Inter-war Period* (New York, 2003).

[56]The initial proposal consisted of revoking the concessions of all emigration agents working for foreign shipping companies. This triggered strong protests from all companies and governments concerned. In the end the law was amended to return the concessions to all emigration agents except those from the Holland America Line.

[57]Frank Broeze, "Dutch Steamshipping and International Competition: The Holland America Line under Foreign Control 1902-1917," in Gordon Jackson and David M. Williams (eds.), *Shipping, Technology and Imperialism* (Aldershot, 1996), 97-119; Thomas Navin and Marian Sears, "A Study in Merger: Formation of the Inter-

company to improve its relations with Red Star. Furthermore, Holland America strengthened its relations with the White Star Line, with which it constantly exchanged inside information on competitors. In short, relations between the companies were subject to constant change.

The interwoven relations between major passenger liner companies in New York were a logical consequence of the concentration of their agencies within a few square miles. Sometimes they even shared the same building. The Head Agent in New York therefore served as a vital information source on competitors and how they related to each other. As David Williams has argued, a focus on the port of arrival, in this case New York, might improve our understanding of conference dynamics. The difficulties of the dispersed location of the different ports encountered in previous studies might be reduced through this approach.[58] Especially in the case of migrant trade, this has an extra dimension because of the system of pre-paid tickets used by between thirty and fifty percent of the migrants who crossed the Atlantic after the American Civil War. Further studies of information flows on business opportunities and competitors flowing back from the Head Agent to the Board of Directors will shed more light on the organization of these companies. The pro-immigration lobby campaign is only one aspect of how these companies tried to influence migration flows. The lack of knowledge about the organization of the market for migrant transport by major passenger lines contributes to the assertion that has stood until now that these companies played only a minor role in influencing migration flows. Little is known about their advertising campaigns and the information they contained. Studies focusing on the organization of the major passenger liners, advertising campaigns and their relation to other companies should contribute to a better understanding of the influence of these shipping enterprises on migration flows in general.

Conclusion

As Carl Strikwerda pointed out, most migration historians who stress the demographic and economic causes of migration have attributed at best a secondary role to the state's influence on migrant flows. During the last two centuries, policies adopted by Western nations have affected migration, despite the

---

national Maritime Company," *Business History Review*, XXVIII, No. 4 (1954) 291-328; and Ville, *Transport*.

[58]David M. Williams, "Recent Trends in Maritime and Port History," in Reginald Loyen, *et al.* (eds.), *Struggling for Leadership: Antwerp-Rotterdam Port Competition between 1870-2000* (Leuven, 2003), 11-26; and Greenhill, "Competition or Cooperation."

lack of an international migration regime, through trade and diplomacy.[59] The consular activity supports this and shows that notwithstanding the lack of migration laws, governments did outline migration policies for their nationals. It proves that they were well aware of chain migration and the significance of information flows on migration opportunities. The slow development of immigration and emigration laws throughout the nineteenth century contrasts with the constant changes in migrant transport legislation which resulted from the competition for migrant traffic. Because of the importance of the migrant trade, some governments tried to attract part of the flow to their ports, and by so doing facilitated migration out of other countries. Consuls occupied a key position to develop the trade by defending the reputation of emigration ports and providing information on rival ports, legal aspects and business opportunities concerning the migrant trade abroad. By juxtaposing the activities of Dutch and Belgian consuls, differences in migration and maritime policies stand out. The opening of a transatlantic steamship line was a vital requirement for the development of migration ports. The efforts of the Belgian government to open such a line and to attract the migrant trade to Antwerp stimulated foreign interest in opening trade routes to the Belgian port. The choice of the American INC to open a line in Antwerp seems a logical consequence of previous failures. The opening of a steamship line further illustrates that competition between ports was a driving force behind the development of the migrant trade. With the establishment of a steamship line the role of the consuls decreased. In the case of the Holland America Line, the transition was gradual. First, both positions were combined; later, the consul introduced shipping agents into the local business community. The consuls would still be called upon to defend the company's interests in legal and tariff matters. Shipping agents followed up the consul's efforts by gathering information on business opportunities and competitors. With the development of the trade, the importance of the reputation of the port shifted in part to the reputation of the company.

Little is known about the activities of the shipping agents and shipping companies in influencing migration.[60] Competition for the migrant trade triggered a propaganda war and widespread networks of agents, about which few beyond Kristian Hvidt and Berit Brattne have written.[61] Moreover, their con-

---

[59]Carl Strikwerda, "Tides of Migrations, Currents of History: The State Economy and the Transatlantic Movement of Labour on the Nineteenth and Twentieth Centuries," *International Review of Social History*, XLIV, No. 3 (1999), 367-394.

[60]Baines, *Emigration from Europe*.

[61]Berit Brattne and Sune Akerman, "The Importance of the Transport Sector for Mass Emigration," in Harald Runblom and Hans Norman (eds.), *From Sweden to America: A History of the Migration* (Minneapolis, 1976), 176-200; and Kristian Hvidt,

clusions about the impact of the shipping companies diverged. The availability of agents across Europe to organize the voyage of the migrant from their village to the final destination and their constant advertising campaigns in local newspapers brought the New World a lot closer in the mental map of many Europeans. The integration of both worlds was further enhanced by the networks of agents in the US selling pre-paid tickets and the increasing number of return migrants. Sources that show how emigration agents linked shipping companies to the individual migrant are nearly non-existent. Nonetheless, studies analyzing the strategies of major shipping lines to position themselves in the migrant trade may shed more light on their influence on migrant movements. The dynamics of inter-firm competition briefly touched upon here shows, for instance, that these companies influenced American public opinion and Congress to prevent the passage of restrictive immigration. Governments involved in the migrant trade and with passenger liners influenced how people migrated. Further research will have to determine the extent to which they affected information flows about migration routes and opportunities, and the impact they had on migration patterns.

Flight to America: The Social Background of 300,000 Danish Emigrants (New York, 1975).

The Role of Foreign-born Agents in the Development of Mass Migrant Travel through Britain, 1851-1924

Nicholas J. Evans[1]

Introduction

Between 1820 – when the United States first began to record immigration – and 1924, when the door was firmly shut, over thirty-six million people are known to have migrated to the US.[2] They represented a substantial proportion of the 19.1 million passengers who left Britain between 1853 and 1913, of whom 13.3 million were British and Irish passengers and 5.3 million aliens.[3] Whether the passengers sojourned, settled permanently or subsequently returned to Europe, their movement to, through and from Britain generated significant income streams for transatlantic shipping companies. The trade benefited not only those who transported the migrants but also companies engaged in ship construction and the port-cities that supported both seaborne travel and associated shipbuilding. This essay examines the ways in which Britain profited from the foreign component of this passenger trade and in particular at the employment of foreign-born agents within Britain and throughout the continent to develop the business. Individuals who worked as commercial agents, translators and lodging-house keepers in Britain, or as Agents General on the continent, proved as pivotal to the development of the passenger operations of the

[1]Earlier versions of this paper were presented at the CHORD Workshop on Migration and Commerce 1500-2000, at the University of Wolverhampton in April 2005 and the international symposium on "The Impact of Maritime and Migration Networks on Transatlantic Labour Migration during the Eighteenth to the Twentieth Centuries" at the European University Institute in Florence in November 2005. The author is grateful for useful feedback from participants at both events.

[2]Imre Ferenczi, *International Migrations* (2 vols., New York, 1929; reprint, New York, 1969), 394-395, noted that 36,242,459 immigrant aliens arrived in the US between 1820 and 1924.

[3]Norman Carrier and James Jeffery, *External Migration: A Study of the Available Statistics, 1815-1950* (London, 1953), 90-91. The data exclude 438,448 passengers whose nationality was "not distinguished."

British merchant marine in the late nineteenth century as the more celebrated use of foreign crew – in particular, Lascar seamen – on the development of long-haul freight routes. German, Danish, Swedish, Norwegian and latter Russian agents all helped British companies such as Cunard, White Star, Anchor, Guion and Union-Castle to develop and maintain a powerful grip on specific transoceanic features of travel, despite the challenges posed by foreign competitors such as Hamburg-America and Norddeutscher Lloyd. Without the use of such foreign-born agents – within and without Britain – it is doubtful whether British companies could have retained their leading role in this highly competitive aspect of seaborne commerce. In turn, the use of such foreign-born agents demonstrates the complex and multi-faceted measures adopted by mid-Victorian shipping entrepreneurs to control transatlantic passenger shipping. Before, during and after shares of steerage traffic had been established through transatlantic passenger conferences, British companies gained a commercial advantage that their European rivals struggled to reduce.[4] Central to this advantageous position, I argue, was the procurement and retention of services offered by foreign-born "agents."

The Emergence of the British Emigrant Market

Britain's share of the mass migrant business comprised three elements: the British, Irish and alien markets. While the first relied heavily upon the expansion of the domestic railway network before ocean travel emerged as a large-scale affair, the latter two necessitated a prior seaborne journey into Britain by would-be emigrants.[5] The use of surplus shipping in the late 1840s for use in the migrant trade initially concentrated upon demand from the Irish market. Later, as rates of Irish emigration lessened, this tonnage was used to meet increasing demand from British emigration – and in particular the exodus from Britain's urban centres that were linked by railway to Liverpool, Glasgow or London. The linkage between out-migration and the expansion of the domestic

---

[4]For a discussion of the cartelisation of the traffic, see Drew Keeling, "The Transportation Revolution and Transatlantic Migration, 1850-1914," *Research in Economic History*, XIX (1999), 39-74; and Keeling, "Transatlantic Shipping Cartels and Migration between Europe and America, 1880-1914," *Essays in Economic and Business History*, XVII (1999), 195-213.

[5]Angela H. McCarthy, *Irish Migrants in New Zealand, 1840-1937* (Woodbridge, 2005), 97-98 and 101-107; and Nicholas J. Evans, "Aliens *en route*: European Transmigration via the UK, 1836-1914" (Unpublished PhD thesis, University of Hull, 2006).

railway network was a vital component in the development of mass migration.[6] The extension of the trans-Pennine rail route across Britain's industrial and manufacturing heartlands – first between Liverpool and Manchester, then to Leeds, before eventually extending to Hull – transformed emigrant flows across the country. British workers in the east of Britain now looked to Liverpool, not Hull or London, as the point of embarkation for the US and, to a lesser extent, Canada. The port of Liverpool, central to both the Irish outflow and out-migration from the trans-Pennine towns and cities of Hull, Bradford, Leeds, Huddersfield, Sheffield and Manchester, emerged as the prime emigration port in Britain and Ireland. Other ports, such as Hull, London and Aberdeen, which had previously handled regional swathes of emigrants, declined rapidly.

The process of migrating through what had become one of Europe's leading emigrant ports provided opportunities for entrance into a labour market that centred on those wishing to relocate from Europe to America. The bulk of the emigrants (at least until 1867) were Irish, many of whom were able to make the crossing as a result of remittances or pre-paid passages from the US.[7] Such remittances supplied migrants with the necessary funds to join relatives already established abroad. Equally important, they also enabled agents engaged in the trade to profit from their fellow countrymen's needs. As David Fitzpatrick and Angela McCarthy have shown, personal connections, and the advice they were able to offer, were a key factor in determining the eventual destination of migrants.[8] Yet such informal networks were also influential in conditioning the development of the mass migrant market as the business became polarised on key maritime centres, such as Liverpool and later Glasgow.

Between the arrival of thousands of Irish emigrants and their subsequent re-embarkation, a residue of the labour flow remained. Liverpool's Irish community had grown to 83,813 by 1851.[9] Two decades later it was still high at 76,761.[10] Irish lodging-house keepers and emigrant runners used their skills

---

[6]J.D. Gould, "European International Emigration, 1815-1914," *Journal of European Economic History*, VIII, No. 3 (1979), 593-677.

[7]Francis E. Hyde, *Cunard and the North Atlantic, 1840-1973: A History of Shipping and Financial Management* (London, 1975), 61.

[8]David Fitzpatrick, *Oceans of Consolation: Personal Accounts of Irish Migration to Australasia* (Cork, 1994); and Angela H. McCarthy, *Narratives of Irish and Scottish Migration. 1921-1965: "For Spirit and Adventure"* (Manchester, forthcoming).

[9]Great Britain, *Census, 1851* (London, 1852), "Population Tables," 664.

[10]Great Britain, *Census of England and Wales, 1871* (London, 1871), "Population Abstracts," 440.

to furnish the needs of British domestic emigration as well as their Irish counterparts. That many of the Irish-born migrants became involved in the emigrant business is not surprising. Running lodging-houses, working as emigrant runners or serving as crew members aboard ocean-going vessels, men such as Dennis Currie and William McDonald typified this trend.[11] As recorded in the 1881 Census, Currie, aged sixty-eight, worked as an emigration agent at 46 Regent Street in Liverpool. He had an Irish-born wife, had children born in Liverpool and employed British and Irish staff to run his emigrant-*cum*-seafarer lodging-house. He housed a multitude of different nationals, but most were British or Irish. McDonald, aged sixty-five, identified himself as both an emigration agent and lodging-house keeper at 45 Regent Street. He had an Irish-born wife but had come to Britain with his young Irish-born family in the 1870s. He kept an all-Irish business that was used by only Irish emigrants at the time of the 1881 census. Moreover, other British migrants, such as Thomas Winmill, a forty-one-year-old Welshman, had already migrated to the US in the late 1860s, where his eldest child was born, before returning to Britain in 1879 to establish himself as an emigration agent. These people profited from a trade that was open to all, but in which each gained from his or her personal knowledge of the market. Crucially to non-British migrants leaving British ports, and thus central to this paper, the rail route across Britain also opened up the market to a new customer – the foreign-born emigrant.

Foreign-born Workers and Alien Emigration from Britain

The role of Britain as a carrier of foreign-born emigrants emerged with the age of the steamship. During the early days of steamship travel, east coast ports such as Hull, Leith and London, along with the south coast port of Southampton, received foreign emigrants before arranging for their subsequent seaborne out-migration. London, as table 1 shows, gained the lion's share of the market in the late 1840s. But this market was of limited scale and variable nature. Passengers were transported to Britain on specially-chartered North Sea steamers before re-embarking on scheduled sailing ships previously filled solely by Irish and British emigrants. The extension of the trans-Pennine rail route to Hull in 1851 changed this. Not only did Liverpool dominate the domestic and Irish markets, but it also increasingly handled the bulk of the foreign-born migrants increasingly arriving in Britain each week aboard scheduled North Sea steamships operating between the Humber and the European ports of Hamburg, Bremen, Antwerp, Rotterdam, Gothenburg, Oslo and Copenhagen.

---

[11]Church of Jesus Christ of Latter-day Saints, *1881 British Census* CD-ROM (Salt Lake City, 1998). The 1881 Census CD-Rom was originally supplied with Viewer 2.0. If a later viewer (Church of Jesus Christ of Latter-day Saints, *Family History Resource File-Viewer 3.0* [Salt Lake City, 1999]) was used, then queries for "emigration agent + Liverpool" or "emigration agent + Hull" are possible.

While Hull declined as an emigrant port, thousands of transmigrants increasingly arrived at its docks *en route* to Liverpool. The additional Liverpool-bound traffic helped the Merseyside port to consolidate its position as the premier emigration port of Europe, a role the city would retain for the next three decades. The scale and regularity of the phenomenon outstripped other transit ports and previous levels of Canada- and US-bound emigrants who had sailed for Québec and New York from Hull.[12] By 1854 more German emigrants left through Liverpool than via any other port, including Hamburg and Bremen. They reached the Mersey port having traversed northern Britain, or transmigrated via the ports of Hull and Grimsby within fourteen days of arrival. Transmigration, or the supply to ocean liners of non-British, third-class European passengers, became an important aspect of British short-sea and transoceanic shipping. In particular, the route between Hamburg and New York (via Hull and Liverpool) emerged as the key artery in transatlantic shipping. As table 1 demonstrates, between 1836 and 1914 over two million Europeans transmigrated through Hull, nearly 500,000 via neighbouring Grimsby and over 100,000 via London.

The role of the foreign-born in the development of this aspect of the British passenger market was essential. The key trading route was between Hamburg and Hull. Not surprisingly, German immigrants quickly became central to the business. Like the Irish at Liverpool, they settled at the British points of entry closest to where they had first landed. Germans such as Henry Hare and James Ellerman, both of Hamburg, not only settled in a port on Britain's east coast but also helped to establish the transmigrant route from Hamburg to Liverpool via Hull. Having developed commercial networks with British companies engaged in the shipment of passengers, freight and goods, many followed the pattern of changing from ships' captains to shipowners and importers to emigration agents. Others established lodging-houses in Hull, or secured roles as translators, clerks or commercial agents. Such middlemen were fundamental to the development of the trade and were to be found at each stage in the migrants' journey westward. The sight of the foreign-born at such ports was impressive. It did not cause alarm among contemporaries, unlike anti-alien sentiment in London and Leeds, where foreign labourers were seen as under-cutting local labour rates and establishing visible alien enclaves. Their presence in key maritime centres such as Hull, Glasgow and London was instead welcomed as contributing to the vitality of a port's commerce. As Joseph Fletcher noted in 1899, at Hull's points of entry:

> There is always a crowd of heterogeneous human elements.
> Here one sees almost every type of the European family, to-

---

[12]John Dixon, "Aspects of Yorkshire Emigration to North America, 1760-1880" (Unpublished PhD thesis, University of Leeds, 1981).

gether with men from the far-off corners of the earth. A Lincolnshire shepherd rubs shoulders with a swarthy Lascar; fair-haired Swedes lounge against the railings beyond which a party of emigrant Russian Jews, greasy and unkempt, are keeping strict watch over a few miserable belongings; Danes, Germans, Spaniards, Italians chatter...in their own tongues to the accompaniment of the louder voices of Yorkshire or Lincolnshire folk who have come into Hull to market. Along the streets leading from the Humber side towards the centre of the town a similarly mixed crowd is always moving.[13]

Table 1
Number of European Transmigrants Arriving at Britain's Three Largest East Coast Ports, 1836-1913

Period	Hull	Grimsby	London
1836-1839	2221	0	250
1840-1844	307	0	101
1845-1849	734	0	21,804
1850-1854	53,884	1,033	28,309
1855-1859	17,873	31	8671
1860-1864	N/A	N/A	N/A
1865-1869	124,052	N/A	N/A
1870-1874	175,533	N/A	N/A
1875-1879	N/A	N/A	N/A
1880-1884	197,932	3769	N/A
1885-1889	271,351	37,829	N/A
1890-1894	237,305	71,168	531
1895-1899	110,015	48,516	896
1900-1904	282,609	120,208	2046
1905-1909	320,258	123,608	32,139
1910-1913	215,252	88,230	27,466
Total	2,009,326	494,392	122,213

Sources: Great Britain, The National Archives, Public Record Office (TNA, PRO), Home Office (HO) 3/1-120, 1836-1860; Hull City Archives, TCM/172-181, minutes of the Kingston upon Hull Town Council Sanitary Committee, 1865-1877, and WHG1/20-46, minutes of the Hull and Goole Port Sanitary Authority, 1888-1913; North East Lincolnshire Archives, 1/113/3-7, minutes of the Grimsby Port Sanitary Authority, 1884-1913; and *British Parliamentary Papers* (*BPP*), "Reports and Statistical Tables Relating to Emigration and Immigration of the United Kingdom," 1890-1905, and "Annual Reports of His Majesty's Inspector, with Statement as to the Expulsion of Aliens," 1906-1913.

---

[13]Joseph Fletcher, *A Picturesque History of Yorkshire* (6 vols., London, 1901), I, 44.

The trade via Hull and Grimsby, and small ports such as Goole, Harwich, Leith and West Hartlepool, was timed to coincide with the scheduled departure of steamships from Liverpool. Thus, most of the transmigrant passengers arrived via scheduled steamers at Hull on a Sunday or Wednesday evening in order to reach steamships leaving Liverpool on Wednesday or Saturday, respectively. By the early 1850s not only were thousands of Germans being transported through Britain but also their needs were being met by their own countrymen who profited from the travellers' ignorance of English. Signs printed in German were produced for the train journey between Hull and Liverpool. Any delay before moving on meant a stay in a lodging-house. These small and overcrowded hovels offered basic accommodation to tired travellers. Generally one-man businesses, they profited from the migrants' need for shelter between their arrival and the train journey across Britain. Such lodging-houses fed the hungry traveller in batches of about eighty. Their owners were typified by men such as Paul Julius Drasdo and Harry Lazarus who established local agencies in the port of Hull during the late nineteenth century. Drasdo, an immigrant from Berlin in 1880, married the daughter of one of Hull's emigration agents (John W. Fett of Germany); after the passage of the Aliens Act, 1905, the Home Office appointed him as Hull's official Immigration Officer for which he met (for a fee) each vessel bringing aliens to Hull and arranged transport for those who had not already paid for onward rail travel. He spoke several languages, including German, Yiddish and Russian, and helped the migrants during their medical inspections and disembarkation.

The use of foreign-born "agents" was restricted to Britain. Other lodging-house keepers at Britain's points of re-embarkation, such as Joseph Jackson, an emigration agent of Earle Street in Liverpool, catered for the needs of foreign migrants at Britain's ports of re-embarkation. Jackson reached the US via Liverpool. He had been born in Denmark, married a German and migrated to the US, before returning to Britain and becoming a naturalised British subject in Liverpool. Austrian Charles Neurkloff, aged forty-eight, a hotel manager at 39 Paradise Street, settled with his Austrian-born wife. They employed a German porter, a Liverpudlian domestic, a cook from Ireland and servants from the Isle of Man, Hampshire and Ireland to cater for the needs of their ninety-three Polish, seventy-three Swedish, eleven German, eight Norwegian and four Danish emigrant customers. Other emigrant hotels were run by British- or Irish-born agents who employed Swedes, Poles, Danes or Germans as translators and interpreters – reflecting the diverse market sailing from Liverpool. In total, the port handled one-third of all immigrants entering the US from all sources, and the role of non-British migrants *en route* and *in situ* was quite evident. As figure 1 demonstrates, at the time of the 1881 Census the Irish played a major part in the Liverpool trade, followed by their English and German counterparts. These three groups represented eighty-nine percent of those listed in the Census as emigration agents.

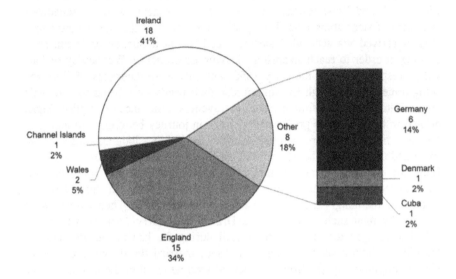

Figure 1:   Country of Birth of Emigration Agents at Liverpool in 1881

Source: Church of Jesus Christ of Latter-day Saints, *1881 British Census and National Index, England, Scotland, Wales, Channel Islands, Isle of Man, and Royal Navy CD-ROM* (Salt Lake City, 1998).

Importance of Continental Agents

The use of foreign-born agents was not restricted to Britain. Other agents on the continent also worked on behalf of British companies and helped British lines to challenge the geographically advantageous position of German, French, Belgian and Dutch shipping companies. They did so alongside the sons of British merchant houses, such as the Wilberforces and Maisters (both of Hull), who had for several generations sent sons to represent British merchant family interests in Scandinavia and Russia.[14] Agencies such as John West Wilson of Gothenburg, Bachke and Co. of Drontheim and Heitmann of Christiania emerged as powerful forces in the development and maintenance of the transmigrant market. Each North Sea shipping company and, in turn, transoceanic shipping firm, became reliant on the successful work of agents to maintain a constant supply of third-class steerage passengers via Britain. Agents-General, a term normally associated with British emigrants bound for parts of the British Empire under assisted schemes promoting the British settlement of

---

[14]Gordon Jackson, *Hull in the Eighteenth Century. A Study in Economic and Social History* (London, 1972), 120-121.

colonial destinations, were employed in key maritime centres and given legal and commercial powers to represent British lines.[15] They managed vast networks of sub-agents who were employed on commission.[16] Robin Bastin has highlighted how lines such as Hamburg-America employed 3200 such agents in 1890.[17] Throughout the 1890s, Cunard spent an average of £50,000 per annum on domestic and foreign agents.[18] Such agents had the local knowledge and personal networks needed to develop sufficient trade. Most also had alternative sources of income and worked part-time on behalf of Agents-General established in major European ports. Their importance in controlling westward-bound emigration was demonstrated in advertising literature produced by British companies. The Wilson Line of Hull stated in its list of mail services for 1907 that:

> The allotment of berths to England has to be left to the Agents at the port of embarkation ... thus passengers from Drontheim, Christiansund, or Aelsund should secure berths through Messrs. Bachke & Co., Drontheim; from Bergen or Stavanger through Mr. Ole R. Olsen, Bergen; from Christiania or Christiansand through Messrs. H. Heitmann & Son, Christiania.[19]

Companies such as the Wilson Line of Hull supplied lines like Cunard and White Star, both of Liverpool, with large numbers of third-class emigrants. Extensive networks of British and European agents assisted Liverpool- and Glasgow-based shipping companies to maximise passenger capacity on transatlantic routes and helped ever-larger ocean liners to run more profitably. The close correlation between the earnings of Agents-General and flows of westward-bound emigrants can be seen by comparing the earnings of the Wilson Lines' Gothenburg-based Agent-General with the number of Scandinavian

---

[15]Marjory Harper, *Emigration from Scotland between the Wars: Opportunity or Exile?* (Manchester, 1998), 41-69.

[16]Kristian Hvidt, "Emigration Agents: The Development of a Business and its Methods," *Scandinavian Journal of History*, III, No. 2 (1978), 185.

[17]Robin Bastin, "Cunard and the Liverpool Emigrant Traffic, 1860-1900" (Unpublished MA thesis, University of Liverpool, 1971), 16.

[18]*Ibid.*

[19]University of Hull Archives and Special Collections, DEW 8/14, *Wilson Line of Steamers – Particulars of Royal Mail Passenger and Cargo Steamers – Summer Season 1907* (Hull, 1907), 8.

transmigrants arriving at Hull and Grimsby for the period 1907-1913 (see figure 2). While it is difficult to ascertain comprehensively whether such "agents" served as a push factor in augmenting rates of emigration, they did channel streams of people who had already taken the decision to leave Europe towards the services of British steamship operators.

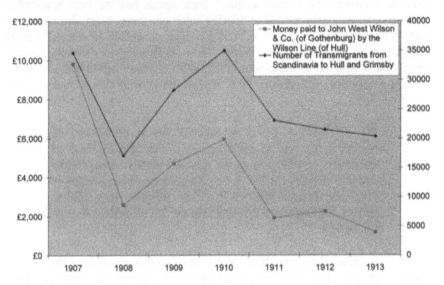

Figure 2:   Earnings of the Wilson Line's Gothenburg Agent-General, 1907-1913, Compared with the Number of Scandinavian Transmigrants Arriving at Hull and Grimsby from Scandinavia

Source: University of Hull Archives and Special Collections, DEW (2)/3/41-48, "Financial Statements of the Thomas Wilson and Sons, Ltd.," 1907-1913; and *BPP*, "Annual Reports of His Majesty's Inspector, with Statement as to the Expulsion of Aliens," 1906-1913.

   The work of such agents therefore cannot be understated. The domestic emigrant market had peaked in the 1880s: the Irish market total crested in 1853 at 162,649; the British in 1883 at 320,118; and the German in 1881 at 220,902.[20] Instead of diverting spare tonnage elsewhere, new passenger markets were opened on behalf of British companies by their foreign-born agents in Scandinavia in the 1860s, Finland in the 1880s and the Baltic in the 1890s. They led to longer-term peaks in the supply of emigrants seeking work predominantly in the US. While it is impossible to calculate the financial benefit

---

[20]All figures are based on total out-migration to all countries from each respective region. Britain's out-migration would grow again in the first decade of the twentieth century; Ferenczi, *International Migration*, I, 386, 417 and 636.

such companies derived from foreign-born agents and individuals, it is clear that they were vital to the long-term success of British-based companies in monopolising the indirect, and thus direct passenger, trades. The passenger operations of Cunard, White Star, Guion, American, Dominion, Anchor and Allan thus saw such migrants as important aspects of their businesses. Aliens seeking to relocate between Europe and North America were an integral feature of transoceanic passenger shipping.

Table 2
Importance of the Alien Market to British Passenger Shipping, 1871-1899

Type of Passenger	United States	%	British North America	%	Australasia	%	All Other Places	%
British	3,844,432	67	648,431	72	788,870	97	529,686	73
Foreigners	1,820,549	32	256,009	28	23,248	3	110,348	15
Not distinguished	37,790	1	1337	0	623	0	85,999	12
Total	5,702,771	100	905,777	100	812,741	100	726,033	100

Source: BPP, "Reports and Statistical Tables Relating to Emigration and Immigration of the United Kingdom," 1890-1905.

The alien market, as shown in table 2, represented thirty-two percent of those bound for the US and twenty-eight percent of those for British North America (Canada). By 1907 the transmigrant business had grown to represent thirty percent of Britain's passenger business. Ten percent of all those arriving in New York had first travelled through the port of Hull, and an even larger number had first migrated via the port of Liverpool. Maritime economies at Hull, Grimsby, Harwich, London, Southampton, Liverpool and Glasgow were bolstered by such business. Between 1890 and 1913, of all those emigrating to Canada and the US, eighty-three percent of Scandinavians transmigrated via Britain, as did twenty-two percent of Russians, twenty-seven percent of Belgians and twelve percent of Dutch migrants. Yet after the entrance of British companies into the transatlantic passenger conferences in 1899 the era of commercial rivalry changed. Agents were still an integral feature of the business; their role in Britain, however, had lessened. Pre-paid tickets reduced the need for agents working in Britain, and references to such agencies virtually disappeared from British trade directories. While the British government employed those with foreign-language skills, companies selling travel directed their energies towards the emerging cruise industry.[21] Agreements on the North Sea and North Atlantic reduced the need for local agents, and only

---

[21]Lorraine Coombs and Alexander Varias, *Tourist Third Cabin: Steamship Travel in the Interwar Years* (New York, 2003), 35-64.

Agents-General retained their status. The commercial significance of monopolies was supplanted by the greater availability (and thus accessibility) of choice. The European labourer choosing to relocate within the transatlantic labour market could thus travel aboard established emigrant services from Hamburg, Bremen, Antwerp, Rotterdam, Le Havre, Liverpool, Southampton, London or Glasgow, or via alternative emigrant ports such as Libau, Oslo, Copenhagen, Trieste, Marseille or several Greek and Mediterranean cities.[22] In Britain the use of lodging-houses at the port of entry lessened as scheduled services and integrated transport systems eradicated the need for port-based lodgings.

The trade in European migrants travelling through British ports peaked in 1907. During that year over 172,438 transmigrants travelled through Britain. With the outbreak of war in 1914 it came to an abrupt end. When the business resumed after the end of the First World War, the market had been transformed. In 1921 the US began to restrict immigration under the Per Centum Act. These reduced flows were further restricted in 1923 under the Immigration Restriction Act. Yet the business of transatlantic shipping changed more markedly – for shipping operators – in July 1923 when passenger shipping began to be increasingly managed by US immigration officials in order to level out the influx of immigrants throughout the year.[23] It prevented a repeat of scenes such as that in May 1923 when too many immigrants arrived in New York, and the US suspended transatlantic immigration from Britain.[24] Under the new rules introduced in 1923, a maximum of one-fifth of the annual quota for each country was permitted to arrive in the US each month. The annual quota, starting in July 1923, was, according to *The Times*, due to have been filled by the end of November.[25] For shipping lines it brought an abrupt end to the regularity of scheduled weekly emigrant services from Britain that had helped to maintain the profitability on transatlantic services during the previous century. Compounded by the Immigration Restriction Act of 1923, it affected an aspect of the trade Britain had once cherished so much – the alien market. Six years after the latter halted the movement of European labour to the US, further immigration restrictions – this time in South Africa – hampered the British alien market yet further. British shipping companies, limited by such

---

[22]See USCIS History Office and Library, US Department of Homeland Security, "Report of the Trans-Atlantic Passenger Movement, 1899-1917."

[23]Marjory Harper and Nicolas J. Evans, "Socio-economic Dislocation and Inter-war Emigration to Canada and the United States: A Scottish Snapshot," *Journal of Imperial and Commonwealth History*, XXXIV, No. 4 (2006), 529-552.

[24]*The Times*, 31 May and 1 June 1923.

[25]*Ibid.*, 2, 17 and 19 July 1923.

foreign and imperial legislation, increasingly used ships that had once carried aliens to or from Britain for the emerging cruise industry. British people increasingly travelled to see the alien in native lands – without disturbing western labour markets – when formerly thousands had journeyed through Britain each week.

Conclusion

Unscrupulous foreigners who preyed upon their unsuspecting fellow nationals are often portrayed in the historiography as an ugly scourge on Britain's migrant past. Yet as this essay has demonstrated, immigrants who worked as emigration agents and lodging-house keepers brought great benefit to the British merchant marine while assisting their fellow countrymen to transmigrate via Britain. The revenue that ports such as Liverpool and Hull gained through passengers is indisputable, but the role of foreigners in encouraging indirect migration is often forgotten. That foreign-born agents had experienced some part of the migrant processes themselves is an obvious – yet equally ignored – feature of life in nineteenth- and twentieth-century passenger shipping. How better for a seller to convince others than through first-hand experience? Foreign-born agents recognised as early as the 1830s that their own experiences could generate income – for either themselves or the companies they represented. The alien profited from the desire of others to relocate overseas. The agencies they developed became vital in maintaining Britain's economic domination of transoceanic travel. Yet their work was also crucial in capturing the market *in situ*. While hundreds of thousands of aliens arrived and settled in Britain, and thousands re-migrated from Britain having remained there for some time, the majority of those arriving, at least several million, used Britain and its ports as transit stations through which to reach transoceanic destinations. Most of them thus arrived as transmigrants and journeyed through Britain alongside thousands of alien tourists. They were lured to Britain by the revolution in transoceanic transport – led foremost by British-based shipping companies. Unlike the alien influx that remained in Britain, which was largely in the hands of foreign merchant fleets, the flow of transmigrants was in the hands of British companies, and until the US immigration acts of the 1920s this represented a significant, if often ignored, aspect of maritime trade on North Atlantic routes.

Transatlantic Emigration and Maritime Transport from Greece to the US, 1890-1912: A Major Area of European Steamship Company Competition for Migrant Traffic

Nicolas Manitakis

"American fever" reached Greece in the 1890s, generating a huge migration towards the US that lasted until 1924 when, due to restrictive measures passed by the American Congress, the stream of migrants slowed. It has been estimated that during this period more than 520,000 Greeks crossed the Atlantic to seek opportunities in the New World.[1] This enormous human relocation produced a large range of migration services, especially in relation to the transatlantic transport of migrants sailing from Greek ports. What is special about the Greek migrant services market is that from its early stages it was highly internationalized and intensively competitive. Since the beginning of the massive outflow, there was fierce competition among the numerous foreign and the few domestic shipping companies that targeted the Greek clientele. This essay defines the various forms of competition between maritime firms in the Greek migrant market and traces its evolution throughout the boom years of massive transatlantic migration from the eastern Mediterranean.

From the Atlantic to the Mediterranean Market for Migration Services

We need first to place the Greek migrant market in its broader regional and continental context within southern Europe. While migration and maritime historians tend to treat the European market for migrant services as heterogeneous, it is more useful to divide it into two broad spheres: the Atlantic (northern Europe) and Mediterranean (southern Europe). The Atlantic migrant market appeared first in the second half of the nineteenth century, and its growth was due to the massive movement from northern, and later central and northeast, Europe. It is well known that the enormous demand for maritime trans-

---

[1] On Greek emigration to the US, see Theodore Saloutos, *The Greeks in the United States* (Cambridge, MA, 1964); Charles C. Moskos, *Greek Americans: Struggle and Success* (New Brunswick, NJ, 1989); and Alexandros Kitroeff, "Transatlantic Emigration from Greece," in Christos Hadziiossif (ed.), *History of Greece in the Twentieth Century* (Athens, 2002, in Greek).

port from this part of Europe led to the creation of a number of prosperous and vigorous steamship companies. These were mainly British, German and French, and they operated from many of the major ports of northern Europe. For example, Cunard and White Star sailed from Liverpool and Southampton; Norddeutscher Linien and Hamburg-America from Bremen and Hamburg; and Compagnie Generale Transatlantique from Le Havre and Cherbourg.[2]

During the last decades of the nineteenth century, the Atlantic market expanded to the emerging Mediterranean emigration zone. Indeed, northern European companies operating from Atlantic ports could count on a rapidly increasing clientele from southern Europe. A growing number of Italian, and later Greek and Ottoman, immigrants heading to the US arrived by sea and rail at the Atlantic departure ports, where they embarked on the transatlantic steam liners of the large northern European shipping companies.

At the turn of the century, as demand for migrant transport declined somewhat in the northern parts of Europe, it rose quickly in the Mediterranean zone, which became increasingly important for the Atlantic providers of migration services. To become more attractive to this new market, these companies made extensive use of advertising and promotional offers. They also organised and financed, at their own expense, the journey from Mediterranean ports to the major Atlantic ports, often covering ship, train and hotel expenses. In so doing they followed a model established in the last decades of the nineteenth century to facilitate the transfer of emigrants from the hinterland of Europe to the western and northern ports of embarkation.[3]

Some northern European steamship companies, however, by the 1890s considered it more reasonable to transfer their transport activities directly to the Mediterranean. To this end they established a direct maritime connection to America, using ports in Italy and France as their major departure points. Their strategy was to bring ships closer to the source of the emigrants. At the same time, some southern European lines also entered the fray.[4] By the turn of the century German, French, British and Italian shipping companies offered regular service from Marseille, Genoa, Naples and Trieste to New

---

[2]Cf. Gunter Moltmann, "Steamship Transport of Emigrants from Europe to the United States, 1850-1914: Social, Commercial and Legislative Aspects," in Klaus Friedland (ed.), *Maritime Aspects of Migration* (Köln, 1989), 313-314.

[3]Pierre-Henri Marin, *Les paquebots ambassadeurs des mers* (Paris, 1989), 73.

[4]Pierre Guiral and Michel Barak, "La navigation française dans l'Atlantique de 1814 à 1914," *Anuario de Estudios Americanos* (1958), 404; and Hubert Guiraud, *Les origines et l'évolution de la navigation à vapeur à Marseille (1829-1900)* (Marseille, 1929), 73-74.

York.[5] As a result, a new market was formed in the south of the continent. The presence of a great number of shipping companies made the new Mediterranean market even more competitive than the Atlantic had been.

Opportunities in Transatlantic Migration from Greece

The first emigrants to migrate from Greece to the US in the 1880s had to travel to ports in northern Europe, mainly in France and England, from where well-established steamship companies operated regular service across the ocean.[6] In so doing, they inaugurated what may be called the "Atlantic migratory route" for Greek emigration to America. This route required a two or three day journey, usually entailing both maritime and rail transport, across Europe to the ports of embarkation. The trip also required the migrants to spend one or more nights in hotels in the port cities while awaiting the departure of the transatlantic liners. During the two following decades, most Greek emigrants sailed from Greek (or Ottoman) ports to Marseille, where they boarded trains for Le Havre or other Atlantic ports. But there were also other ways to reach western ports. In 1902, for example, the French consul in Laurium reported that there were "persons asking to be introduced to captains of steamers sailing to England or Belgium, from where they planned to embark on ships going to New York."[7]

Once ports in Italy and the south of France became points of embarkation in the 1890s, what may be called the "Mediterranean migratory route" became available for Greek emigrants. Migrants bound for New York now could leave from Genoa, Naples or Marseille, ports they could reach solely by sea. While this new route shortened the preliminary journey, it did not totally eliminate the need to change vessels or to stay for a day or two in port of embarkation.

The growing number of Greek emigrants arriving in Italian, French or northern European ports in search of a steamer on which to sail to America caught the attention of western steamship companies. Interested in the potential of this new market, they tried to attract Greeks by appointing sales representa-

---

[5]Paul Bois, *La Transat et Marseille* (Marseille, 1996), 68-72; Tomasso Gropallo, *Navi a Vapore ed armamenti italiani dal 1818 ai giorni nostri* (Cuneo, 1958), 139-141 and 247-248; Georg Bessel, *Norddeutscher Lloyd 1857-1957. Geschichte einer bremischen Reederei* (Bremen, 1957), 83; Aimé Dussol, *Les grandes compagnies de navigation et les chantiers de constructions maritimes en Allemagne* (Paris, 1908), 34 and 44; and Roderick Scott McLellan, *Anchor Line 1856-1956* (Glasgow, 1956), 36.

[6]Saloutos, *Greeks in the United States*, 24-28.

[7]Archives Diplomatiques de Nantes (ADN), Athènes/240, French Vice-Consul, Piraeus, to French Ambassador, Athens, 13 March 1902.

tives, agents and sub-agents in the country, first in the main ports and later throughout the country. Once this network was in place, a migrant could purchase tickets for steamers sailing from Atlantic and Mediterranean ports in Greece. Often, a single ticket could cover the entire trip.

As table 1 shows, at the beginning of the twentieth century many well-known northern European transport companies, interested in the promising Greek emigrant market, had their own representatives in Greece, many of whom were recruited from the many new travel and emigration agencies.

Table 1
Foreign Transatlantic Steamship Companies and
Their Greek Representatives, c. 1905

Steamship Company	Greek Representative
Holland America Lines	P. Tsibis
Hamburg America Lines	Th. Nicolaidis
France Line	Tsilimikras
Red Star Lines – Fabre Lines	Ch. Christofis
Navegazione Generale Italiana	Vellas
White Star Lines – Prince Lines	Gastaldi
Norddeutscher Lloyd	Rot and cie
Austro-Americana	G. Morfi

Source: *Ebros* (Athens), 24 September 1906; and *Sfaira* (Piraeus), 4 January 1905.

Dutch, German, French, Belgian, British, Italian and Austrian shipping companies tried to penetrate the Greek market for transatlantic transport by finding local partners and launching advertising campaigns to attract potential migrants. At least ten foreign companies from seven European countries were active in Greece, without counting the Greek operators which appeared later. Such a concentration of economic actors seems to constitute a rather unique case and was due mainly to the late emergence of the Greek migratory market.

Some of these European companies provided a journey to America through Atlantic ports (Havre, Southampton, Amsterdam and Antwerp), while others operated through Mediterranean ports (Marseille, Naples, Genoa and Trieste). Thus, until 1905 competition for Greek migrants was mainly between companies using the Atlantic and Mediterranean routes.

The Importance of Greek Emigrants for French Shipping Companies

For some of these European maritime companies the Greek migrant market was not just an additional opportunity but rather a crucial source for their development (or even survival). This was mainly the case with the French transporters. France was a maritime power but not a country of emigration. Indeed,

its emigration rate was particularly low in the late nineteenth and early twentieth century. To fill their transatlantic steamers, French lines relied mainly on
foreign demand and either had to attract (or transfer) foreigners to French
ports or serve foreign harbours, especially those close to important zones of
emigration.[8] In either case, they tended to exploit emigration markets abroad.

As a result, the emerging Mediterranean emigration zone proved to be
of great importance for French maritime interests. During the last decades of
the nineteenth century, Italian emigrants filled the steerage decks of the Compagnie Générale Transatlantique and Fabre liners. But in the 1890s the Italian
market became extremely competitive, as a growing number of transatlantic
steamship companies, foreign and national, started to sail from Italian ports.
The unification of the competing Italian companies into a single national line
posed a serious threat to the French carriers. The passage of laws in 1888 and
especially in 1901 that regulated the activities of emigrant transporters wors-
ened the situation.[9] French shipowners considered that these measures favoured Italian shipping interests to the detriment of foreign firms.[10] The increased competition also squeezed profits for French operators.

It was in this context that the Greek market appeared to present rewarding opportunities for French shipping companies. Archival materials and
articles in the press both testify to the initial success of the French shipping
lines. The newspaper *Ebros* in February 1901 reported the departure of 1000
emigrants on steamships owned by the French company Messageries Maritimes.[11] In one of his reports in 1902, the French consul in Piraeus stated that
"the last Messageries liner had taken on board around 1000 emigrants from
Piraeus bound for Marseille, heading for the USA." He also reported that an
equal number of emigrants had been booked for a sailing a fortnight later. The
consul further commented that the transport of Greek emigrants was extremely
advantageous for Messageries.[12] Similar information can be found in the
monthly reports of the French consuls in Greece in the following years.[13] In

---

[8]Moltmann, "Steamship Transport," 314.

[9]Gropallo, *Navi a Vapore*, 190.

[10]Chamber of Commerce, Marseille, to Minister of Commerce, 22 September
1898, in Chambre de Commerce de Marseille, *Compte-rendu des travaux pendant
l'année 1898* (Marseille, 1898), 70-71.

[11]*Ebros* (Athens), 26 February 1901.

[12]ADN, Athènes/240, French Vice-Consul, Piraeus, to French Ambassador,
Athens, 13 and 19 March 1902.

[13]Archives du Ministère des Affaires Etrangères (AMAE), French Ambassador to French Secretary of Foreign Affairs, 26 March 1908.

1903, a captain of the same French steamship company remarked that he had taken 1338 emigrants from the port of Piraeus bound for the US, of whom 395 disembarked in Naples and 943 in Marseille.[14] Thus, at the beginning of the twentieth century Messageries enjoyed a significant rise in passenger numbers due to Greek transatlantic migration. Many of these emigrant-passengers were transferred to Marseille, where they boarded the transatlantic liners of the Compagnie Fabre. Others joined the clients of the Compagnie Generale Trans-atlantique, whose steamers sailed from Le Havre.[15] Collaboration was estab-lished between French carriers: the Mediterranean lines provided the transat-lantic lines with regular flows of passengers. Thus, both made a profit out of this new migrant stream.

French consuls and vice-consuls in Piraeus, Patras, Volos and other ports closely followed the emigrant traffic from Greece, reporting regularly to the French Minister of Foreign Affairs and to the Chamber of Commerce of Marseille and representing the interests of Fabre and other French shipown-ers.[16] During the first years of the massive outflow to America, French ship-pers gained a significant part of the Greek market for transport services. In-deed, it is not an overstatement to argue that for French shipowners the grow-ing Greek emigration market compensated for losses in the Italian market, which became more regulated and subject to state control. It is obvious that Greek demand for overseas transport was of great importance for French ship-ping companies. Since vital economic interests were at stake, the French were unlikely to leave even when competition in the Greek market intensified.

Austro-Americana: Establishing a Direct and Regular Sea Route to the US

French companies seem to have taken great advantage of the massive Greek emigration during the first years of the twentieth century. But as early as 1905 a serious rival appeared: the Austrian transatlantic steamship company Austro-Americana, sailing from Trieste to New York. The port of Patras, located on the northwestern edge of the Peloponnesus, was turned into one of its points of embarkation. Austro-Americana entered the Greek migrant market with seri-

---

[14]Patrick Boulanger, "Témoignages sur le transport des immigrants en Méditerranée: les rapports des capitaines des Messageries maritimes (1871-1914)," in J-L. Miege (ed.), *Navigation et migrations en Méditerranée. De la préhistoire à nos jours* (Paris, 1990), 352.

[15]Marthe Barbance, *Histoire de la Compagnie Générale Transatlantique. Un siècle d'exploitation maritime* (Paris, 1955), 235-236.

[16]For a similar role played by Belgian consuls in providing information for the government and shipping companies, see Torsten Feys, "The Battle for the Migrants: The Evolution from Port to Company Competition, 1840-1914," *this volume*.

ous economic goals. The decision to use Patras and Trieste was wise, since although emigration was a nation-wide phenomenon, "the greatest outflow came out of the Peloponessus."[17] Patras became a regular port of call for Austro-Americana liners both going to and coming from the US, making the company the first to launch a regular direct route from a Greek port to America.

By offering a direct voyage to New York, Austro-Americana obtained an advantageous position in the race to conquer the Greek emigrant market. This position was strengthened when stories surfaced of the ways in which emigrants who travelled through foreign ports were exploited. Press reports revealed cases of Greek emigrants who never reached their final destination and were left unattended and helpless in foreign ports, victims of wily fraud artists. Such incidents even aroused discussion in Parliament. For example, during the session on 16 May 1905 a deputy denounced the sufferings of a group of emigrants who had been deceived by steamship companies and their agents. He referred to the case of some Greeks bound for America who had travelled from Volos to Piraeus, where they embarked for Trieste. Arriving at the Austro-Hungarian port, they were abandoned, as the steamship company had no liners serving the Atlantic. Not only were the emigrants obliged to return to Piraeus but they also were denied reimbursement by the emigration agency that had booked their tickets.[18]

The issue of emigrant transport and its dangers attracted a great deal of publicity. To choose an indirect voyage to the US was increasingly considered a risky option that could easily be avoided by using Austro-Americana between Patras and New York. In fact, the Austro-Hungarian steamship company became one of the most popular transatlantic carriers in the region in large part due to its direct service. The company introduced a new element of competition and forced its competitors to consider new tactics to protect their market share.

New Competitors: Greek Transatlantic Companies

Until 1907, four or five foreign companies dominated migrant traffic from Greece, including Austro-Americana and the French Cyprien Fabre and Com-

---

[17]The "currant crisis" fuelled the exodus from this region, especially from the northwestern provinces bordering the city of Patras. See Saloutos, *Greeks in the United States*, 35.

[18]Greece, Parliament, *Journal of Parliamentary Debates*, Session of 16 May 1905, 311.

pagnie Générale Transatlantique.[19] Although the idea of a Greek transatlantic company specialising in emigrant transport appeared as early as 1901, it was not until June 1907 that such a project was launched when Moraitis inaugurated a direct line between Piraeus and New York. The delay in the entry of Greek shipowners is puzzling since an important fleet of Greek steam freighters already participated in international maritime trade.[20] Still, the collapse of this first Greek transatlantic company one year later due to its enormous debts and the effects of the economic crisis of 1908 on migration flows underscores the significant difficulties Greek capitalists had in entering the foreign-dominated migration business. Although this proved a demanding and hazardous market, two new Greek operators, "tempted by the important exodus that was offering them emigration from their country and from their neighboring countries," soon entered the fray.[21] These were the Greek Transatlantic Steam Navigation Company and the National Greek Line, both of which were founded in 1908 to serve the regular, direct service from Piraeus inaugurated by their predecessor. The option of a direct service to America, already offered by Austro-Americana, was reinforced. Operating on the same route, the two Greek companies engaged in a keen rivalry that only ended in 1912 when they merged.[22] As a consequence of the appearance of the first Greek steamship companies to target the emigrant market, competition soon entered its most intense phase.

Fare Wars and Aggressive Advertising: The Rise of Antagonism

A rate war soon broke out as companies sought to gain a competitive advantage. The French vice-consul in Piraus, who closely followed the matter, estimated in 1909 that companies had gone too far in lowering prices and that their profit margins had become insignificant.[23] In 1907, Fabre was selling tickets from Greek ports to America for 240 *francs*; in response, in 1909 the

---

[19]Archives Nationales (AN), F/12/7469, French Consul, Piraeus to Secretary of Commerce and Industry, 15 May 1909.

[20]See Gelina Harlaftis, *A History of Greek-Owned Shipping. The Making of an International Tramp Fleet, 1830 to the Present Day* (London, 1995).

[21]Archives de la Chambre de Commerce de Marseille (ACCM), M Q55/046, Company Cyprien Fabre to Chamber of Commerce, Marseille, 21 June 1907.

[22]For an in-depth study of the first Greek passengers companies that provided Atlantic passages, see A. Tzamtzis, *The Greek Transatlantic Liners, 1907-1977* (Athens, 1996), 34-47.

[23]AN, F/12/7469, French Consul, Piraeus, to Secretary of Commerce, 15 May 1909.

Greek Transatlantic Steam Navigation Company reduced the price of this same voyage to 100 *francs* and Austro-Americana dropped its fare to eighty *francs*.[24] Here, as elsewhere, a price war is an undeniable sign of fierce competition. The intensity of this competition was also apparent in advertising campaigns. Foreign companies had used advertising since the beginning of the twentieth century to publicize their timetables.[25] Yet company advertising during the price war became much more aggressive. In 1909, for example, Fabre advertised in Chicago's Greek newspaper that

> By using this line, passengers avoid the long and tiring railway journey to Europe. Within two days passengers arrive at Naples from Piraeus, from where they immediately leave for New York, under the protection of the French company Fabre. The journey from Piraeus to Naples lasts two days and from Naples to New York eleven and a half days. The Company Fabre uses big and new steamers.

The same year, North German Lloyd placed an advertisement in a Greek newspaper in Bucarest claiming that it was "the fastest line between Piraeus-Naples-New York operated by new and magnificent ships. Excellent seats. Unique service, food served with wine. The only line operating directly from Piraeus to New York."

In an effort to attract customers, each company tried to highlight its own advantages and to draw the attention to its rivals weaknesses using short evocative texts. For example, Fabre's ad stressed the inconveniences of the combined ship-rail journey to America through the Atlantic ports used by some of its rivals. It also specified that trip would not exceed fourteen days. In addition, it emphasized the age and size of its liners. In the same way, North German Lloyd stressed speed, convenience, new vessels and the quality of its services. It also emphasized its direct route to New York, knowing how much this influenced the decision of prospective Greek emigrants. The firm even pretended to be the only company offering such a service, though this was untrue. Advertising acquired an aggressiveness that was practically unknown before.

---

[24]*Ibid.*, and ACCM, M Q55/046, French Vice-Consul, Volos, to Secretary of Commerce, 20 May 1907.

[25]See *Sfaira* (Piraeus), 15 March 1901; and *Acropolis* (Athens), 23 September 1905.

Appealing to Economic Patriotism: The Greek Companies

Greek companies also resorted to advertising which pointed to their assets
while drawing attention, directly or indirectly, to the disadvantages of their
competitors. One of their main arguments was nationalism. Greek companies
emphasized their "Greekness" to attract their compatriots, as an advertisement
placed by the Hellenic Transatlantic Steam Navigation Company stressed.

> A direct line between America, Greece and Egypt. A new
> steamer, the fastest, powered by two helices. What do you
> gain by leaving on the *Themistoclis*? Reduction of fares, di-
> rect journey, expenses relating to transshipment, security for
> your luggage, Greek food, excellent service, free facilities
> and the most important, you give your money to a newly
> created Greek company and not to foreigners.[26]

This ad referred explicitly to the threats and costs of journeys to America from
foreign ports. Its aim was to deprecate the itinerary used by many of its rivals.
The low fare was another argument, mostly to compensate for the absence of
the big, fast, comfortable and luxurious steamers possessed by many of the
western transatlantic companies. But most striking is the clear appeal to national sentiment: preference should be given to Greek shipowners, not to foreigners. Reference to the Greek food served on board emphasized the "Greekness" of the emigrant's choice. In a period of strong nationalism, the effect of
an appeal to national sentiment should not be underestimated.

Greek transatlantic companies were strongly supported by the Greek
press. The idea that emigration should contribute to the development of national shipping became popular after the appearance of the first Greek transatlantic companies. Greek newspapers urged emigrants to favour Greek rather
than foreign ships on the grounds that domestic businessmen should be the first
to profit from the economic activity generated by the massive exodus.[27] Indica-
tive of this pro-national attitude is the advice to travellers in a *Greek-American
Guide to Emigrants*, published in 1909. Its author wrote that

> We recommend inexperienced emigrants to prefer travelling
> by direct lines, avoiding changes and loss of time. The newly
> established Greek company Moraitis has saved many inexpe-

---

[26]*O Astir tou Sikagou* (Chicago), 15 June 1909.

[27]A similar development can be observed in Italy at the end of the nineteenth
century; see Ercole Sori, *L'emigrazione dall'Unita alla Seconda Guerra Mondiale* (Bo-
logna, 1979), 315-318.

rienced migrants from difficulties and misadventures that their compatriots were experiencing previously, not knowing how to communicate with the foreign crew of the ships.[28]

To choose a national company was considered less risky. As shown in this passage, national preference was linked with a stronger feeling of security. Thus, a new axis of competition appeared among maritime companies active in the Greek migrant market, favouring Greek over foreign transporters.

In a short period of time, the overall situation changed radically. Foreign companies transporting emigrants through ports such as Naples, Marseille and Le Havre rapidly lost ground. In response, some attempted to establish direct lines from Greece to America, but not on a regular basis. By 1909 it was clear that companies providing a regular direct service to the US were dominating the Greek migrant market. These included at first Austro-Americana with its service from Patras and later the two Greek companies sailing from Piraeus. If Greek emigrants preferred domestic companies, it was mostly because they felt safer on direct journeys which avoided the risks entailed in travelling through foreign ports. The fear of being "cheated or mistreated in transit" haunted them, as was the case with other European emigrants.[29] The presence of a Greek crew and, more generally the existence of a familiar ambience like Greek food, strengthened the feeling of security offered by Greek companies. Thus, despite their late entrance into the market, their lack of experience and their relative financial weakness, the Greek maritime carriers managed finally to prevail over most of their powerful northern European rivals.

Conclusion

Following the era of intense competition, it is possible to pinpoint two distinct periods. The first spanned the years 1890-1906, when emigrant transport was operated exclusively by foreign companies, mainly French, German, English and Italian carriers. The second was the era 1907-1912, when the first Greek transatlantic companies appeared and competition escalated. Subsequently, company antagonism increased as the Greek migrant market gradually became dominated by Greek companies that offered a direct route to the US.

During the 1890-1912 period, the main focus of competition among shipping companies shifted from the port of embarkation (an Atlantic or Mediterranean city), to the type of itinerary (with or without transit) and finally to

---

[28]Seraphim Kanoutas, *Greek-American Guide* (New York, 1909), 42.

[29]Drew Keeling, "The Economics of Migrant Transport between Europe and the United States, 1900-1914" (Unpublished paper presented to the World History Workshop, University of California, 2005), 7.

the national origin of the carrier (Greek or foreign). The issue of company competition in the Greek maritime market was determined to a great extent by the emigrant's quest for security, not from accidents at sea, as one might think, but rather from human fraud and deception. Indeed, emigrants bound for America from Greek ports tended to prefer firms offering a direct voyage, thus avoiding the perilous transit in foreign harbours. For the same reason, they were inclined to favour companies providing a familiar ambiance (a Greek-speaking crew, Greek food, and the like) that provided this sense of comfort. Although company competition for migrants has been a rather common phenomenon in the history of transatlantic migration, but few places in Europe experienced as high a degree of entrepreneurial antagonism as did Greece.

The "Relatives and Friends Effect:" Migration Networks of Transatlantic Migrants From the Late Habsburg Monarchy

Annemarie Steidl

Transatlantic migration may begin from a desire for income gain, a strategy to avoid economic loss, a recruitment programme by employers, shipping lines or the state to satisfy demands for low-wage workers, or some combination thereof. Although wage differentials, relative risks, recruitment efforts and market penetration may continue to cause people to move, new conditions that arise in the course of migration come to function as independent causes. Migrant networks, for example, increase the likelihood for further migration because they lower the costs and risks and increase the expected net returns resulting from migration. These networks are a set of interpersonal ties that serve to connect migrants, former migrants and non-migrants in common origin and destination areas through ties of kinship, friendship and shared community origin. Once the number of migrants reaches a critical threshold, the expansion of networks causes the probability of migration to rise, which inspires further movement and expands the networks.[1]

Within migration research the so-called "effect of relatives and friends" as support for information networks is widely argued. As Adam Walaszek stated, "[m]igration was typically organized by families, relatives, or friends. Recent migrants to America invited their relations and friends to follow in their shoes. Close ties existed between those who left for America and those who remained in European villages."[2] Although most migration historians emphasize the importance of these networks, there has been relatively little systematic analysis of the roles of family and kin in the process. While economists and sociologists have done some important studies on the impact of close and more expanded kinship groups, historical studies are

---

[1] See Douglas S. Massey, *et al.*, "Theories of International Migration: A Review and Appraisal," *Population and Development Review*, XIX, No. 3 (1993), 448.

[2] Adam Walaszek, "Preserving or Transforming Role? Migrants and Polish Territories in the Era of Mass Migration," in Dirk Hoerder and Jörg Nagler (eds.), *People in Transit: German Migrations in Comparative Perspective, 1820-1930* (Washington, DC, 1995), 104.

close and more expanded kinship groups, historical studies are mostly limited to the impact of the nuclear family.[3]

The first attempt to analyze the relationships among migration and kinship groups was made in the context of movements to North America in the nineteenth century. This analysis was achieved through statistical sources. But such records are inadequate in addressing the question of whether the Atlantic was crossed mainly by individuals or family groups, since the identification of families is limited mostly to the family name and place of origin.[4] According to Jürgen Schlumbohm, those studies which reconstruct family ties according to a common name and origin underestimate the importance of kinship, leading to a systematic misinterpretation.[5]

Two themes have been the centre of recent migration studies: the role of familial support in decision-making and the impact of former migrants in the process of chain migration.[6] The importance of these new approaches is that they demonstrate that migration decisions are not made by isolated individual actors but by larger units, such as families or households, in which people act collectively not only to maximize expected income but also to minimize risks.[7]

---

[3]See, for example, Douglas S. Massey, "Social Structure, Household Strategies and the Cumulative Causation of Migration," *Population Index*, LVI (1990), 3-26; and S.C. Joshi, *Sociology of Migration and Kinship* (New Delhi, 1999).

[4]For a rather uncritical reconstruction of family ties, see Simone A. Wegge, "Chain Migration and Information Networks: Evidence from Nineteenth-century Hesse-Cassel," *Journal of Economic History*, LVIII, No. 4 (1998), 971.

[5]Jürgen Schlumbohm, *Lebensläufe, Familien, Höfe. Die Bauern und Heuerleute des Osnabrücker Kirchspiels Belm in proto-industrieller Zeit, 1650-1860* (Göttingen, 1994), 281.

[6]Jon Gjerde, "Chain Migrations from the West Coast of Norway," in Rudolph J. Vecoli and Suzanne M. Sinke (eds.), *A Century of European Migrations, 1830-1930* (Urbana, IL, 1991), 158-181; Dudley Baines, "European Emigration, 1815-1930: Looking at the Emigration Decision Again," *Economic History Review*, XLVII, No. 3 (1994), 525-544; Wegge, "Chain Migration;" and Tamara K. Hareven, *Families, History, and Social Change. Life-Course and Cross-Cultural Perspectives* (Boulder, CO, 2000), 37-39.

[7]See, for example, Rose Duroux, "Emigration, Gender and Inheritance: A Case Study of the High Auvergne, 1700-1900," in David R. Green and Alastair Owens (eds.), *Family Welfare. Gender, Property, and Inheritance since the Seventeenth Century* (Westport, CT, 2004), 47-71; and Marie-Pierre Arrizabalaga, "Migration Patterns and Destinies among Basque Men and Women in the Nineteenth Century," in Annemarie Steidl, *et al.* (eds.), *Relations among Internal, Continental, and Transatlantic Migration in the Nineteenth and at the Beginning of the Twentieth Century* (Göttingen, forthcoming).

Especially important is the effect of relatives and friends, which acts as an information network.[8] That there was regular and intense communication among families and friends on the two continents can be shown by the large number of letters exchanged between Europe and North America.[9] At the end of the nineteenth century, transatlantic routes were anything but unidirectional. The intention of most migrants, especially those from south and central Europe, was not permanent emigration to North America but rather a temporary sojourn to earn money with the intention of returning to Europe after several years. The economic and socio-cultural transfers of migrants and return-migrants are discussed in recent historical research.[10]

While most historical research is concentrated on the impact of the nuclear family, sociologists in particular have emphasized the role of extended kin groups in the support of migration: "The extended family is well suited to aid its members in migrating both in sending them from the community of origin and receiving them in the community of settlement."[11] Networks should not be restricted to family ties but expanded to include friends as well: "After family members, friends provide the second most important source of help for all kinds of problems. Friends help more often in intermediary ways, such as in finding jobs and providing information, than in supplying material needs."[12] According to Leslie Page Moch, the nuclear family is not always the appropri-

---

[8]Timothy J. Hatton and Jeffrey G. Williamson, *The Age of Mass Migration: Causes and Economic Impact* (New York, 1998), 38; and Mildred C. Levy and Walter J. Wadycki, "The Influence of Family and Friends on Geographic Labor Mobility: An International Comparison," *Review of Economics and Statistics*, LV, No. 2 (1973), 198-203.

[9]See, for example, Charlotte Erickson, *Invisible Immigrants: The Adaptation of English and Scottish Immigrants in Nineteenth Century America* (Coral Gables, FL, 1972); Wolfgang Helbich, et al. (eds.), *Briefe aus Amerika. Deutsche Auswanderer schreiben aus der Neuen Welt, 1830-1930* (München, 1988); and David Gerber, *Authors of their Own Lives: Personal Correspondence in the Lives of Nineteenth Century British Immigrants to the United States* (New York, 2005).

[10]See, for example, Ewa Morawska, "Return Migrations: Theoretical and Research Agenda," in Vecoli and Sinke (eds.), *Century of European Migrations*, 277-292; Walaszek, "Preserving or Transforming Role?" and Jon Gjerde, "Transatlantic Linkages: The Interaction Between the Norwegian American and Norwegian 'Nations' during the Century of Migration, 1825-1920," *Immigration and Minorities*, XX, No. 1 (2001), 19-35.

[11]Harvey M. Choldin, "Kinship Networks in the Migration Process," *International Migration Review*, VII (1973), 163.

[12]*Ibid.*, 169, see also Hareven, *Families*, 22.

ate unit of analysis; instead, she argues for broadening the concept to include both kin and friendship ties.[13] Likewise, Laurence Fontaine insists upon an extended network concept: "Migrants are seen as individuals, or at best, as small families...Thus, migrant membership in other social configurations, such as kinship groups or clientele structures...remains either hidden or outside comprehension."[14]

While this research has only recently attracted widespread scholarly attention, we can look to the seminal work of the American sociologist Mark Granovetter, who in the 1970s published his theory on what he called the "strength of weak ties."[15] His theory divides social networks into individuals with strong and weak ties to each other. Strong ties, he asserts, are common among close friends and relatives, while a range of alliances, including distant acquaintances and friends of friends, comprise the networks with "weak ties." The absence or minimal number of weak ties deprive individuals of information from distant parts of the social system and consequently limit exposure to the views of close friends and relatives. "The network, for migration as well as in other cases, is based on 'the strength of weak ties': secondary relationships that can be mobilized and to which individuals have access...will provide the most important possibilities for expansion."[16] While Granovetter's theory is widely accepted by sociologists, migration historians have taken little notice. One of the rare exceptions is Leslie Page Moch, whose study on the social networks of Bretons moving to Paris acknowledges it specifically: "The second observation, which interlocks with the first, is Mark Granovetter's 'strength of weak ties,' that come to bear when contacting someone one hardly knows, which are especially useful when one wants to move outside of one's ordinary circle to leave home or find a new job."[17]

The present essay concentrates on the transatlantic ties of migrants from the Austrian part of the Habsburg Monarchy in the decades before World

---

[13]Leslie Page Moch, *et al.*, "Family Strategy: A Dialogue," *Historical Methods*, XX, No. 3 (1987), 114.

[14]Laurence Fontaine, "Migration and Work in the Alps (17th-18th Centuries): Family Strategies, Kinship and Clientelism," *History of the Family*, III, No. 3 (1998), 352.

[15]Mark S. Granovetter, "The Strength of Weak Ties," *American Journal of Sociology*, LCCVIII, No. 6 (1973), 1361-1380.

[16]Christophe Z. Guilmoto and Frederic Sandron, "The Internal Dynamics of Migration Networks in Developing Countries," *Population: An English Selection*, XIII, No. 2 (2001), 150.

[17]Leslie Page Moch, "Networks among Bretons? The Evidence for Paris, 1875-1925," *Continuity and Change*, XVIII, No. 3 (2003), 432.

War I. Which person was contacted first after entering the United States? After family members, friends provided the second most important source of assistance for newcomers to the US.[18] How important were family networks for Polish, Ruthenian, Czech, Jewish and German-speaking migrants from the Habsburg Monarchy, and when did these people draw upon their friends' contacts?

Sources on Transatlantic Migration

Data for analyzing socio-cultural differences in migration networks come from a sample of passenger ship records collected by American immigration authorities and stored in the National Archives (NARA) in Washington and New York.[19] These documents have been used only in rare instances for migration studies from the Habsburg Monarchy.[20] In collaboration with the Centre for Immigration Research at the Balch Institute in Philadelphia, it was decided to take a sample from 1910 to create a computerized database (1910 was a census year for the Austrian Empire as well as for the US). At the beginning of the twentieth century, the Austrian Empire's transatlantic migrants left Europe via different ports, but some of these harbours handled more migrant traffic than others, with Bremen and Hamburg at the top, followed by Antwerp and Rotterdam.[21] Since nearly two-thirds of all Austrian migrants chose a German departure port for their transatlantic move, our database contains information on all the passengers on twenty ships from Bremen and two ships from Hamburg.[22] Some transatlantic migrants, especially Slovenians, Croatians and Dal-

---

[18]Choldin, "Kinship Networks," 169; and Hareven, *Families*, 22.

[19]United States, National Archives and Records Administration (NARA), Record Group (RG) 85, T715, Immigration and Naturalization Service (INS), 1891-1957, Passenger and Crew Lists of Vessels Arriving at New York, 1897-1957.

[20]See, for example, Heinz Faßmann, "Auswanderung aus der österreichischungarischen Monarchie 1869-1910," in Traude Horvath and Gerda Neyer (eds.), *Auswanderungen aus Österreich. Von der Mitte des 19. Jahrhunderts bis zur Gegenwart* (Wien, 1996), 33-55.

[21]Johann Chmelar, "The Austrian Emigration, 1900-1914," *Perspectives in American History*, VII (1973), 318-378.

[22]NARA, RG 85, T715, INS, Passenger and Crew Lists, 1910. The creation of the database was part of the research project "Migration to North America, Internal Migration, and Demographic Structures in Late Imperial Austria" (P14733 – HIS), financed by the Austrian Research Council (FWF) and the DFG (Deutsche Forschungsgemeinschaft) and conducted by Josef Ehmer. I would like to thank Imogen Zimmer for

matians, preferred the Mediterranean ports of Trieste, Genoa and Fiume (currently Rijeka, Croatia). It is important to be aware, therefore, that our data do not fairly represent overseas migrants from the southern parts of the Habsburg Monarchy.

I am fully aware of the criticisms raised, especially by German historians, against research based on previously computerized passenger lists, but I believe that any mistakes made in the first phase of entering data can be easily mitigated.[23] By choosing a sample chronologically delimited to the first decade of the twentieth century, we can avoid problems that have occurred in transatlantic migration studies in the second half of the nineteenth century based on American passenger records.[24] Ship lists from the early twentieth century were more carefully written and much more detailed than earlier documents.

Depending on the size of the immigrant vessels, between 500 and 2000 passengers were transported on vessels departing from Bremen and Hamburg in the early twentieth century; the journey lasted from a week to ten days. My sample includes data for 23,996 individuals, of whom 7521 originated from the Austrian part of the Habsburg Monarchy. Therefore, my analysis is based on a significant sample of six percent of the entire US-bound migration for the year 1910. About 5600 of the remaining passengers originated from the Hungarian part of the Monarchy, nearly 2000 were German citizens and about 1600 left Russia *en route* to the US. For about twenty percent of the passengers, the last place of residence was not documented, while the remainder originated from other parts of Europe or were already born or nationalized in the US.

The records contain a range of personal information for each passenger: name, details on accompanying family members, sex, age, marital status, professional qualifications, regional and ethnic origin and, crucial for our purposes, information about their nearest relative or friend in the region of origin and the name and address of a contact person in the US.[25] These documents

---

creating the ship passenger database and Heidi Sherman for ironing out Germanic touches in this article.

[23]See Antonius Holtmann, "Germans to America, Lists of Passengers Arriving at U.S. Ports. Deutsche nach Amerika – Fallstricke für Genealogen und Historiker," *Studies in Indiana German Americana*, II (1995), 88-99.

[24]Charlotte Erickson, *Leaving England: Essays on British Emigration in the Nineteenth Century* (Ithaca, NY, 1994); and Simone A. Wegge, "Occupational Self-Selection of European Emigrants: Evidence from Nineteenth Century Hesse-Cassel," *European Review of Economic History*, VI (2002), 367.

[25]See Ira A. Glazier and Robert J. Kleiner, "Comparative Analysis of Emigrants from Southern and Eastern Europe from U.S. Ship Passenger Lists: 1910," in

thus provide systematic information on the social networks of the migrants. All the newly arrived were asked whether they were going to join a relative or friend in the US and, if so, "what relative or friend, and his name and complete address." Even though this information can only be used as an indicator of social relationships, I will attempt in this essay to shed new light on the "strong and weak ties" exercised by immigrants from the Habsburg Monarchy.

From the Austrian Empire to the United States

In comparison with other European states, such as the German Reich or the Scandinavian countries, inhabitants of the Habsburg Monarchy were latecomers to transatlantic migration. Few people from the Austrian provinces migrated to North America during the eighteenth and nineteenth centuries.[26] Massive migration to the US began only in the decades preceding the outbreak of the First World War. In the period 1890-1914, approximately fifteen million people migrated from Europe to the US; the vast majority was born in Southern and Eastern Europe, and more than twenty percent originated in the Habsburg Monarchy.[27] During the first decade of the twentieth century in particular, some Habsburg provinces became major sources of labour migrants for the US. According to the port records of Bremen and Hamburg, only 7626 inhabitants of the Austrian part of the Monarchy (which does not include the Hungarian Crown lands) headed overseas in 1876. By 1900, the number of passengers reached 62,605, and by 1910, one of the peak years of emigration, the numbers increased dramatically to 113,218.[28] Between 1870 and 1910, roughly

---

Aubrey Newman and Stephen W. Massil (eds.), *Patterns of Migration, 1850-1914* (London, 1996), 255-265.

[26]In the eighteenth century many groups fled Europe due to religious persecution. See Heinz Durchhardt, "Glaubensflüchtlinge und Entwicklungshelfer: Niederländer, Hugenotten, Waldenser, Salzburger," in Klaus J. Bade (ed.), *Deutsche im Ausland – Fremde in Deutschland. Migration in Geschichte und Gegenwart* (München, 1992), 284-301. The US was also one of the main destinations for political refugees following the revolutions in 1848/1849; Gerda Neyer, "Auswanderung aus Österreich. Ein Streifzug durch die 'andere' Seite der österreichischen Migrations-geschichte," in Horvath and Neyer (eds.), *Auswanderungen*, 14. See also Michael Kurz, "'Nun ist die Scheidestunde da...' Die Emigration aus dem Salzkammergut im 19. Jahrhundert nach Nordamerika" (Unpublished PhD thesis, University of Salzburg, 1999).

[27]Angelika Schwarz "'Send the Homeless, Tempest-tost to Me?' Das viktorianische Amerida und die 'neue Einwanderung' am Ende des 19. Jahrhunderts," *IMIS-Beiträge*, VII (1998), 37.

[28]Faßmann, *Auswanderung*, 33.

three million people from the Habsburg Monarchy settled in the US, with fifty-two percent originating from Austrian territory. About 240,000 Austrian immigrants were recorded in the 1890 US census, and by 1910 the figure had reached 1.2 million.[29] The great wave of nineteenth and early twentieth century transatlantic population movement declined sharply with the outbreak of the First World War.

It is important to note here that Austrian overseas migration should not be reduced to only one pattern of transatlantic mass migration. Different forms of overseas mobility can be identified among the various ethnic and cultural groups who lived within the borders of the Empire. Demographic, social and ethno-cultural characteristics were important in determining patterns of migration. Inhabitants from Bohemia, Moravia and the most westerly part, Vorarlberg, were after 1850 the first group to move to the US in large numbers. By the 1890s, the geographic core of transatlantic migration shifted to the eastern part of the Empire, especially the western part of Galicia. According to the port records of various European harbours, the proportion of overseas migrating Galician Poles (18.6 percent) and Slovenes from Carniola (16.1 percent) was above average for the general population. Similarly, the proportion of Jewish migrants was also above average, while Ruthenians (6.6 percent), Czechs (4.3 percent) and German speakers (11.8 percent) took part in the transatlantic move to a lesser degree.[30]

In economic, as well as in social and cultural terms, the Habsburg Monarchy can be characterized as one of the most heterogeneous European states around 1900. Its economic development, both in the industrial and agricultural sectors, was strongly determined by regional processes. Despite the Monarchy's relatively early industrialization, it has often been described as "backward" because of rather slow rates of economic growth during the nineteenth century.[31] The Bohemian lands and the provinces of Galicia and Bukovina were at opposite ends of the spectrum in terms of economic devel-

---

[29] Michael John and Albert Lichtblau, "Vienna around 1900: Images, Expectations, and Experiences of Labor Migrants" in: Dirk Hoerder and Horst Rössler (eds.), *Distant Magnets. Expectations and Realities in the Immigrant Experience, 1840-1930* (New York, 1993), 55.

[30] Karl Englisch, "Die österreichische Auswanderungsstatistik," *Statistische Monatsschrift*, XVIII (1913), 90; and Heinz Faßmann, "Emigration, Immigration, and Internal Migration in the Austro-Hungarian Monarchy 1910," in Dirk Hoerder and Inge Blank (eds.), *Roots of the Transplanted: Late Nineteenth-Century East Central and Southeastern Europe* (New York, 1994), 55-79.

[31] On the history of industrialization in the Habsburg Monarchy, see David F. Good, "Modern Economic Growth in the Habsburg Monarchy," *East Central Europe*, VII (1980), 248-268.

opment. In the second part of the nineteenth century, the northern districts of Bohemia, as well as some regions of Moravia and Austrian-Silesia, underwent an early transition to mechanized production and formed the industrial core of the Habsburg provinces.[32] By contrast, at the end of the century Galicia and Bukovina were still predominantly rural, relying on traditional methods of agricultural production with relatively little industrial penetration. According to the census of 1890, seventy-seven percent of the Galician population still relied on agriculture, while only forty-one percent of the Bohemians made their living as peasants or agricultural servants.[33]

People from the Czech lands were first to migrate to the US in relatively high numbers. Between 1876 and 1885, more than half of all international migrants from the Habsburg provinces, either to North America or to other European countries, were born in Bohemia, especially in the south and southwestern areas of the province.[34] In the mid-nineteenth century, nearly eighty percent of all overseas migrants from the Austrian Empire originated in Bohemia, with the US as the primary destination. Whereas by 1850 only about 500 Bohemians had settled in the US, this figure reached 85,000 by 1880. The Bohemian movement to the US decreased around the turn of the century, and by 1900 their proportion dropped below five percent. In 1910, the American immigration office recorded only 8162 Czech-speaking immigrants.[35]

By 1900, the economy of the mainly agricultural provinces of Galicia and Bukovina had not undergone much change. In comparison with the other Polish territories in the German Reich and the Russian Empire, Galicia was in economic terms the least advanced region. At the end of the nineteenth century, economic growth occurred due to the new railroads, which spurred an

---

[32]On the economic and demographic development in Bohemia, see Ronald Smelser, "German-Czech Relations in Bohemian Frontier Towns: The Industrialization/Urbanization Process," in Keith Hitchins (ed.), *Studies in East European Social History* (2 vols., Leiden, 1981), II, 62-87; and Josef Ehmer, *Heiratsverhalten, Sozialstruktur, ökonomischer Wandel. England und Mitteleuropa in der Formationsperiode des Kapitalismus* (Göttingen, 1991), 136.

[33]Results of the Austrian Census in 1890. See Jiří Kořalka, "Some Remarks on the Future Model of Czech Emigration (1848-1914)," in Julianna Puskás (ed.), *Overseas Migration from East-Central and Southeastern Europe, 1880-1940* (Budapest, 1990), 11.

[34]"Auswanderung nach den Vereinigten Staaten von Nord-Amerika," in *Statistische Monatsschrift*, XI (1886), 423-424; and Jiří Kořalka, *Tschechen im Habsburgerreich und in Europa 1815-1914* (Munich, 1991), 79.

[35]Kořalka, "Some Remarks," 12.

increase in trade with other provinces of the Monarchy.[36] With about 8.5 million inhabitants in 1910, Galicia was the most populous Habsburg province; the mother tongue of about half of the people was Polish. Polish-speaking people dominated the population of the western regions, comprising the majority of urban inhabitants, albeit with a significant Jewish and a small German-speaking minority, while the rural eastern part (today's Ukraine) was primarily populated by Ruthenians.

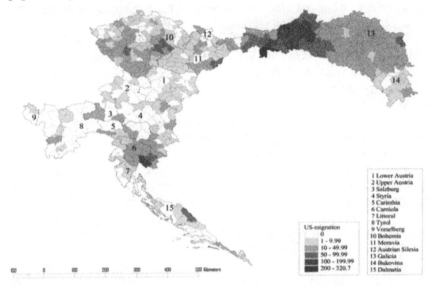

Figure 1: Regional Distribution of Migration to the US from the Austrian Empire, 1910

Note: US migration is equal to the number of people who migrated to the US divided by the population of the respective district multiplied by 100,000.

Source: United States, National Archives and Records Administration (NARA), Record Group (RG) 85, T715, Immigration and Naturalization Service (INS), Passenger and Crew Lists, 1910; and *Österreichische Statistik*, 1912-1915.

Figure 1, which is based upon our sample of passenger records from 1910, demonstrates a dramatic shift concerning provinces with high overseas migration. From 1890, transatlantic migration from the Austrian Empire was mainly a movement from Galicia and the provinces bordering the Mediterranean. In the sample nearly seventy percent of all Austrian migrants to the US

---

[36]Ewa Morawska, "Labor Migration of Poles in the Atlantic World Economy, 1880-1914," in Dirk Hoerder and Leslie P. Moch (eds.), *European Migrants: Global and Local Perspectives* (Boston, 1996), 170-210.

were born in Galicia. At the turn of the century, Polish-speaking people from Galicia dominated transatlantic migration from the Austrian Empire.[37] In contrast, Ruthenians from the east began to migrate in appreciable numbers later than the Poles, with Canada as their main destination.[38] Ewa Morawska has estimated that between 1880 and 1914 migration to America involved about seven to eight percent of the rural population of all three Polish partitions combined, and that between 1899 and 1914, the main overseas migration period, approximately 200,000 Ruthenians braved the long trip to America.[39] The number of migrants from the Czech lands increased quite slowly, whereas transatlantic migration from other provinces rose dramatically, causing a continuous decline of the proportion of Bohemians and Moravians. At the beginning of the twentieth century, migrants from the Austrian Empire were principally Poles and Ruthenians, followed by Slovenians, Jews and Czechs.

Expanded Networks of Kin and Friendship Ties

An overwhelming majority of migrants who moved to the US did so not as isolated individuals but as members of family, kin or friendship groups.[40] At the start of the twentieth century, transatlantic migrants were not "crowds of helpless people," moving in a disorganized fashion into completely unknown territory. They had already received some first-hand descriptions of the place to which they were going, and a fortunate number had someone awaiting them upon arrival.[41] Relatives or friends who were accustomed to the new society facilitated quick adaptation for the newcomers. They would have needed lodging and some form of work immediately, since most had exhausted their savings on the transatlantic passage. Already established migrants most likely had reliable and up-to-date information on local or regional job opportunities and could help the newly arrived find work. Indeed, the more seasoned migrants may even have had a working knowledge of English, which certainly was

---

[37]Chmelar, "Austrian Emigration," 318.

[38]See Stella M. Hryniuk, *Peasants with Promise: Ukrainians in Southeastern Galicia, 1880-1900* (Edmonton, 1991).

[39]Morawska, "Labor Migration," 184.

[40]See Yukari Takai, "The Family Networks and Geographic Mobility of French Canadian Immigrants in Early-Twentieth-Century Lowell, Massachusetts," *Journal of Family History*, XXVI, No. 3 (2001), 387.

[41]Hareven, *Families*, 37.

valuable. All these support mechanisms significantly reduced the new migrant's variable costs of establishing him or herself in America.[42]

It is well known that the US imposed no quantitative limitations on immigration until the 1920s. But it is often forgotten that the federal government sought to impose a variety of qualitative controls on migration prior to the Quota Act of 1921.[43] The shift of migrants' origin from northwestern to southeastern Europe, and the rising number of newcomers from the 1880s onward, was accompanied by attempts by American trade unions to obtain legislation to ban the contract labour system. Until the 1880s, many unskilled inexperienced European migrants were recruited by mining operators or building entrepreneurs, if not always on a preliminary contract, at least according to terms devised to undermine the skilled American workers' efforts towards unionization and rising pay scales. In response to the fear of the union workers of being displaced by an "alien workforce," the Foran Act was passed in 1885. According to this act, migrants were forbidden to sign contracts with an American company prior to entering the US.[44]

But the contract labour law did not halt immigration. At the end of the nineteenth century, in response to the rapid increase of southern and eastern European migrants who had been helped by a decrease in transportation costs, the federal government took direct responsibility for immigration control with the Immigration Act in 1891.[45] Even so, the restrictions applied only to criminals, prostitutes, the "insane," anarchists and contract labourers – in short, only to a small number of people. In 1907, the rejection rate was about five percent of all arriving people.[46] Even though the rejection rate of migrants seems low, however, the restrictions touched larger numbers in disconcerting ways, as when single women were readily suspected of being or becoming prostitutes. An unaccompanied woman of any age, marital status or background might be questioned as a potential public charge because she appeared

---

[42]Wegge, "Chain Migration," 962.

[43]Gerald L. Neuman, "Qualitative Migration Controls in the Antebellum United States," in Andreas Fahrmeier, Oliver Faron and Patrick Weil (eds.), *Migration Control in the North Atlantic World: The Evolution of State Practices in Europe and the United States from the French Revolution to the Inter-War Period* (New York, 2003), 106.

[44]Chaterine Collomp, "Labour Unions and the Nationalisation of Immigration Restriction in the United States, 1880-1924," in *ibid.*, 245.

[45]Michael Bass, *Das "Goldene Tor:" Die Entwicklung des Einwanderungsrechts der USA* (Berlin, 1990), 61.

[46]Dirk Hoerder, "From Migrants to Ethnics: Acculturation in a Societal Framework," in Hoerder (ed.), *European Migrants*, 225.

to lack a male provider. Indeed, Ellis Island officials regularly detained women travelling on pre-paid tickets to join husbands in New York if men failed to appear in person to claim their "dependents."[47]

The growing number of "new immigrants" led to an increasing number of measures to prevent them from becoming dependent and to dreadful inspections, which were both hurtful and degrading, at Ellis Island and other American ports. All incoming passengers were asked an increasing number of questions upon entry to the US. According to the passenger records of 1910, all migrants had to answer twenty-nine different questions. Since newcomers had to prove that they could support themselves, and because it was now forbidden to possess a work contract before one's arrival into the country, relatives and friends already in the US served as guarantors for immigration authorities that the migrants would find housing and employment.

While immigrants increasingly needed contact persons to enter the US in the first decade of the twentieth century, we should not assume that all newcomers were welcomed with open arms by kith or kin. Not all successful migrants were pleased at the prospect of assisting helpless friends or relatives. According to our sample from 1910, nearly all migrants from the Austrian Empire stated that someone awaited their arrival in the US, but we have no way of confirming whether those meetings actually materialized. Moreover, possessing a name and address of someone in the US did not necessarily mean that these persons knew one another. Historically, migrants have devised a number of means to avoid immigration controls, as can be seen today in immigration to Europe and the US. While keeping such potential limitations in mind, analyzing the relationship of immigrants to first contact persons can nevertheless prove useful in gaining deeper insight into migration networks.

On the eve of World War I, nearly eighty percent of migrants bound for the US had a relative awaiting them, while fifteen percent were joining friends.[48] As shown in table 1, which is based upon the sample of passenger records, first-person contact in the US was not restricted to members of the nuclear family. When asked by officials, migrants declared affiliation with other relatives and friends. Gender also appears to have played a role in the people named as the first person of contact. There is an even distribution between husbands and brothers, but in contrast to men, females bound for America more often listed female relatives, such as sisters (ten percent), aunts and sisters-in-law as the primary contact person. An analysis of Canadian migrants to Lowell, Massachusetts, reveals similar results:

---

[47]Donna Gabaccia, *From the Other Side: Women, Gender, and Immigrant Life in the U.S., 1820-1990* (Bloomington, IN, 1994), 37.

[48]Leslie Page Moch, "The European Perspective: Changing Conditions and Multiple Migrations, 1750-1914," in Hoerder (ed.), *European Migrants*, 125.

The above findings may suggest that the presence of a female sibling, probably more than a male sibling, at the destination was a determinant factor for a minority of unmarried women to carry out the project of crossing the border. Sisters at the destination must have been expected to provide their female siblings who traveled alone with emotional support, immediate help in finding a job, and the economic foundation for joint households.[49]

Table 1
Relationship to the Contact Person in the US of Migrants from the Austrian Part of the Habsburg Monarchy, 1910

Contact Person	Female		Male	
	Number	Percent	Number	Percent
Husband/wife	396	17.9	20	0.5
Brother	395	17.8	904	23.1
Brother-in-law	340	15.3	970	24.8
Cousin	293	13.2	645	16.5
Uncle	227	10.2	290	7.4
Sister	217	9.8	152	3.9
Other kin	244	11.0	360	9.3
Friend	103	4.7	564	14.5
Total	2215	100.0	3905	100.0

Note: Includes only migrants older than fifteen years.

Source: NARA, Immigration and Naturalization Service (INS), Passenger and Crew Lists, 1910.

In contrast to women, the male contact persons tended towards brothers, brothers-in-law and cousins. Only twenty male migrants from Europe were awaited by their wives in the US. These men had either migrated to the US with their wives on a previous occasion and had returned to Europe alone for a brief period, or their wives had made the transatlantic crossing alone at an earlier time. It is necessary to be careful not to draw rash conclusions; even married women did not necessarily follow their husbands.[50] More than fourteen percent of male migrants planned to be met by a friend upon their arrival to the US, while fewer than five percent of women had a friend awaiting them.

---

[49]Takai, "Family Networks," 389.

[50]For more information on female migration from the Habsburg Monarchy to the United States, see Annemarie Steidl, "Young, Unwed, Mobile, and Female. Women on their Way from the Habsburg Monarchy to the United States of America," *Przeglad Polonijny*, IV (2005), 55-76.

The data from passenger lists also permit a breakdown for the first contact person according to the migrant's ethno-cultural background (see table 2). In 1910 many transatlantic migrants from the Austrian part of the Habsburg Monarchy had brothers, husbands, sisters or cousins in the US who could provide support. For Polish and Ruthenian migrants, the most important first contacts were brothers-in-law. Since most Galician migrants intended to stay in the US only temporarily, it can be assumed that most of these brothers-in-law left their families in Europe.[51] At the beginning of Southeast European mass migration, these migrating men often lived together in boarding houses. In contrast, the contact persons of German speakers, Jews and migrants from the Czech lands were more evenly distributed between extended kin and friends.

In the 1850s people from the Czech lands were the first to migrate to the US in fairly large numbers, while transatlantic migration was not a characteristic feature in Galicia prior to the 1880s. Since Czech transatlantic migration had a longer tradition, support networks were well developed by 1910. In contrast to Poles and Ruthenians, more than half of the Czechs left Europe as family groups with the intention of settling permanently in the US, a factor that facilitates relatively rapid adaptation.[52] Similarly, German speakers and Jews could use well established networks of kin and friends.

The support via friendship ties greatly depended on the ethno-cultural origin of the migrants. While for Jews the extended family was most supportive, more than twenty percent of German-speaking migrants declared friends as the person of first contact. Similarly, an even higher percentage of other ethnicities, such as Slovenes, Hungarians, Slovaks and Croatians, who started their transatlantic migration from the Austrian part of the Monarchy, used friends as the first contact person. Hungarians, Slovaks and Croatians are especially good candidates for characterization as so-called "stage migrants," since prior to their transatlantic move they had already made an internal migration from the Hungarian to the Austrian part of the Monarchy. Continuous moves might have weakened their family ties, but in return they strengthened contacts to friends.

---

[51]For more information on Polish return migrants, see Walaszek, "Preserving or Transforming Role?" and Morawska, "Return Migrations."

[52]Even in the 1850s and 1860s, as many Czech women as men headed overseas. Franz von Meinzingen, "Die Wanderbewegung auf Grund von Gebürtigkeitsdaten der Volkszählung vom 31. Dezember 1900," *Statistische Monatsschrift*, VIII (1903), 133-161.

Table 2
Relationship to First Contact Person in the US of Migrants from the Austrian Part of the Habsburg Monarchy, 1910, by Ethnic Origin

Contact Person	Polish		Ruthenian		Czech		German		Jewish		Others	
	N	%	N	%	N	%	N	%	N	%	N	%
Brother-in-law	835	24.3	197	23.4	123	15.6	55	13.7	56	18.5	44	12.8
Brother	782	22.7	185	21.9	140	17.8	58	14.5	59	19.5	75	21.7
Cousin	592	17.2	141	16.7	69	8.8	43	10.7	47	15.5	46	13.3
Sister	231	6.7	53	6.3	34	4.3	22	5.5	14	4.6	15	4.3
Husband	211	6.1	55	6.5	65	8.3	29	7.2	26	18.6	12	3.5
Uncle	198	5.8	64	7.6	138	17.5	44	11.0	46	15.2	27	7.8
Other kin	321	9.3	64	7.6	110	14.0	66	16.5	37	12.2	24	7.0
Friend	271	7.9	84	10.0	108	13.7	84	20.9	18	5.9	102	29.6
Total	3441	100.0	843	100.0	787	100.0	401	100.0	303	100.0	345	100.0

Notes: Includes only migrants older than fifteen years. The classification of ethnicity is based upon the variable "race" in the ship passenger records. While it can be assumed that this information is based mostly upon the mother tongue of the migrants, the source does not give any information about how Jews were counted or whether these migrants declared themselves as being Jewish. By the eighteenth century, East European Jews had their own identity and built their own culture, and it therefore seems warranted to classify them as an ethnicity. See Heiko Haumann, *Geschichte der Ostjuden* (München, 1990), 56.

Source: See table 1.

Table 3

Relationship to the Contact Person in the US of Migrants from the Austrian Part of the Habsburg Monarchy, 1910, by Occupation

Contact Person	(1)		(2)		(3)		(4)		(5)	
	N	%	N	%	N	%	N	%	N	%
Brother-in-law	668	21.8	75	20.7	30	23.8	69	16.7	11	12.0
Brother	735	23.9	89	24.6	32	25.4	73	17.7	14	15.2
Cousin	560	18.2	36	9.9	12	9.5	64	15.5	13	14.1
Sister	208	6.8	42	11.6	4	3.2	12	2.9	4	4.3
Uncle	271	8.8	48	13.3	13	10.3	53	12.9	11	12.0
Other kin	337	11.0	33	9.1	15	11.9	59	14.3	19	20.7
Friend	292	9.5	39	10.8	20	15.9	82	19.9	20	21.7
Total	3071	100.0	362	100.0	126	100.0	412	100.0	92	100.0

Notes: (1) = landless agrarian workers; (2) = industrial workers; (3) = peasants; (4) = artisans; and (5) = merchants and those with higher qualifications. Includes only migrants older than fifteen years. The occupational classification is based upon the variable "occupation" in the ship records and refers to the occupation of the migrant prior to the transatlantic move.

Source: See table 1.

Our sample raises the question of whether the strength of family ties depended on the ethno-cultural origin of the migrants. Following Granovetter's theory of the "strength of weak ties," the formation of networks is determined by socio-economic and not by ethno-cultural characteristics.[53] This theory is supported by sociological research projects on the patterns of job finding.[54] Weak ties provide people with access to information and resources beyond that which is normally available in their own narrow social circle. Better-qualified individuals, such as skilled labourers and office workers, most often draw upon these weak ties while people of lower status mostly depend on the strong ties of their families.[55]

In table 3, I have grouped the occupations given in the passenger ship records according to five distinct categories which serve as indicators of the social status of the migrant. Three-quarters of the migrants worked as farm labourers, maids and servants prior to their transatlantic move. The category of "industrial workers" consists mainly of labourers, factory workers and miners. While groups three and four are self-explanatory, I included merchants as well as those with higher skills, such as engineers, secretaries or doctors, in the fifth category due to their low frequency. Contemporary occupational terms can only be considered a weak indicator since vague terms, such as "farm labourer" or "servant," do not specifically indicate where and if the person was employed. We can only infer the actual status of these persons in their respective society. Until the twentieth century, people most often had several occupations to make ends meet but mentioned only the one that seemed to satisfy the questions of migration officials.[56] But even vague terms suggest something about a subject's social situation. Although we have to bear in mind this limitation, the figures in table 3 paint a clear picture that is consistent with Granovetters' theory. While male and female agricultural labourers depended mostly upon close kin during the first years of their migration to the US, friends functioned as the most important first contact group for merchants and

---

[53]Mark Granovetter, "The Strength of Weak Ties: A Network Theory Revisited," *Sociological Theory*, I (1983), 201-233.

[54]See for example, Simon Langlois, "Les Reseaux Personnels et la Diffusion des Informations sur les Emplois," *Recherches Sociographiques*, II (1977), 213-245.

[55]Granovetter, "Strength of Weak Ties," 209.

[56]For an historical discussion of terms, norms and practice of work, see Josef Ehmer and Peter Gutschner, "Befreiung und Verkrümmung durch Arbeit," in Richard van Dülmen (ed.), *Erfindung des Menschen. Schöpfungsträume und Körperbilder 1500-2000* (Wien, 1998), 296-298; and Ehmer, "Die Geschichte der Arbeit als Spannungsfeld von Begriff, Norm und Praxis," *Bericht über den 23. Österreichischen Historikertag* (Salzburg, 2003), 35.

highly-skilled migrants. Migrating artisans fall between the two extremes, with an even distribution between close family and friends as their primary contacts upon arrival in the US.

Transatlantic migrants from the Habsburg province of Galicia, mainly Poles and Ruthenians, most often cited near relatives as their primary support in the US. When asked about their occupational status by immigration authorities, eighty-five percent answered that they had been employed in agriculture. Even though making the transatlantic crossing suggests that these agricultural labourers did not necessarily belong to the poorest stratum of society, their social position was nevertheless inferior in the late Austrian Empire.[57] Only six percent of Galician migrants were industrial labourers and four percent trained artisans. By way of contrast, less than half of all transatlantic migrants from the Czech lands, as well as German speakers and Jews, were employed in agriculture prior to their transatlantic move. While around one-quarter of the Czechs in the passenger lists were recorded as artisans, German speakers and Jews possessed still more prestigious skills or crossed the Atlantic as merchants.[58] Ernest Spaulding points out that according to American statistics very significant numbers of "German-Austrians" were employed as skilled craftsmen, highly-trained industrial workers or employees in commerce and trade, such as merchants and tailors, and 4.5 percent were "professionals" (doctors, lawyers, architects, artists and musicians).[59] It is important, therefore, to emphasize that social networks of kin and friendship are not necessarily formed by different family patterns but are mainly based on the continuity of a migration process and the social status of the migrants involved. Since my sample of passenger records also contains information on transatlantic migrants from other European countries, it will be possible to compare the "relatives and friends effect" for transatlantic migrants from the Austrian and the Hungarian part of the Habsburg Monarchy, as well as with the German Reich and the Russian Empire.

According to our sample, a close relative in the US expected the majority of transatlantic migrants from the Austrian and the Hungarian parts of the Monarchy as well as those from the Russian Empire (see table 4). Brothers, brothers-in-law, cousins, sisters and husbands comprised sixty-five percent of all contact persons. Since the number of married women who crossed the

---

[57]For a discussion of the effects of income on transatlantic migration, see Engelbert Stockhammer, Annemarie Steidl and Hermann Zeitlhofer, "The Effect of Wages and 'Demographic Pressure' on Migration from the Habsburg Monarchy to the United States of America in 1910" (forthcoming).

[58]NARA, RG 85, T715, INS, Passenger and Crew Lists, 1910.

[59]Ernest W. Spaulding, *The Quiet Invaders. The Story of the Austrian Impact upon America* (Wien, 1968), 68-72.

Atlantic was highest among migrants from the Hungarian part of the Monarchy, it is not a surprise that many expected to join their husbands in the US. These east and southeast European migrants were part of the so-called "Proletarian Mass Migration" which lasted, according to Dirk Hoerder, from 1870 to 1920.[60] Men and women from rural backgrounds with little or no property made their way from south and southeastern Europe to America. More than three-quarters of the migrants from Austria-Hungary and the Russian Empire worked in non-technical positions in agriculture and as labourers in other sectors prior to their transatlantic move.[61] Since in 1910 most of these migrants were still newcomers to transatlantic movements, they were excluded from access to social resources and relied on support from close family networks.

Table 4
Relationship of Migrants from Various European Countries to Contact Persons in the US, 1910

Contact Person	Austria		Hungary		Russia		Germany	
	N	%	N	%	N	%	N	%
Brother-in-law	1310	21.4	947	22.4	295	22.9	118	9.2
Brother	1299	21.2	707	16.7	286	22.2	184	14.3
Cousin	938	15.3	481	11.4	198	15.4	91	7.1
Sister	369	6.0	113	2.7	22	1.7	57	4.4
Husband	398	6.5	528	12.5	82	6.4	39	3.0
Uncle	517	8.4	338	8.0	146	11.3	195	15.2
Other kin	622	10.2	515	12.2	152	11.8	256	19.9
Friend	667	10.9	596	14.1	107	8.3	347	27.0
Total	6120	100.0	4225	100.0	1288	100.0	1287	100.0

Note: Includes only migrants older than fifteen years.

Source: See table 1.

Migrants from the German Reich had already started to move to the US in great numbers in the 1850s, and the German transatlantic movement declined sharply in the 1890s.[62] Only forty-four percent of the passengers in our sample originating in the German Reich were part of the agricultural workforce or industrial labourers. The majority consisted of merchants (twenty-one

---

[60]Dirk Hoerder, *Cultures in Contact: World Migrations in the Second Millennium* (Durham, NC, 2002), 344-365.

[61]NARA, RG 85, T715, INS, Passenger and Crew Lists, 1910.

[62]See Klaus J. Bade, "Massenwanderung und Arbeitsmarkt im deutschen Nordosten von 1880 bis zum Ersten Weltkrieg. Überseeische Auswanderung, interne Abwanderung und kontinentale Zuwanderung," *Archiv für Sozialgeschichte*, X (1980), 271.

percent), artisans (fourteen percent) or were part of better-skilled occupational groups, such as engineers, doctors or secretaries.[63] Whether all these passengers from the German territories can be accurately characterized as "immigrants" is uncertain since the sources I am using for this study may also be describing salesmen who travelled to America on business. Regardless, broad social networks were well established by 1910 due to the long tradition of transatlantic movements from the German Reich. When they first arrived in the US these newcomers could rely on extended networks consisting of parents, children, uncles, aunts, nephews and nieces. The most important contacts in the US were no longer restricted to the family; friends were now key. According to Granovetter, the person to whom a migrant is only weakly tied has better access to occupational information not already available to the migrant or his or her family. These highly-skilled migrants therefore had a deeper well of support for adapting to the receiving society.[64]

Conclusion

This essay contributes to the effect of networks of relatives and friends in providing information and other supports to transatlantic migrants from the Austrian part of the Habsburg Monarchy. It is a key contribution that migration decisions are made not by isolated individual actors but by larger units of social networks in which people act collectively not only to maximize expected income but also to minimize risks. The main part of the chapter is devoted to an analysis of passenger ship records. At the beginning of the twentieth century, European migrants were required to provide the names and addresses of relatives and friends whom they intended to contact upon their arrival in the US. The analysis of the information on relatives and friends is based on a sample of passenger records from the ports of Bremen and Hamburg in 1910.

Much of the current historical debate on migration networks is based on studies which deal with special migrant groups, small communities or slightly broader regions. While these micro-studies are of considerable value, my analysis sheds new light on the effect of relatives and friends on overseas migration on a much broader scale by using data for the entire Austrian part of the Habsburg Monarchy. Following the theory of the "strength of weak ties," formulated by Mark Granovetter, I asked about the importance of family networks for Polish, Ruthenian, Czech, Jewish and German-speaking migrants from the Habsburg Monarchy, and when they draw upon friends as the primary contact person.

---

[63]NARA, INS, Passenger and Crew Lists, 1910.

[64]Granovetter, "Strength of Weak Ties," 205.

The main conclusion that can be drawn is that social networks of kin and friendship are not necessarily formed by different family patterns but are based mainly upon the continuity of a migration process and the social status of the migrants involved. In 1910, the greater part of Polish and Ruthenian transatlantic migrants, mostly from Galicia, was on average poorly qualified and came mostly from the landless agrarian classes. Overseas migration from these Habsburg areas started rather late in comparison with other European regions, and as a result their information networks had a brief history and were poorly developed. Therefore, when asked for the names of their first contact persons, Poles and Ruthenians provided names of close family members, which, according to Granovetter, limited their chances on the American labour market. "German Austrians," Czechs, and Jews from the Austrian provinces, on the other hand, had higher qualifications and on average better jobs prior to their transatlantic move. Overseas migration patterns of these migrants had a much longer tradition; Czechs, for example, started to move to the US in the 1850s. According to first-person contact names given in the ship records, their social networks were highly developed, composed of close and more remote relatives as well as friends.

Although the importance of migration networks is widely argued by historians, there has been relatively little systematic analysis of the impact of family and kin in the process of migration. Even if a quantitative approach has its limitations in analyzing social networks, we can nevertheless acquire fresh insights into the decision-making process, the course of migration and the integration of newcomers into the host society, especially when we compare results of quantitative with qualitative analysis. We must await further research before such results can be generalized.

Crossing the Last Frontier: Transatlantic Movements of Asian Maritime Workers, c. 1900-1945[1]

G. Balachandran

It is well known that the introduction of steam in international merchant shipping coincided with a rapid increase in the employment of Asian maritime workers. Foreign-born labour was especially prominent on British vessels after the Navigation Laws were repealed, accounting by 1891 for more than a fifth of the crews. This proportion rose to nearly one-third in 1904 before declining to about twenty-seven percent on the eve of World War I.[2] By the early years of the twentieth century foreign crews on British vessels largely came from southern Europe, Asia, Africa and the Caribbean. Though there were Arabs, Malays and Sinhalese as well, the majority of Asian seamen came from India, followed by China. Britain was not the sole employer of Asian men, who also worked on French, German, Italian, Dutch, Norwegian and other vessels.

This essay focuses on an Asian maritime "migration" network that linked Asia and the US through Europe. (I use the term "migration" because in legal terms Asian seafarers staying on in the US were not migrants.) It is based on my research on Indian seafarers in the British merchant marine and reflects this bias. In 1891, ten percent (or 24,000) seamen on board British vessels were roughly classified as "lascars." Though commonly understood to describe seamen from India, "lascars" was still a fluid category that included many Chinese, Arab and African seamen. This fluidity did not disappear until the 1920s, though by 1914 Chinese and Arab seamen were largely excluded from the definition unless they happened to have signed on under special contracts (or "articles of agreements") known as "lascar articles." By 1914 there were some 52,000 Indian seamen by this stricter definition, representing 17.5

[1]A grant from Fonds National Suisse for the research in this paper is gratefully acknowledged.

[2]Conrad Dixon, "Lascars: The Forgotten Seamen," in Rosemary Ommer and Gerald Panting (eds.), *Working Men Who Got Wet* (St. John's, 1980), 281; and Ronald Hope, *A New History of British Shipping* (London, 1990), 383 and 392.

percent of the total employment on British vessels. According to an admittedly unreliable source, the fleet also employed an estimated 8000 Chinese seamen.[3]

The numbers of Indian seamen remained stable during the First World War or declined slightly because of competition from safer shore jobs in India and Mesopotamia. But the employment of Chinese seamen rose sharply during the same period. British vessels employed over 50,000 Indian seamen on the eve of the depression, about 40,000 during the 1930s and nearly 60,000 at the height of the Second World War. The employment of China-born seamen, on the other hand, declined after 1919 and was unlikely to have exceeded 7000 during the interwar years. According to Tony Lane, some 5000 Chinese seamen were employed on British vessels in 1939. This figure reportedly doubled after the loss of Hong Kong added Chinese seamen on Hong Kong-registered vessels to the British merchant navy.[4]

The Asian Maritime Migration Network to Britain

The so-called "lascar articles" under which Indian seamen were engaged precluded their discharge anywhere except at ports in British India; shipowners dispensing with their services abroad had to arrange for their return to India under articles or as passengers. There was no such requirement in Chinese seamen's contracts, though immigration restrictions in the US from the end of the nineteenth century onwards, and in Britain after the First World War, made their discharge at American and British ports progressively more difficult. Nevertheless Chinatowns in ports such as Cardiff and London, not to mention San Francisco and New York, beckoned Chinese seamen arriving at these ports. Whatever their origins, by the early twentieth century the channels of circulation, supply, and the renewals of these settlements were linked closely to seafaring and the sea.[5]

The growing presence of Chinese seamen in Britain drew bitter protests from local unions alleging a "Chinese Invasion" of the hapless island.

---

[3]Dixon, "Lascars," 281. The Chinese figures are from C.E. Tupper (written by Ernest F. Charles), *Seamen's Torch: The Life Story of Captain Edward Tupper, National Union of Seamen* (London, 1938), 240. Tupper was virulently anti-Chinese and prone to take wild liberties with facts.

[4]Tony Lane, *The Merchant Seamen's War* (Manchester, 1990), 162.

[5]On Chinatowns in London and Cardiff, see Stan Hugill, *Sailortown* (London, 1967), 123-130; and Robert Sinclair, *East London: The East and North-east Boroughs of London and Greater London* (London, 1950), 119-125. For a recent work on Chinese communities in San Francisco, see Yong Chen, *Chinese San Francisco, 1850-1943: A Trans-Pacific Community* (Stanford, 2000).

According to a union pamphlet, in 1913 more than 9000 Chinese seamen were employed on British vessels under European articles. In the same year there were reportedly 2355 "engagements" of Chinese seamen for foreign-going British vessels at six ports in the UK.[6]

Indian seamen had been employed for far longer on British vessels trading with Europe and outnumbered the Chinese. But only a small handful appear to have made Britain their home by the turn of the twentieth century. In the beginning, Indian seamen lived among Arab and African seafarers, and if the name adopted by one Indian seaman Jiwan – Ji Wan – offers any clue, also among Chinese mariners. The first Indian seamen's boarding house in London was probably set up only about 1913, the second about 1919, and distinct communities of Indian seamen do not appear to have formed in Britain until shortly before the First World War.[7]

Neither relative wages nor network resources (such as information) provide a clue to this mystery. Many seamen from Calcutta found themselves ashore in Britain for long periods during the war and came into possession of P.C. 5 tickets entitling them to employment on British vessels at National Maritime Board rates. Yet most returned to India after the war even though the wage of an ordinary Indian seaman was now only one-sixth of that paid to a British AB.[8] Nor is an explanation to be found in their articles, since Indian seamen broke them with greater regularity in the 1920s despite the adoption of more rigorous procedures to trace and punish deserters and deprive them of alternative livelihoods.

The propensity of Indian seamen to desert was not uniform across the various regions of the sub-continent to which they belonged. Even during the Second World War, remarkably few seamen from coastal India, including Goa, deserted. And the same was true for deck and cabin crews.

The majority of Indian deserters were engine-room crews hailing from interior regions, such as Punjab, the northwest frontier province in pre-

---

[6]University of Warwick, Modern Records Centre (MRC), MSS 175/3/14/2, "Chinese Invasion of Great Britain: A National Danger. A Call to Arms," draft British National Transport Workers Federation pamphlet, n.d. [1914], 3-4. It is not known how many seamen these engagements represented. The ports were Blyth, Cardiff, Barry, Penarth, Glasgow and Hull.

[7]Caroline Adams, *Across Seven Seas and Thirteen Rivers: Life Stories of Pioneer Sylheti Settlers in Britain* (London, 1987), 41-44. In contrast, the union pamphlet cited above claimed (p. 8) that ten Chinese boarding houses had been opened in London's East End and a dozen in Cardiff between October 1906 and March 1908 alone.

[8]National Archives of India (NAI), Commerce Department, June 1922, 1-30A, note of the Department of Industries, n.d. [September 1921].

sent-day Pakistan, and Sylhet in present-day Bangladesh. A British official observed in 1931 that "desertion is now seemingly a recognised means" for men from these regions of "getting in to this country and settling down here." Hardy peasants who probably had their first glimpse of the sea through the portholes of their forecastles, Punjabi seamen were mainly migrants in search of urban employment. Many were said to be "one voyage men," sailing "in the guise of seamen" to circumvent Indian passport restrictions and land in Britain. Once in the UK they sought employment in mines and factories, or tried their hand at petty peddling: "the Punjabi looks to peddling only and does not seek sea service." A small minority engaged as firemen or were "smuggled in by boarding-house masters among Arab stoke-hold crews."[9]

Sylheti seamen, on the other hand, were more likely to have been petty owner-cultivators.[10] Some Sylhetis had established themselves in Britain by the end of the First World War – the first two Indian seamen's boarding houses were both owned by Sylhetis – and Sylhetis began to desert in fairly significant numbers from the 1920s. Once in Britain they seem to have been willing to return to sea on European wages, only resorting to "hawking and peddling as an interim measure."[11] From the 1930s more of them began to run or work in cafés and boarding houses. Britain's ubiquitous curry houses owe their origins to these Sylheti seamen-entrepreneurs and ships' cooks.[12]

The number of Indian seamen ashore in Britain rose sharply during the Second World War, though not all the increase was due to desertions. In the early months of the war Indian seamen staged prolonged strikes for higher wages in India and at ports round the world, including in Britain, where hundreds were sent to gaols for varying terms. The demoralization caused by the strike, wartime labour shortages in Britain, and the long spells that Indian seamen spent on land in the UK between engagements encouraged a drift towards shore-based jobs. While most Indian seamen sought work in factories in

---

[9]British Library (BL), Oriental and India Office (OIOC), L/E/9/962, notes at the Indian High Commission on the Home Office letter of 31 December 1931. The quotes are from the same source.

[10]Katy Gardner, *Global Migrants, Local Lives: Travel and Transformation in Rural Bangladesh* (Oxford, 1994).

[11]BL, OIOC, L/E/9/962, notes at the Indian High Commission on the Home Office letter of 31 December 1931.

[12]The London agents of the British India Steam Navigation Company noted, for example, that "the men who have deserted from...[its] vessels are all connected with the preparation of food." BL, OIOC, L/E/9/962, 30 July 1930.

the Midlands, others enlisted in the British merchant navy. A wartime intelligence report noted that Indian workers were remitting:

> phenomenally...large sums to India. To those who are prepared to face the perils of the sea, this is naturally a big temptation and it may well be that Indians are joining ships' crews with the sole intention of deserting as soon as they arrive in these islands.[13]

Desertions by Indian seamen in wartime Britain did not acquire prominence, however, because of any increase in numbers. While there were over 600 desertions in 1938, fewer than 400 Indian seamen deserted each year during the war despite the steep increase in their numbers and the length of their stays in Britain. But this decline meant little to local officials alarmed by the visible concentration of Indian workers in their areas. Many measures were adopted to deal with them, including denying suspected seamen the identity papers required to secure jobs and rations. While the overt aim was to improve the supply of merchant seamen, the 1945 amendments to section 47AAD of the defence regulations allowed any police constable or officer of the armed forces to arrest suspected Indian seamen and enabled magistrates to imprison them until a ship was found to take them to India, recalling the post-First World War deportation of Indian and Arab seamen and anticipating the forcible deportation of Indian and Chinese seamen in 1945-1946.[14] More than helping to overcome the wartime shortage of merchant seamen, such measures reflected fears of racial miscegenation and contamination that grew as the end of the war approached and an anxiety to prepare the "home front" for men returning from the conflict.[15]

---

[13]Great Britain, The National Archives, Public Record Office (TNA, PRO), HO213/2085, "Desertion of Indian Seamen," note by Richard Butler, MI5.

[14]These paragraphs are based on BL, OIOC, L/PJ/12/630 and L/PJ/12/645; and TNA, PRO, HO 213/2085, HO 213/820 and HO 144/22144.

[15]For an example of wartime fears of racial miscegenation and contamination, see TNA, PRO, Board of Trade, MT 9/3952/6457/1944, "An Investigation into Conditions of the Coloured Population in a Stepney Area," May 1944. Similar investigations were carried out in several other towns. For the 1919-1920 deportations, see BL, OIOC, L/F/7/1102, F. 8227 and L/E/7/1103, F. 8230 and 8231; on Chinese deportations after the Second World War, see Maria Lin Wong, *Chinese Liverpudlians: History of the Chinese Community in Liverpool* (London, 1989); and for some materials dealing with the problem of postwar "control" of Chinese seamen, see TNA, PRO, HO 213/808. For a recent discussion of post-First World War fears of miscegenation that twinned sexual and racial anxieties, see Lucy Bland, "White Women and Men of Col-

Maritime employment and migration also helped create the infrastructure and resources that later supported postwar Sylheti migration to Britain. Its principal champion was Aftab Ali, the Labour Minister in the first post-Partition East Pakistan government. Son of a small Sylheti landowner, Ali went to sea as a fireman in the early 1920s, only to desert in the US where he worked for nearly three years before returning to Calcutta to become a leader of the principal port union and a leading representative of Indian seamen. Sylheti-owned seamen's boarding houses and cafés were often the first stop in Britain for postwar Sylheti migrants.[16] But the direct links between the two migratory processes were otherwise tenuous, with the better educated migrants who came later attempting to distance themselves from "peasants who jumped off the boat possessing only the lice on their heads."[17]

Transatlantic Crossings

Since their earliest days on British and other merchant vessels, Indian and Chinese seamen sailed to US ports. While the latter frequented ports along both coasts, until the Second World War vessels with Indian seamen called mainly at points along the Atlantic coast. There were thus two routes for Asian maritime labour flows to the US – one leading more or less directly across the Pacific from China to the US west coast and the second, more indirect route, linking the maritime labour markets of China and India with those of the US east coast through intermediate markets in European ports.

There were fewer restrictions on the engagement of Chinese than on Indian seamen. Chinese, Malay, Sinhalese and Arab crews could be engaged on agreements lasting up to two (later three) years on vessels plying to any part of the world year round. Ocean-going agreements for Indian crews typically lasted one year and could be extended for up to eighteen months. From the 1890s ships carrying Indian crews were not allowed to go north of $60°$ N or south of $60°$ S. Voyages around Cape Horn required special agreements. Most important, Indian seamen could not sail to ports north of $38°$ N (i.e., north of

---

our: Miscegenation Fears in Britain after the Great War," *Gender and History*, XVII, No. 1 (April 2005), 29-61.

[16]Yousuf Choudhury, *Roots and Tales of Bangladeshi Settlers* (London, 1993).

[17]Monica Ali, *Brick Lane* (London, 2003), 34. See also 28 for the novel's male protagonist Chanu's idea of a "respectable" Bangladeshi settler in the UK. In his own words, Chanu had "stepped off an aeroplane with a degree certificate."

Chesapeake Bay) on the US Atlantic coast (and 43° N or up to Boston for engine and cabin crews) between October and March.[18]

Intended originally to protect Indian seamen from the severe north Atlantic winter, these restrictions survived until 1939 because British seamen's unions opposed their removal. They affected Asian seamen's transatlantic crossings in one of two ways: either by forcing owners of vessels trading between India and the US to turn to other Asian crews in the winter or by compelling masters of vessels with Indian crews during winter transatlantic voyages to leave them behind for several days at ports such as Newport while making voyages to the more northerly ports with local crews.[19]

Not much seems to be known about the movement of Asian seamen to the US before the 1920s. It is not clear, for example, whether or how far the exclusion acts affected the landing of Chinese seamen in America. But wartime labour shortages in the US, and its 1915 renunciation of the 1892 Anglo-American treaty on deserters, emboldened Asian seamen to jump ship at US ports, notably New York. The treaty renunciation took effect in 1916. But the Immigration Act of 1917 denied persons from an "Asian barred zone," which included China and India, entry into the US. The conflict between the two measures opened a window of opportunity for Asian seamen wishing to enter the US. In 1919 an Indian seaman, Jan Mohamed, jumped ship in New York, worked there and in Detroit for some years, and became a naturalized American. He remained until 1923 when his citizenship was annulled after the US Supreme Court ruled in the Bhagat Singh Thind case that its 1922 definition of "Caucasian" (in the famous 1922 Ozawa vs. the United States case) could not be applied to persons born in India.[20]

Jan Mohamed was perhaps unique in having secured and lost his US papers in such rapid order. But he was not the only Indian merchant seaman in the US at the time. A Public Broadcasting System (PBS) documentary on Niaz Mohamed (who arrived the year Jan Mohamed left) reported that he worked in

---

[18]And ports south of 38°S in the southern winter. The restrictions described here pertain to 1902-1903 and differ slightly from the preceding decade. These restrictions were suspended between 1916-1919, somewhat refined in the 1920s and lifted in 1939.

[19]From the mid-1930s ships sailing from India to the US east coast that headed due west from Gibraltar on a course between 33 and 37°N latitudes (and crossing 38°N a day or two before reaching Boston) were allowed to employ Indian deck crews as far as 38°N. At this latitude riggers were taken on board from a tug. Indian deck crews became passengers, remaining in this capacity until the return crossing.

[20]This is based on BL, OIOC, L/E/7/1390 F. 2503, L/PJ/12/645; and TNA, PRO, HO 45/13750.

Ford's Detroit factory "along with several of his Muslim countrymen."[21] Niaz
Mohamed (and others, such as the Sylheti seaman-turned politician Aftab Ali)
appears to have recognized that after the 1917 Immigration Act maritime employment offered the only means for Asians from the barred zone to enter the
US for employment. Niaz Mohamed's fellow Muslim workers in Detroit
probably took the same route. To judge from shipowners' growing preoccupation with the problem of Chinese desertions in New York in the late 1910s and
early 1920s, many Chinese seamen also apparently reasoned likewise.[22]

After "shuttling between New York and Detroit" for seven years,
Niaz Mohamed went on to become a successful farmer in California and
Texas. He married a local woman, raised four children and became a US citi-
zen three decades after the Bhagat Singh Thind ruling.[23] In 1920-1921 US immigration authorities refused British requests to apprehend deserters on the
ground that immigration laws did not apply to them unless they had demonstrably ceased to be seamen by taking up another occupation. Yet according to
the British ambassador, efforts to persuade officials to arrest and deport Asian
seamen who had taken up other jobs did not succeed "owing to the [latter's]
lack of enthusiasm."[24] Such attitudes may help explain the contrasting fates of
Jan Mohamed and Niaz Mohamed, and the opportunities that still awaited en-
terprising Asian seamen willing to jump ship in the US.

In 1922 the US authorities sought a bond against desertion of $500
(later $1000) for each "detained" Asian seaman taking shore leave. Employers
and British officials welcomed this, the former because they could now deny
leave to Asian crews and the latter because they feared that deserting Indian
seamen would be replaced by "undesirable" political elements "passing
as...Lascars in order to get to India."[25] Though court rulings barred masters
from prohibiting shore leave, and shipowners were rarely fined for missing
Asian crews, the bond proved handy for employers of Indian, Malay and some

---

[21]See http://www.pbs.org/rootsinthesand/f_moh_home1.html (viewed 9 April
2005).

[22]BL, OIOC, L/E/7/1142 F. 4817, British Ambassador to the Foreign office,
7 June 1923.

[23]See http://www.pbs.org/rootsinthesand/f_moh_home1.html (viewed 9 April
2005).

[24]BL, OIOC, L/E/7/1142 F. 4817, British Ambassador's to the Foreign Office, 3 August 1923.

[25]*Ibid.*, L/E/7/1142 F. 4817, Indian government to India Office, 5 December
1922; and note by C.E. Baines, 5 December 1922. "Undesirables" were Indian revolu-
tionary nationalists abroad.

Chinese seamen who used it to justify a clause in the articles under which the crews "voluntarily" forsook shore leave in the US. Thereafter, many Asian seamen were not allowed off their ship at US ports, except for an excursion or two "under escort for shopping and other purposes."[26] Indian seamen left behind at ports such as Norfolk and Newport were also not given advance wages but only small allowances that were entrusted to the charge of the local British consul.[27] But desertions continued because not all Asian seamen were covered by the voluntary clause and US immigration authorities did not always order Asian seamen to be "detained" on board their vessels.[28]

Consequently, from the mid-1920s American seamen's organizations resumed protests against the landing of "Oriental" crews at US ports. In 1927 William Henry King tabled a bill in the US Senate, reportedly as a *"beau geste"* to Andrew Furuseth, the formidable leader of US seamen and of the International Seamen's Union, to bar foreign vessels coming to the US from employing "aliens" excluded under US immigration law. The bill's aim was to prevent the entry "of undesirable aliens, particularly Orientals, who escaped" from boats at US ports. Or in Furuseth's words, it aimed "to make the Chinese exclusion law applicable to the sea." Despite swift progress through various committees, the bill was not brought to a vote. In 1929 Robert La Follette, Jr. introduced a bill making it illegal for a ship in the US to engage seamen ineligible to become US citizens. Both bills were introduced in virtually every session of Congress for the next few years. They acquired momentum and powerful interdepartmental support in 1931/1932 because of the depression and in 1933 during the breakdown of international economic cooperation.[29]

The repeated airing of the bills and the support they gained in the 1930s drew two responses from shipowners. First, the Trans-Atlantic Steamship Conference and the Shipping Federation promoted an alternate draft allowing Asian crews to be brought to US ports if they were not allowed ashore.[30] Second, many shipowners employing Chinese crews began to replace them with Indian and Malay seamen. According to the owners of the Silver

---

[26]*Ibid.*, L/E/7/1142 F. 4817, Indian government telegram to India Office, 5 December 1922; and L/E/9/974, Ellermans to Foreign Office, 11 October 1935.

[27]*Ibid.*, L/E/7/1345, Government of India to India Office, 14 May 1925.

[28]*Ibid.*, L/E/9/974, British Embassy, Washington, to Foreign Office, 6 January 1936.

[29]This is based on *ibid.*, L/E/7/1458 F. 4454.

[30]*Ibid.*, L/E/7/1458 F. 4454, British Embassy to Foreign Office, 19 November 1931.

Line who replaced Chinese crews with Indian and Malay crews shipped from
Singapore on nineteen vessels, the former were quite efficient, but

> we were forced to incur very considerable costs at United
> States ports in watching services. At that time there was a
> great danger of an Alien Seamen Bill being passed into law
> in the United States...[T]he Bill in question imposed serious
> restrictions on Oriental seamen and was particularly levelled
> at Chinese.

Though the bill had not become law, "there is a definite chance of it being
resurrected at any time...Being faced with these difficulties, we decided to dis-
continue employing Chinese and to use Malays on deck, Goanese in the Saloon
and Lascars in the engine-room."[31]

War Passages

In the first two years of the Second World War, nearly 2800 allied seamen
other than British reportedly deserted their vessels in the US. Norwegian seamen (847) were the most numerous, followed by Greek (439) and Dutch na-
tionnals (268).[32] America's entry into the war and its massive shipbuilding
programme were further expected to boost demand for seamen and shore
workers and to encourage desertions.[33] Britain managed to enforce some control over its own seamen, including by restricting discharges in the US (yet
over 650 British seamen deserted between 1939 and 1941). But governments-
in-exile of the smaller allies found it far more difficult to check desertions
among their seamen in the US. Once America entered the war the manpower
requirements of the US economy clashed with the logic of not undermining the
control of allied governments over their own people. Finally, under pressure
from Britain, whose trade unions demanded the same strictures on desertions
by all allied seamen and whose government feared losing control over its own
shipping crews, the US convened an inter-allied conference on manning in

---

[31]TNA, PRO, ADM 1/22978, Stanley and John Thompson Ltd.'s reply, 19
July 1934, to admiralty enquiry, 18 July 1934. Other companies also responded along
similar lines.

[32]*Ibid.*, MT 9/3570, memorandum of 30 September 1941. There were an
estimated 20,000 Norwegian, 11,000 Dutch and 6500 Greek seamen on British vessels.

[33]*Ibid.*, MT 9/4341, Richard Snedden, Shipping Federation, to Julian Foley,
Ministry of War Transport, 5 February 1942.

February 1942 at which, among other things, it was agreed to arrest and deport allied seamen deserters to the UK if their governments were in exile there or if they had originally been engaged at British ports. Nearly 2900 allied seamen were thus deported between April and July 1942.[34]

The "deplorable conditions" of Indian crews on British ships aroused the interest of the National Maritime Union in the US and its paper, the *Pilot*. Union officials made contact with Indian seamen who were also regular visitors to the New York offices of the union and its paper.[35] Yet up to this point there were very few Indian merchant seamen deserters in the US; a MI5 "Hollerith Machine Analysis" of some 1000 seamen yielded the name of just one Indian deserter. There also appear to have been only about 160 Chinese deserters among the 3400 allied seamen of all nationalities who deserted in the US during the first two years of the war.[36]

In general, Indian seamen do not appear to have deserted in large numbers in the US during the war. Dimock's testimony to the House Immigration Committee claimed that 10,000 merchant seamen had deserted in the US since August 1939, of whom thirty percent were Chinese and twenty-five percent were "seamen of the British empire including Lascars." But I have found no evidence to support these figures. To the contrary: arguing for unrestricted shore leave for Indian seamen in the US, the Indian government noted in 1945 that "so few" of them had deserted during the war that they did not "present any problem to the authorities."[37] Indian seamen nevertheless spent long spells on land in the US as members of allied merchant seamen pools, usually awaiting lend-lease vessels allotted to Britain. Their presence attracted the interest of local trade unions.[38] Many Indian seamen also entered local labour

---

[34]*Ibid.*, MT 9/4370, statement of Marshal E. Dimock of the US Recruitment and Manning Organization to the House Committee on Immigration and Naturalization, 3 March 1943. For British unions' complaints about allied desertions, see MT 9/3570, note by the International Mercantile Marine Officers' Association, the International Transport Workers Federation, and the Allied Shipowners' (Personnel) Committee, 30 September 1941.

[35]BL, OIOC, L/PJ/12/630, Indian political intelligence note for Silver, 12 November 1941.

[36]TNA, PRO, MT 9/3570, R. Duthy to N.A. Guttery, 23 September 1941.

[37]BL, OIOC, L/E/9/974, Indian government to India Office, 21 July 1945. Shore leave for Indian crews was until then voluntary, with all but one shipping company reportedly allowing Indian seamen to go ashore, though it is not clear whether freely or under guard.

[38]*Ibid.*, L/PJ/12/630, censor's copy of letter from Clifford M. Gale, Shipping Federation, New York, to Richard Snedden, 20 October 1944.

markets, taking up all kinds of jobs ashore to supplement their incomes, from picking oranges and grapes in California to lending "atmosphere" as extras for the film *Calcutta*.[39]

Desertions by Chinese seamen were a far greater concern, particularly from the late summer of 1942. Tense since at least the First World War, relations between Chinese crews and officers on British vessels deteriorated during the Second World War and became a source of frequent confrontations. Disparities in wages and war bonuses between Chinese and British crews also led to endless disputes which the British government first attempted to settle using force, including arrest and forcible deportations to China. But the fall of Singapore, Hong Kong and Shanghai to the Japanese ruled out this option and strengthened the bargaining position of Chinese seamen, so that in April 1942 the British government and shipowners were forced to concede higher wages and war bonuses. Still, the new wages were still a quarter to a third below those of British seamen.

> The differential was never subsequently reduced and this, accompanied by unrelenting British intransigence and heavy-handed behaviour by everyone from ships' officers, through senior civil servants, senior partners in ship-owing firms to diplomats, produced unending conflicts with Chinese seamen.[40]

Chinese crew desertions were partly a result of such conflicts. The denial of shore leave in the US, or leave only under armed guard, led to a rash of strikes during which scores of Chinese seamen were turned over to immigration authorities for "safekeeping" at various detention centres including Ellis Island. The April 1942 wage agreement was overshadowed in the US by one such strike in Brooklyn in which the master of *Silverash* shot and killed a Chinese seaman, Ling Yang-chai, for refusing orders in protest against not being allowed to go ashore or sign off. It took a grand jury ten minutes to acquit the master of manslaughter.[41]

This incident drew attention to the restrictions under which Chinese seamen laboured in American ports, and in August 1942 the US government managed to overcome British and Dutch resistance to allow them to go ashore

---

[39]*Ibid.*, L/E/9/974, British Ambassador to Indian government, 26 July 1945.

[40]The above account generally follows Lane, *Merchant Seamen's War*, 164-166. The quote is on page 165.

[41]There are some reports of this incident in TNA, PRO, MT 9/4370. It is also discussed in Lane, *Merchant Seamen's War*, 167.

unguarded. The next few months saw a haemorrhage of Chinese crews from British and Dutch vessels in New York – though not in Boston or Philadelphia – with nearly a third of them deserting between August and December 1942.[42] Pressed into action, the Immigration Service periodically raided cafés, restaurants and clubs in New York's Chinatown and other places and rounded up dozens of suspected deserters for despatch to Ellis Island and other detention centres.[43] In May 1943, only seven months prior to the repeal of the Chinese exclusion laws, US immigration laws were amended to allow Chinese deserters to be deported to India to join the Chinese labour corps or the army.[44] Despite such measures, desertions continued to occur in New York, where during the course of 1943 and the first half of 1944 an estimated fifth to a quarter of Chinese crews exchanged their jobs at sea for lives ashore.[45]

A reason commonly offered for Chinese desertions in New York was the abundance of higher-paid employment opportunities, "especially now that labour is so scarce and so many openings exist in Chinese and other restaurants, sandwich-bars, laundries, and farms." There was also "no shortage" of agents ashore at New York offering "inducements" to Chinese seamen to desert.[46] Such agents included federal offices recruiting workers for Californian and midwestern farms and jobs in the city's hospitals through open advertisements in New York's Chinese-language press.[47]

Wages were only part of the story. Other factors cited to explain desertions included poor conditions on board, "harsh treatment" and "discrimination against Chinese seamen by white officers." Similar views were expressed in New York's Chinese-language press, which described as characteristic of the British attitude a consular official's statement that "the only way to

---

[42]TNA, PRO, MT 9/4370, Combined Shipping Assistance Board memorandum, 3 January 1943.

[43]There are some graphic descriptions of such raids in the above file.

[44]TNA, PRO, MT 9/4370. But several difficulties came in the way of British efforts for speedier arrests and deportations, including shipping shortages, lack of detention spaces and Indian opposition to a large Chinese labour corps.

[45]*Ibid.*, MT 9/4370, Scott to Shaughnessy, 16 January 1944; and Hopwood to Rowbotton, 30 August 1944.

[46]*Ibid.*, MT 9/4370, "Survey of the Chinese Seamen Situation in the United States," intelligence memorandum, 26 May 1943, paragraph 13.

[47]*Ibid.*, reproducing an advertisement in the *China Daily News*, 22 May 1943 that promised Chinese seamen the "freedom to stay" if they took up jobs in the city's hospitals.

get the Chinese to work...[was] to get tough," and that Chinese seamen "were coolies before they became seamen and they are still coolies."[48]

The Chinese seamen's growing sense of resentment at their treatment puzzled British officials; an intelligence report blamed it on the self-respect of Chinese seamen having been boosted by "propaganda on behalf of China and praise of China's fighting stand against Japan."[49] The report acknowledged, however, the impossibility of drawing firm conclusions:

> Desertions have occurred from Panamanian ships where the crews were receiving Panamanian wages [$104 per month]; they have occurred on certain British ships where the seamen were receiving normal British rates of pay; and they occur on ships where seamen are receiving the British rates as applicable to Chinese seamen. Perhaps the only fact that definitely stands out is that desertions are considerably more frequent in New York than in any other port.[50]

Another reason for the high rate of Chinese desertions in New York mentioned in passing in the above report perhaps deserves further attention. This was the Chinese seamen's loss of contact with home and their virtual homeless status after 1942. The former acted as a strong inducement to put down roots at a place such as New York with a large Chinese community in the hope of getting news about families in China and re-establishing contact with them. Their homeless status also meant long and repeated re-engagements since Chinese seamen were prevented from remaining for any length of time in Britain without shipping out again, or at other ports without facing immigration restrictions of various kinds. It is therefore not surprising that so many hundreds of Chinese seamen sought refuge in New York, preferring even incarceration on Ellis Island to returning to sea, because besides abundant work at good wages, the city offered these men who had been cut adrift from their

---

[48]*Ibid.*, MT 9/4370, letter to *P.M.* by Chinese philosopher Lin Yutang, 16 May 1943.

[49]*Ibid.*, "Survey of the Chinese Seamen Situation," paragraphs 4-7. See also press cuttings from the *Pilot* and *P.M.* in the file, and enclosures to Dimock's memorandum to the British Shipping Mission, 31 March 1943; and the note by W.S. Johnston of the Ministry of War Transport, 9 June 1943. Shipowners feared the impact of war propaganda on the self-images of their Chinese employees, and "strongly opposed...anything [such as propaganda films] that flattered the Chinese!" See *ibid.*, MT 9/4370, note of a meeting on "Chinese crew problems," 15 January 1943.

[50]*Ibid.*, "Survey of the Chinese Seamen Situation," paragraph 10.

homes the priceless possibility of a communal life and respite from toiling ceaselessly as "coolies" of the sea for European colonial powers in Asia.

Conclusion

The transatlantic circulation and movements of seafarers is an under-researched aspect of the history of Asian labour flows to the United States. Seafarers are also ignored more generally in histories of Asian migration to the US even though some of the earliest protests against racial immigration policies surfaced in the 1920s and during the Second World War in the context of their treatment of Asian seamen. In a preliminary effort to shed some light on these subjects, this essay has attempted to outline the routes, processes and logic of maritime labour flows from Asia to the US east coast, and the response of governments, employers and trade unions to this maritime breach of US immigration policies and its social and racial premises during the first half of the twentieth century.

There is no doubt that the US was an attractive destination, especially for Chinese seafarers, and that hundreds of Chinese seamen and perhaps scores of Indians used the maritime route to arrive in that country in search of employment. But the story of Asian maritime labour flows to the US also serves as a warning against focussing too closely on wage differentials to the exclusion of political, social and cultural factors in explaining migration decisions, or in this case the decision to jump ship. Although Indians were paid lower wages than Chinese seamen, fewer Indian seamen crossed the last frontier permanently. The propensity of Indian seafarers to live and work abroad also appears to have varied depending upon where they came from in the vast subcontinent and what kind of work they did on board the ship. It also seems to be worth asking how far desertions by Chinese seamen in the US were affected by the way they were treated on British and Dutch vessels, and the gap between their actual treatment and the seamen's own perceptions of the proper treatment owing to them as proud members of a great and heroic nation. If the Irishman, in Marx's famous words, crossed the Atlantic to become a Feinian, did desertions by Chinese seamen in the US reflect a self-conscious embrace of nation and nationalism, and their growing recognition of parallels between their own subjugation on the ship and their nation's subjection to foreign occupation?

Costs, Risks and Migration Networks between Europe and the United States, 1900-1914

Drew Keeling

Migration between Europe and the United States during the period 1900-1914 occurred at the peak of an Atlantic century of open borders, globalization and massive human relocation. About eleven million European migrants entered the US through its four largest ports over the course of these fifteen years, constituting ninety-six percent of all migrants arriving from Europe and sixty percent of all transatlantic migrants during this period.[1] The volume of these Atlantic traverses fluctuated cyclically but rose over the period as a whole and represents, by any reckoning, one of the greatest and most diverse voluntary mass migrations of all time.[2]

With rare exceptions, however, prior historical investigation into the general causes of this migration has been hampered by inadequate attention to the processes of the organized networks which physically carried out the relocation.[3] The objective here is to redress this imbalance by examining four sets

---

[1]These eleven million comprise the set of migration flows which are the main focus of this analysis. In order of migrant volume, the four largest ports were New York, Boston, Baltimore and Philadelphia. In addition to first-time westward crossings of the Atlantic, the eleven million also made about five and a half million "return" crossings eastward to Europe and two and a half million "repeat" westward crossings to the US. Annual volumes of these "gross" flows are closely approximated by the measures shown in appendix 1. See also Drew Keeling, "The Business of Transatlantic Migration between Europe and America, 1900-1914" (Unpublished PhD thesis, University of California at Berkeley, 2005), iii, 329 and 345-346, for further particulars on the derivation of these statistics. They differ slightly from the figures compiled by the US Bureau of Immigration (BI, see also appendix 2) which undercounted repeat migrants for part of the period; see Drew Keeling "Repeat Migration between Europe and the United States, 1870-1914" (Unpublished working paper, University of California Institute of European Studies, July 2006).

[2]See appendices 1-4.

[3]Useful insights covering the entire region and period, and some aspects of migrant transport, can be found, however, in Erich Murken, *Die großen transatlantischen Linienreederei-Verbände, Pools und Interessengemeinschaften bis zum Ausbruch des Weltkrieges: Ihre Entstehung, Organisation und Wirksamkeit* (Jena, 1922); Philip

of networks: kinship and community groupings of migrants; steamship agents functioning as travel intermediaries; networks of steamship lines and "conferences;" and the various governmental entities which regulated their businesses and the overall migration.[4] The analysis of the causes of the migration here focuses primarily on the role of risks and costs as intervening obstacles that had to be overcome by the migrants.

Migrants moving *en masse* to the US from Europe in the early 1900s came in pursuit of what they perceived to be better opportunities. It is not easy to generalize about what those perceptions were, however, in a manner which accounts for both the record number of Europeans choosing to relocate overseas and the even greater number deciding to remain in Europe, while also being applicable across the remarkable ethnic and linguistic diversity of those who did move across the ocean. "Seen through a magnifying glass," historian Frank Thistlethwaite noted, "this undifferentiated mass surface breaks down into a honeycomb of innumerable particular cells, districts, villages, towns, each with an individual reaction or lack of it to the pull of migration."[5]

Standard general causal explanations for the high level and strong growth of this migration, such as continued higher real wages in America and falling costs of travelling there, do not explain, for instance, why fifty-two percent of Irish immigrants in this period were women while only twenty percent of Italians were, or why twenty-five percent of Jews moving to the US were under fourteen years of age, whereas for Poles, travelling on much the same routes, that proportion was only ten percent.[6] A myriad of other ethni-

---

Taylor, *The Distant Magnet: European Migration to the USA* (New York, 1972); Günter Moltmann, "Steamship Transport of Emigrants from Europe to the United States, 1850-1914: Social, Commercial and Legislative Aspects," in Klaus Friedland (ed.), *Maritime Aspects of Migration* (Köln, 1989), 309-320; Maldwyn Allen Jones, "Aspects of North Atlantic Migration: Steerage Conditions and American Law, 1819-1909," in *ibid.*, 321-331; and Walter Nugent, *Crossings: The Great Transatlantic Migrations, 1870-1914* (Bloomington, IN, 1992).

[4]After 1900, the main impact of immigrant assistance organizations, cooperatives, trade unions, labour agents, newspapers, political "machines," etc., occurred *after* migrants had arrived in the US; see Maldwyn Allen Jones, *American Immigration* (Chicago, 1960; 2nd ed., Chicago, 1992), 87-207. These "networks" are discussed only intermittently here to the extent they were also involved in physical movements of migrants across the Atlantic and the political determination of US immigration policy.

[5]Frank Thistlethwaite, "Migration from Europe Overseas in the Nineteenth and Twentieth Centuries," in Rudolph Vecoli and Suzanne Sinke (eds.), *A Century of European Migrations, 1830-1930* (Urbana, IL, 1991), 28.

[6]United States, US Immigration Commission, 1907-1910, *Reports* (*Dillingham Report*) (41 vols., Washington, DC, 1911), III, 47 and 89ff.

cally correlated characteristics, including occupation, marital status, timing of the move and the rate of later return back to Europe, also impede an overall assessment of migration motives.

"How can we make sense of this diversity?" economic historian Dudley Baines asked.[7] Most migration historians have not tried to do so, preferring to focus instead on fractional subsets of the entire movement, but there is something of a consensus that family, kinship and community networks were somehow significant factors across the wide heterogeneity of the entire transatlantic population transfer.[8] Historians' references to these networks, and to the "chain migration" they fostered, come more often in the context of destination choices, timing of the relocation, settlement clustering and "assimilation" or "identity" issues than in any discussion of ultimate causes.[9] There is nonetheless general agreement that network-mediated migration was self-replicating or self-reinforcing, or, as Baines put it, "emigration causes emigration."[10]

Traditionally, the causes of migration have been catalogued as "pushes" and "pulls," which roughly translate as the benefits of moving out of one area and into another. Costs of migrating have received far less attention in previous historical literature, and that may be one reason why costs are often assumed, based on little or no comprehensive evidence, to have constituted the operative "filter" determining who migrated across the North Atlantic and who did not. Whatever the general validity of suppositions that travel costs were the primary operative constraint upon transoceanic migration during the nineteenth century, any hypothesis that applies this to the European flow to

---

[7]Dudley Baines, *Emigration from Europe, 1815-1930* (London, 1991). See also Hasia Diner, "History and the Study of Immigration. Narratives of the Particular," in Caroline B. Brettell and James F. Hollifield (eds.), *Migration Theory: Talking across Disciplines* (New York, 2000), 27-28 and 36-37.

[8]A discussion of networks in the context of group decisions on migration can be found in John Bodnar, *The Transplanted: A History of Immigrants to Urban America* (Bloomington, IN, 1985), especially 51-53.

[9]Examples include Ewa Morawska, "The Sociology and Historiography of Immigration," in Virginia Yans-McLaughlin (ed.), *Immigration Reconsidered: History, Sociology, and Politics* (New York, 1990), 214-215; Yans-McLaughlin, "New Wine in Old Bottles: Family, Community, and Immigration," in David A. Gerber and Alan Kraut (eds.), *American Immigration and Ethnicity* (New York, 2005), 39-47 (excerpted from Yans-McLaughlin, *Family and Community: Italian Immigrants in Buffalo, 1880-1930* [Ithaca, NY, 1977]); and Leslie Page Moch, "The European Perspective: Changing Conditions and Multiple Migrations," in Dirk Hoerder and Leslie Page Moch (eds.), *European Migrants: Global and Local Perspectives* (Boston, 1996), 125.

[10]Baines, *Emigration*, 29. See also Timothy J. Hatton and Jeffrey G. Williamson, *The Age of Mass Migration* (New York, 1998), 14, 17 and 41.

America in the period 1900-1914 is questionable at best, as will be shown below. Most in-depth analyses of the migration's causes have, moreover, tended
more towards Thistlethwaite's alternative suggestion that "the ultimate problem of immigration is psychological."[11]

The "extended" approach proposed by Dirk Hoerder is one persuasive general explanation of migrant self-selection that does not presume relocation costs to be the prevailing barrier.[12] This model of migration decision-
making takes into account not only "measurable material benefits or losses"
but also "non-quantifiable but subjectively considerable emotional and spiritual
benefits and losses." Here the prospective migrant, or his larger personal network, is seen as deciding, in effect, "how much of the old-culture customs,
values, and habits to surrender in return for new job and income opportunities."

It is certainly plausible to think of potential migrants going through
some such calculation before deciding whether to leave home. It is questionable, however, whether intangible, non-measurable and uncertain concerns,
such as "loss of relationships, sadness, homesickness (or "network depriva-
tion" in Hoerder's term), happiness and social contacts," are best described as
benefits (or negative benefits), as Hoerder classifies them, or whether risks
might be a more accurate way of describing many of these "non-material"
factors, especially those most critical to decisions to migrate overseas.

Risks are central, for example, to the formulation of migration advanced by Charles Tilly:

> Long-distance migration entails many risks: to personal secu-
> rity, to comfort, to income, to the possibility of satisfying
> social relations. Where kinsmen, friends, neighbors, and
> work associates already have good contacts with possible
> destinations, reliance on established interpersonal networks
> for information minimizes and spreads the risks. Implicitly
> recognizing those advantages, the vast majority of potential
> long-distance migrants anywhere in the world draw their
> chief information (including the decision to stay put) from
> members of their interpersonal networks, especially to the
> extent that by migrating they acquire the possibility and the
> obligation to supply information and help to other potential
> migrants. Constrained by personal networks, potential mi-

[11]Thistlethwaite, "Migration," 42.

[12]See Dirk Hoerder, "Segmented Macrosystems and Networking Individuals:
The Balancing Functions of Migration Processes," in Jan Lucassen and Leo Lucassen
(eds.), *Migration, Migration History, History. Old Paradigms and New Perspectives*
(Bern, 1997), 75-78.

grants fail to consider many theoretically available destinations, and concentrate instead on those few localities with which their place of origin has strong links. The higher the risks and greater the cost of returning, the more intense the reliance on previously established ties.[13]

Tilly does not explicitly state that the risks of migration and how they are dealt with determine who migrates and who does not, but he lists all the pieces necessary for such a logical conclusion: risks are numerous in migration, interpersonal networks reduce those risks, the greater the risks the more the reliance on networks, which shape decisions regarding whether and where to migrate.

Of course, the unusual diversity and massive scale of American immigration in this period practically guarantee numerous individual counterexamples to any general pattern. There were certainly instances, for example, of migration networks being a source of risk to migrants as well as a mechanism for ameliorating risk. Nevertheless, risk considerations offer considerable explanatory potential for the causes of mass migration. They help explain why migrants are often considered "gamblers," and why large majorities of Europeans might have preferred the less remunerative but less uncertain alternative of staying in Europe a century ago. The likely higher risk of not finding employment, for example, is probably one reason why unmarried Italian women migrated to the US at a much lower rate than single Irish females.[14] Certainly the relatively significant risks of remaining in western Russia faced by Jews at least partly explain why their emigration was more dispersed across age brackets than were Polish departures from the same general regions.

To understand how networks dealt with migration risk, and how this helped shape migration decisions and patterns, however, it is important to recognize that kinship or community affiliations formed only one of several kinds of mediating networks involved in this overall relocation. The most common denominator of the highly heterogeneous eleven million migrants of this period and area is that nearly all were fare-paying customers of a far-flung, regulated, international travel industry. In addition to the personal networks of migrants,

---

[13]Charles Tilly, "Transplanted Networks," in Yans-McLaughlin (ed.), *Immigration Reconsidered*, 84.

[14]Slightly more unmarried Irish females than unmarried Italian females entered the US during the period, despite the fact that Italian immigrants to America, overall, were five times as numerous as Irish immigrants; *Dillingham Report*, III, 47. The stereotypical Irish "Bridget" had the double advantage of joining a greater stock of prior arrivals (due to heavy Irish migration earlier in the nineteenth century) than was the case for Italians, and of fluency in English – a useful skill for domestic service. See, for instance, Roger Daniels, *Coming to America: A History of Immigration and Ethnicity in American Life* (Princeton, 1990), 130-132.

three other groups of actors played important roles in carrying out the large-scale physical relocation across the North Atlantic a century ago: the agents of the steamship lines through which most migrant passages were booked, the steamship companies themselves and the governmental regulators of migration – the US authorities being of foremost importance in this regard. How these networks might have shaped the factors behind the mass migration is a subject treated only sporadically in past migration histories, however, and this has led to misunderstandings.

Facilitating Agents

The idea that steamship agents significantly "stimulated" migration across the Atlantic in the late nineteenth and early twentieth centuries has not been substantiated by subsequent historical research. Definitive conclusions are difficult to reach because these agents numbered in the many thousands and left little documentary evidence behind, but scholarly studies tend to indicate that kinship networks, particularly in the form of migrants returning from America to fetch relatives and encourage neighbours, were much more important than the persuasive powers of professional intermediaries in the formation of decisions to migrate.[15]

There are no shortage of contemporary claims about the power of steamship agents to provoke "unnatural" emigration, such as this investigator's communique which found its way into the 1904 annual report of the US Bureau of Immigration (BI):

> I am fully convinced that the volume of immigration into the
> United States would not exceed one-half of the present figure
> but for the activity of the transportation companies in their
> hunt for the business...the most remote agricultural valleys
> [in Europe] are invaded by agents with advertising matter of
> every description...It is one of the best organized, most en-
> ergetically conducted branches of commerce in the world.[16]

The findings of relevant scholarship have not confirmed such depictions, however.

Olaf Thörn discovered the papers of the Larsson Brothers agency of Gothenburg, Sweden, stored in a barn and printed colourful excerpts of their

---

[15]See, for instance, Jones, *American Immigration*, 156-157; and Kristian Hvidt, "Emigration Agents: The Development of a Business and Its Methods," *Scandinavian Journal of History*, III (1978), 187-192.

[16]United States, Bureau of Immigration (BI), *Annual Report, 1904* (Washington, DC, 1905), 133-134.

correspondence (mostly from the 1880s) in his 1959 article. It contains numerous examples of what he referred to as "propaganda" proffered by "proselytizers," but no indication that such efforts were either intended to or succeeded in convincing people to leave Sweden. A more comprehensive analysis of this material presented by Berit Brattne in 1976 concluded that "the emigrant agent was more of a travel agent than an emigrant recruiter." Kristian Hvidt's analysis of Danish agents, based mostly upon archival records from the 1870s and 1880s, and first published in 1971, suggested that steamship agents "could to a certain degree raise the level of emigration beyond normal 'push and pull,'" but also concluded that by the turn of the century "old fashioned" agents, "restless and somewhat unscrupulous" salesmen, had been replaced by travel bureau directors and administrators.[17]

In his 1988 analysis of agents handling migration from southeast Europe between 1881 and 1914, Michael Just found it difficult to "precisely isolate" their effects on migrants' decisions to leave their homelands. He thought it possible that the agents tipped the balance towards departure in the minds of some ambivalent prospective emigrants but, based upon his scrutiny of official investigative files, concluded that a more important function was the agents' solutions to "organizational problems" of the "migration process." Odd Lovoll, writing in 1993, but citing two additional Scandinavian studies from the 1970s, also concluded that agents had a "minimal impact on the volume of emigration," although they "did have some influence on the choice of transportation" (e.g., with which shipping company to travel).[18] While these studies are not exhaustive, their general thrust supports the judgement of Walter Kamphoefner that "agents should be seen as mediators and facilitators, who eased the process of emigration. But they could do little to promote it where a predisposition did not already exist or a firm decision to emigrate had not already been made."[19]

---

[17]Olof Thörn, "Glimpses from the Activities of a Swedish Emigrant Agent," *Swedish Pioneer Historical Quarterly*, X (1959), 3-24; Berit Brattne and Sune Akerman, "Importance of the Transport Sector for Mass Emigration," in Harald Runblom and Hans Norman (eds.), *From Sweden to America: A History of the Migration* (Minneapolis, 1976), 194; and Hvidt, "Emigration Agents," 202-203.

[18]Michael Just, *Ost- und südosteuropäische Amerikawanderung 1881-1914: Transitprobleme in Deutschland und Aufnahme in den Vereinigten Staaten* (Stuttgart, 1988), 61 and 260; and Odd S. Lovoll, "'For People Who Are Not in a Hurry:' The Danish Thingvalla Line and the Transportation of Scandinavian Emigrants," *Journal of American Ethnic History*, XIII, No. 1 (Fall 1993), 50 and 66. More recent studies largely corroborate these findings; see, for instance, the articles by Nicolas Evans and Torsten Feys in this volume.

[19]Walter Kamphoefner, "German Emigration Research, North, South, and East: Findings, Methods, and Open Questions," in Dirk Hoerder and Jörg Nagler

A number of factors appear to have perpetuated an exaggerated view in some more general histories of the influence steamship agents had upon migration.[20] It is clear that agents were at times important in affecting steamship lines' market shares of migrants who had already decided to leave Europe.[21] Nonetheless, some later observers may have leapt a bit too readily to the conclusion that this implied an influence by agents over the total size of the migration market as well.[22] Many individual agents or subagents were returned (former) emigrants, and some went on later to turn agencies into steamship lines, so the image of agents' activities may be overstated to some extent by their overlap with steamship companies and with "chain migration" networks.

(eds.), *People in Transit: German Migrations in Comparative Perspective, 1820-1930* (New York, 1995), 28. See also Brattne and Akerman, "Importance of the Transport Sector," 194; and Isaac Hourwich, *Immigration and Labor* (New York, 1912), 96-99.

[20]See, for instance, Mark Wyman, *Round-Trip to America: The Immigrants Return to Europe, 1880-1930* (Ithaca, NY, 1993), 25-31: "...on the local scene, where immigrants made their final decisions, the major instrument...of emigration was the steamship company agent. They were ubiquitous...winning converts in numbers that would have made an evangelist drool...The agent's commission was the motor behind this activity." Note, however, that the role of steamship agents is tangential to Wyman's topic, which is return migration. Among many other answers to Wyman's query "if the agents were not necessary to stir up business, why did the shipping lines employ them in such numbers?" See also Taylor, *Distant Magnet*, 109: "they stored emigrants' baggage. They arranged the transmission for their money to America. They handled tickets prepaid by relatives abroad;" and Keeling, "Business," 191. By essentially sub-contracting ticket sales through geographically dispersed networks of part-time ticket-sellers, shipping lines could more readily and economically reach would-be migrants, than through a centralized apparatus of full time employees. Networks of grocers, shoemakers, and other middlemen merchants handling ticket sales on the side, could also weather severe seasonal and cyclical fluctuations in migration flows. By contrast, if a shipping company handled ticket sales "in-house," it would have required a large staff to handle peak periods that then would have been largely redundant during slack periods. On the general reliance of the inherently far-flung shipping industry upon agents, see, for example, Stephanie Jones, "The Role of the Shipping Agent in Migration: A Study in Business History," in Friedland (ed.), *Maritime Aspects of Migration*, 349-353; and Gordon Boyce, *Information, Mediation, and Institutional Development: The Rise of Large-scale Enterprise in British Shipping, 1870-1919* (Manchester, 1995), 26-43.

[21]See, for instance, Murken, *Die großen transatlantischen Linienreederei-Verbände*, 12-14, 47-49, 53, 285, 359-360 and 403-404.

[22]This is described, for example, by Marcus Lee Hansen, *The Atlantic Migration 1607–1860: A History of the Continuing Settlement of the United States* (Cambridge, MA, 1940), 198: "Many mistakenly saw [in the activities of the agents] the principal cause of the exodus."

Earlier in the nineteenth century there were, furthermore, a large number of well-publicized efforts at private and public promotion of migration: colonization schemes, solicitations by railroad and real estate boosters and so forth. These efforts were less significant in shaping the volume of migration than appeared to some contemporary observers, and historians may have assigned undue weight to those contemporary accounts and implied a later applicability than would be warranted based upon their historical concentration in the second and third quarters of the nineteenth century. Finally, a great deal of commentary about steamship agents after 1900 came from committed anti-immigration interests in the US which were demonstrably more interested in decrying the unhealthy power of these intermediaries to "artificially stimulate" the inflow of "undesirables" than in a sober assessment of their actual "recruiting" power. The fact that a clause in the US Immigration Act of 1891 made it illegal for shipping companies or their agents to "invite, solicit, or encourage the immigration of any alien" is, moreover, no more proof of its actual relevance to migration volumes than is another provision of that same act banning polygamists from entry to America.[23]

Two caveats should nonetheless be noted here. First, although networks of steamship agents were a facilitating adjunct to the processes of human transfer across the Atlantic rather than a determinant of its volume, they were indispensable in many cases. No account of the physical processes of this mass relocation, including the choice of destination, the hazards encountered *en route* and precautions taken against such hazards, can be complete without at least acknowledging the presence of these agents. Second, when it comes to causes of migration within a long-lasting, self-reinforcing movement, all migrants are not equal. To the extent that agents played a greater role in encouraging earlier nineteenth-century "pioneer" migrants, many "links" in the subsequent "chains" of followers may in some sense be indirectly attributable to a relatively small number of initial "recruitments" by agents.

The steamship lines represented by these agents were undeniably more important than the agents themselves to the processes of mass physical relocation. Although most migrants apparently dealt with steamship agents, it was entirely possible to bypass them altogether. By contrast, there was no crossing the Atlantic a hundred years ago without first boarding a steamer.[24] The role of transatlantic steamships in mass migration has long been on the fringes of historians' traditional specialties, however: not quite on the radar screens of experts in migration, shipping, American or European history. Here

---

[23]See Jones, *American Immigration*, 104-109 and 161-165; Keeling, "Business," 187-195 and 238; and *Dillingham Report*, XXXVIII, 98-99.

[24]Transatlantic passenger service by sailing ships came to an end in the 1870s. See Raymond L. Cohn, "The Transition from Sail to Steam in Immigration to the United States," *Journal of Economic History*, LXV, No. 2 (June 2005), 470-476.

again, care is needed to identify and distinguish between anecdotal drama and fundamental underlying patterns, causes and effects.

Human versus Freight Cargoes

Passenger travel across the early twentieth-century North Atlantic was carried out by a privately-owned but government-regulated and supported oligopoly. Taking into account shipping line mergers over the period, two-thirds of migrants between Europe and the US between 1900 and 1914 travelled on ships of the four largest corporations, and ninety percent of migrants travelled with the largest ten.[25]

Migration was both the largest and riskiest contributor to the revenues and earnings of this early twentieth-century North Atlantic shipping industry. Travel by tourists and businessmen, which also grew markedly between 1900 and 1913, was both less frequent and less volatile in its fluctuations.[26] Freight

---

[25]These measurements were derived by ranking shipping companies by the number of second and third class passengers transported in both directions between Europe and the US, 1900-1914, as compiled in US Citizenship and Immigration Services Historical Reference Library, Reports of the Transatlantic Passenger Conferences. In descending order, the ten largest (merged) groups were White Star (twenty percent); North German Lloyd (nineteen percent); Cunard (fifteen percent); Hamburg American (thirteen percent); Compagnie Générale Transatlantique (seven percent); Navigazione Generale Italiana (seven percent); Holland America (four percent); Fabre (three percent); Austro-Americana (three percent); and Scandinavian American (two percent). These percentage figures total more than ninety percent due to rounding.

[26]The revenues, by business segment, of shipping lines carrying migrants between Europe and the US during 1900-1913 are estimated in Keeling, "Business," 368-369: fifty percent migrant passengers; twenty-five percent freight; twenty percent non-migrant passengers; and five percent mail. The total annual revenues to which this sectoral breakdown applies rose from just over $50 million in 1900 to just under $150 million in 1913, not including lucrative but sporadic wartime transport. Differentiating within these revenue streams between physical shifts and changes in prices, the rates of growth between the four-year averages of 1900-1903 and 1910-1913 were:

	Migrants	Non-Migrants	Freight
Number of Passengers	72%	39%	
Average Fares	23%	43%	
Revenues	111%	99%	98%

Migrant revenues fluctuated more than did non-migrant revenues. The coefficient of variation of the deviation from trend (as per Roderick Floud, *An Introduction to Quantitative Methods for Historians* [London, 1973], 82 and 114) were twenty-one percent for migrant revenues and thirteen percent for non-migrant revenues. The coefficients of variation for physical volumes differed more markedly by passenger class: twenty-six

shipments were sizable as well, and rose over the period as a whole, but were handled much more independently of migrant passenger traffic during these years than has often been assumed.

Historical discussions of how shipping companies influenced North Atlantic migration have often suggested that competition between the transport lines helped increase migration over the period by lowering fares; that the companies prospered by exploiting and overcharging migrants; or that some mixture of both occurred.[27] None of these stand up to careful analysis, however, and all have taken inspiration from another often overstated belief, expressed forthrightly by none other than Frank Thistlethwaite in his frequently-

---

percent for second and third class versus but only seven percent for first class, since fares were more stable than physical volumes, especially in second and third class. See Keeling, "Business," 368-369. About seventy-five percent of second class passengers between 1900 and 1914 were migrants, accounting for about thirteen percent of all migrants (Keeling "Business," 286). Coefficients for the Cunard Line's revenues from non-migrants, freight and migrants during 1885-1907 show a similar pattern: twenty-five, twenty-nine and forty-nine percent, respectively; University of Liverpool (UL), Cunard Archives (CA), Cunard Voyage Accounts, 1885-1914 (CVA), AC 12/1-6. Because nearly all costs associated with the generation of these revenues were fixed and jointly incurred (that is, they were little affected by either how full the ship was with passengers and freight or how big these two revenue segments were relative to each other), profit rates by segment are difficult to estimate. Clearly, however, a stream of revenues which fluctuates greatly (e.g., from migration passengers) produces under conditions of fixed costs a greater degree of fluctuation in earnings after deduction for those costs than does a less volatile revenue source (e.g., tourist passengers). This riskiness of migration flows shows in the annual reports of the North Atlantic steamship lines, which registered high overall corporate profits in migration boom years such as 1906-1907 and losses during migration slumps, as in 1908. (These results are shown more fully in Keeling, "Business," 257-263 and 336-337.) An analysis based upon available expense data and deck plan configurations revealing the allocation of carrying capacity by travel class indicates that while the margin over cost charged on tickets to migrants exceeded that of non-migrant passengers, this difference was in line with the demonstrably higher volatility (higher risk) and lower prestige value of migrant traffic. It also seems that shipping line executives believed (not unjustifiably) that decisions to travel made by non-migrants (mostly US tourists) were more sensitive to both fare levels and on-board conditions than was the case for migrants; see Drew Keeling, "Transport Capacity Management and Transatlantic Migration, 1900-1914," *Research in Economic History*, XXV (2007, forthcoming).

[27]For example, David M. Brownstone, *et al.*, *Island of Hope, Island of Tears* (New York, 1979), 118, wrote of how shipping lines "jammed migrants into quarters unsuited for any habitation at all...and made enormous profits in doing so," whereas John Lewis Gaddis, *We Now Know: Rethinking Cold War History* (Oxford, 1997), 3, wrote that "cheap steamship fares greatly increased the flow of emigrants from Russia to the United States...during the decade preceeding World War I."

quoted article "that emigrants were essentially valuable bulk cargo for unused shipping space in raw cotton or timber ships on the return voyage is a basic fact."[28]

It is entirely possible that this sort of "backhaul" may have taken place on some sailing ships of some routes at some periods during the eighteenth and nineteenth centuries, but there can be little doubt that this occurred rarely on passenger steamships after the 1890s.[29] Over thirty million migrants reached America on steamships, a number far in excess of the less than eight million voluntary and involuntary arrivals by sailing ship.[30] Migration historians have not always appreciated how different the physical circumstances of migration travel were on sailing ships in comparison with steamships which, after 1900, were roughly five or six times as fast and twelve times as voluminous as their sailing counterparts of five or six decades earlier.[31]

---

[28]Thistlethwaite, "Migration," 32.

[29]Hans-Jürgen Grabbe, *Vor der großen Flut: Die europäische Migration in die Vereinigten Staaten von Amerika 1783-1820* (Stuttgart, 2001), 115, refers specifically to this remark of Thistlethwaite saying it could not be generally applied across the whole early national period. Herbert S. Klein, *The Atlantic Slave Trade* (New York, 1999), 97 and 143-144, states categorically that "the belief in a triangular trade (European goods to Africa, slaves for America and sugar for Europe all on the same voyage) is largely a myth. The majority of American crops reached European markets in much larger and specially constructed West Indian vessels designed primarily for this shuttle trade; the majority of slavers returned with small cargoes or none at all." Robert G. Albion, *Square-Riggers on Schedule: The New York Sailing Packets to England, France, and the Cotton Ports* (Princeton, 1938), 79, points out the multiple use of early nineteenth-century sailing ships' 'tweendecks for migrants or "fine freight" (not bulk goods which were placed below the 'tweendecks and not interchanged with migrants) but does not indicate how often such multiple use may have occurred in different directions of the same voyage. Regarding the tendency of steamship lines to have specialized separate vessels for freight and for passengers, see also Thomas Sowell, *Migrations and Cultures: A World View* (New York, 1996), 41; and Cohn, "Transition," 485.

[30]Figures from *Historical Statistics of the United States from Colonial Times to 1970* (2 vols., Washington, DC, 1975), 105-106; and Cohn, "Transition," 472.

[31]Based on vessels during 1900-1914 averaging 13,000 gross tons in size and an oceanic crossing time of one week (see Keeling, "Business," 15 and 299) versus ships in the 1850s averaging about 1000 gross tons and taking five or six weeks to cross the Atlantic (see Albion, *Square-Riggers on Schedule*, 274-317; and Terry Coleman, *Passage to America: A History of Emigrants from Great Britain and Ireland to America in the Mid-nineteenth Century* [London, 1972], 92). Based on these sources, and the Commissioners of Emigration of the State of New York, *Annual Reports of the Commissioners of Emigration of the State of New York from the Organization of the Commission, May 5, 1847 to 1660* (New York, 1861), table A, the number of vessels in

Ellis Island and the Peopling of America: The Official Guide, is not atypical in its conflating of sail and steam travel. Immigrants to Ellis Island, this otherwise useful volume indicates, "spent ten days to three weeks traveling in the uncomfortable steerage class across the sea...filling the space taken by the cotton, wood, and crop cargoes...[shipped in the opposite direction]."[32] A vivid drawing of huddled masses, "Between the Decks in an Emigrant Ship," presented on the same page (64) of that book, is dated 1872 – twenty years before the first immigrant ever walked off a steamer to be processed on Ellis Island. The ship in that drawing is not identified, but the interior appears to be that of a large sailing ship, although by 1872 ninety-four percent of steerage passengers arriving at New York actually came on steamships.[33]

Transatlantic cargo traffic in the early twentieth century was indeed massive, but most went by freight-only carriers.[34] Freight transported by major passenger lines went mostly on freight-only vessels or freight-only voyages.[35] Voyages from Italy, which became the largest source of migrants to America after 1900, were accompanied by little freight flow, and the contemporary elite express liners between Britain and America took high-value, speed-dependent "fine freight" but few bulk cargoes.[36] If substantial quantities of bulk goods left early twentieth-century America in underused eastward steerage spaces of Atlantic steamers, they must have been part of the US exports to Germany and

---

regular service may have been about three times higher in the 1850s than during 1900-1914.

[32]Virginia McLaughlin and Marjorie Lightman, *Ellis Island and the Peopling of America: The Official Guide* (New York, 1997), 64.

[33]New York Commissioners of Emigration reports.

[34]Most notably Phoenix (Belgium). Leyland (England), the biggest freight transporter, according to Thomas R. Navin and Marian V. Sears, "A Study in Merger: Formation of the International Mercantile Marine Company," *Business History Review*, XXVIII, No. 4 (December 1954), 296, also carried migrants on a small percentage of its ships (based on Transatlantic Passenger Conference reports).

[35]Navin and Sears, "Study in Merger," 296; and Murken, *Die großen transatlantischen Linienreederei-Verbände*, 125.

[36]Murken, *Die großen transatlantischen Linienreederei-Verbände*, 373; and Francis E. Hyde, *Cunard and the North Atlantic, 1840-1973: A History of Shipping and Financial Management* (London, 1975), 68.

have been shipped on the HAPAG and Holland America lines, but even on those routes this was not the dominant pattern of freight movements.[37]

An oft-cited example of freight and steerage working in tandem is HAPAG's "cyclopean" *Pennsylvania* of 1896, designed with "huge migrant dormitories for use outbound, transformed into massive cargo compartments for the homeward return."[38] The more circumscribed actual extent of such freight-steerage interchange can be gauged by the detailed surviving deck plans of *President Lincoln*, the 1907 successor to *Pennsylvania*.[39] Fully half the cargo space was cargo-only (the other half was the stereotypical "cargo or passengers"). This was clearly an extreme case; most ships carried nearly all freight in cargo-only holds. The physical layout reinforced such practices.[40]

---

[37]Half of US exports went to Germany and Britain (but the latter mainly on freight lines); Navin and Sears, "Study in Merger," 296. Thus, the biggest use of "combined" freight-and-steerage ships occurred between the US and Germany. Of major passenger lines in the German-US goods traffic, NDL was well behind HAPAG in freight, while the American and Red Star lines to Antwerp faced competition from freight-only lines, such as Phoenix. Of the north European passenger lines, Holland America (Rotterdam) and HAPAG (Hamburg) took the most freight. See Murken, *Die großen transatlantischen Linienreederei-Verbände*, 28, 125, 130 and 584.

[38]See Lamar Cecil, *Albert Ballin: Business and Politics in Imperial Germany, 1888-1918* (Princeton, 1967), 24; and Kurt Himer, *Geschichte der Hamburg-Amerika Linie* (Hamburg, 1927), 35-36: *"vielseitige Verwendbarkeit...als Auswanderermassenquartiere auf der Ausreise und als Massengütertransportschiffe auf der Heimreise."*

[39]N.R. Bonsor, *North Atlantic Seaway: An Illustrated History of the Passenger Services Linking the Old World with the New* (5 vols., Newton Abbot, 1975-1980), I, 373. The deck plan for *President Lincoln* is in Hamburg Staatsarchiv (HSA), HAPAG Ship Plans (HSP), 3914/1.

[40]A variety of deck plans were consulted in repositories such as Merseyside Maritime Museum; University of Glasgow, Modern Business Records Centre; Hamburg Staatsarchiv; Deutsches Schiffahrtsmuseum; Museum Maritime (Rotterdam); and the CGT Archives (Le Havre). See also John Maxtone-Graham, *Crossing and Cruising: From the Golden Era of Ocean Liners to the Luxury Cruise Ships of Today* (New York, 1992), 2; Drew Keeling, "The Transportation Revolution and Transatlantic Migration, 1850-1914," *Research in Economic History*, XIX (1999), 52; and Murken, *Die großen transatlantischen Linienreederei-Verbände*, 11. In a sample of forty-three vessels in use during 1900-1914, it was calculated that using one hundred percent of open-berth steerage space for freight transport would have increased total freight carrying capability by only fifty percent (comparable figures for eight HAPAG and eleven Holland America vessels included therein are lower, however: thirty-two and forty-one percent, respectively), i.e., two-thirds of maximum freight volume fit in the cargo-only sections of these ships. But this two-thirds measure is effectively too low, since steerage areas were often physically too high up in the ship for bulk freight to be conveniently loaded

As a capacity-management technique, moving over-booked steerage passengers "up" into otherwise unused cabin quarters had few negative repercussions, since the available empty cabin berths would normally be the least desirable and least-wanted spaces of that portion of the ship.[41] Even in the other (less frequent) "shifting" direction, steerage passengers would not normally mind if an occasional over-booked cabin passenger was given an empty berth in steerage, since such berths, unlike those in the cabin class, tended to be equally desirable in terms of comfort and price.[42] By contrast, moving freight "up" into steerage quarters risked cluttering passenger areas, and quartering even lowly migrant passengers in below-steerage cargo holds was a technique to which companies competing on the size, grandeur and spaciousness of their vessels did not resort.[43] The largest North Atlantic steamers, most heavily travelled by migrants, tended to be the faster "express" vessels which also tended not to be in port long enough to load bulk freight in large quantities, even if they had had enough empty dormitory-style steerage space for grain, cotton, timber or other high-volume, low-value cargoes.[44]

Another common assumption is undermined by actual financial trends showing that freight and migration movements were more correlated cyclically than not.[45] Indeed, service diversity and geographic scope tended to increase

---

and carried. More typical would be NDL's "*Barbarossa* class," c. 1900, where eighty percent of maximum freight capacity was in cargo-only areas and only twenty percent in steerage. Even this, though, measures only German "combi" ships (see Keeling, "Business," 329 and 369). Elsewhere, the steerage-freight exchange was lower still and in decline. UL, CA, CVA, for instance, shows "alternation of passenger fittings" (removal of steerage bunks for cargo loading) at three percent of total voyage costs in 1890 but only 0.1 percent by 1910.

[41]See Keeling, "Capacity," section 3.

[42]This is based on an examination of deck plans; see note 40.

[43]This practice was illegal anyway by 1909, when regulations requiring all passengers to be quartered above the waterline came into force. See, for example, *Dillingham Report*, XXXIX, 374; and *New York Times*, 9 May 1912.

[44]See Keeling, "Capacity," section 5.

[45]Suggestions that freight transport was a cyclical hedge to fluctuations in migration can be found in Hyde, *Cunard and the North Atlantic*, 134; Edwin Drechsel, *Norddeutscher Lloyd, Bremen, 1857-1970: History, Fleet, Ships, Mails* (Vancouver, 1995), 134; and Birgit Ottmüller-Wetzel, "Auswanderung über Hamburg: Die H.A.A.G. und die Auswanderung nach Nordamerika, 1870-1914" (Unpublished PhD thesis, Freie Universität Berlin, 1986), 139. On the other hand, a weighted average of available data of Cunard, HAPAG, Holland America and CGT (based upon company

cyclical risk.[46] Shipping lines combined transatlantic freight with migration, not primarily as an eastbound "backhaul" or as a cyclical offset but in accordance with strategies to rent out all compartments of their large oceanic vessels remuneratively and conveniently.[47]

The finding that the interchange of ship space between migrants in one direction and freight cargoes in the other was rare after 1900 has three implications which warrant brief mention. First, although a widely-noted and truly dramatic decline in freight rates during the nineteenth century helped spur the rapid growth of exports from North America (and this, in turn, had significant and far-flung effects internationally, especially in Europe),[48] migration to the US was essentially de-coupled from this process in at least two respects: migrant passenger fares did not fall between the 1850s and 1910s (although European and US wages trended higher over these decades) and the overall level of migrant flows (which rose several-fold over this time for other reasons) was not very sensitive to changes in ticket prices. Second, the steamship lines found it expedient increasingly to interchange carrying capacity between migrants and tourists. Third, this practice meant that increasing numbers of migrants between Europe and the US after 1900 travelled not in the old-fashioned, open-berth steerage with its removable wooden bunks but in more modern and private enclosed second and third class cabins.[49]

---

annual reports and archival records) shows a seventy percent positive correlation between freight and passengers on volume and a thirty percent correlation on price.

[46]See Murken, *Die großen transatlantischen Linienreederei-Verbände*, 121 and 354-355; Deutsches Schiffahrtsmuseum (DSM), *Norddeutscher Lloyd* (NDL), Annual Report, 1908, 4; and Frank Broeze, "Albert Ballin, The Hamburg-Bremen Rivalry and the Dynamics of the Conference System," *International Journal of Maritime History*, III, No. 1 (June 1991), 1-32.

[47]See Drew Keeling, "Transatlantic Shipping Cartels and Migration between Europe and America, 1880-1914," *Essays in Economic and Business History*, XVII (1999), 197.

[48]See, for example, Kevin H. O'Rourke, "The European Grain Invasion, 1870-1913," *Journal of Economic History*, LVII, No. 4 (December 1997), 775-801. Interestingly, one effect was to increase the incentives for European peasants to emigrate overseas because their agricultural output was no longer competitive against cheaper imports from America.

[49]By 1913 over one-third travelled in such enclosed rooms; Keeling, "Business," 288. Open-berth steerage was an area of the vessel which could also be used for carrying freight, although (as discussed above) it rarely was after 1900. On fare trends, see Keeling, "Transportation Revolution," 42-43.

The newer form of on-board accommodation was less discomforting and provided better protection against disease and violations of personal privacy. The conversion to "closed berths," which was complete on routes from the British Isles by 1913 and well underway on others, is one example of several wherein a strategy by one network (e.g., the transport oligopoly's efforts to reduce the risk of costly unused capacity) indirectly helped reduce the risks to another network (e.g., of migrants facing discomfort and lack of privacy on their oceanic crossings).[50]

A similar sort of overlapping risk reduction applied to the rather more coordinated and networked interaction between steamship lines and governments. Before that can be examined, however, it is first necessary to identify and discuss briefly the government entities most centrally involved.

Regulating the Atlantic Door to Keep It Open

Across the transatlantic labour markets of 1900-1914, the most crucial political actors were the public authorities in the US. There were two main reasons for the paramount importance of US entities within the network of regulators establishing legal and institutional rules and operating guidelines for mass migration in this period.

First, the US was the dominant country involved with transoceanic relocation from Europe during these fifteen years. Nearly two-thirds of European emigrants crossing the Atlantic were destined for US ports. The second largest New World recipient country, Argentina, took only about thirteen percent of the total.[51] The largest exporter of labour across the Atlantic, Italy, contributed twenty-three percent, a volume barely one-third of that which entered the US over that same time span. The two largest countries of "transit migration," Britain and Germany, each handled about twenty percent of the total flow.[52] Because of the sheer size and weighting of the U.S. within the

---

[50]The growth and regional use of closed berths to house transatlantic migrants after 1900 is outlined by Taylor, *Distant Magnet*, 150-164; and Maxtone-Graham, *Crossing and Cruising*, 11. See also *New York Times*, 6 March 1905; Edward Steiner, *On the Trail of the Immigrant* (New York, 1906), 112; and *Dillingham Report*, XXXVII, 5-13.

[51]See appendix 4.

[52]The 22.5 million westward transatlantic migrants of 1900-1914 (see appendix 3) broken down by source, destination and route were as follows:

total relocation, therefore, even a relatively improbable possibility of a partial closing of its "open door" to European population inflows was a matter for international concern.

The possibility of a shift towards noticeably greater barriers against foreigners coming to work and live in the US was the second source of American importance in the political formulation of transatlantic migration policy and practice. Although the actual trend in the two decades preceding the First World War was toward the incremental raising of minor barriers by the US government, which reduced the total inflow from Europe by less than ten percent, there were regular calls for much more drastic action.[53] In 1897 and again in 1913, laws which would have blocked the entry of all migrants unable to "read and write the language of their native country" passed both houses of Congress and were only stopped by presidential vetoes.[54]

During 1900-1914, no comparably severe impediment to America-bound migration was ever seriously considered by European countries. To be sure, there were recurring regrets that able-bodied young workers were leaving

	From All of Europe			From Italy
	Direct	Indirect	All	
To US:	32%	33%	65%	16%
To Canada:	5%	4%	9%	1%
To Rest of Western Hemisphere	21%	5%	26%	7%
Total by route (direct/indirect):	58%	42%	100%	23%

The source, destination and route totals come from the time series used in appendices 1 and 4. "Direct" means from a port in the migrant's home country to a country in the Western Hemisphere. Indirect means via a third country. The direct-indirect division for "rest of Western Hemisphere" was derived as follows: seventy-five percent of migrants to this large "remainder" area moved to Argentina and Brazil. Eighty percent of migrants to Argentina and Brazil came from Italy and Spain. It is assumed that those eighty percent travelled direct, that all others travelled indirect and that this eighty percent/twenty percent ratio applies to the remaining twenty-five percent of the "rest of Western Hemisphere" region as a whole.

[53]Most of these were blocked in Europe, according to BI, *Annual Report, 1907* (Washington, DC, 1908), 8-10 and 138. Ninety-nine percent of European migrants who traversed the Atlantic to the US were admitted (BI, *Annual Report, 1914* [Washington, DC, 1915], 106).

[54]These measures would have blocked about half of "new immigrants" from southern and eastern Europe from entry to the US, given that their self-reported illiteracy rate (recorded on manifests of arriving passengers) of thirty-three percent (based on *Dillingham Report*, III, 84) was probably an underestimate. On the legislative actions and presidential vetoes, see John Higham, *Strangers in the Land: Patterns of American Nativism, 1860-1925* (New Brunswick, NJ, 1988), 101-105 and 190-191.

European labour forces, and there was an active interest in the repatriation of their earnings and experience, if not their physical persons. There was also a periodic hue and cry about *how* migrants reached the Americas (e.g., whether by national or foreign steamship carriers) and, in "transit countries," frequent concerns over diseases and other unpleasantries which might accompany "third country" migrants. With the exception of a ban on departures of males of military age imposed by many European countries (but widely evaded), however, no major barrier on overseas relocation was seriously contemplated.[55] Most changes in European policy and procedure towards overseas emigration came as networks there adapted to and coordinated with gradually tightening American rules designed to preserve the essentially unrestricted nature of transatlantic migration by regulating its hazards and deficiencies.

The US Bureau of Immigration (BI) reflected this regulatory "risk management" approach to migration in its 1901 *Annual Report* when it commented on the "necessity, as a means of self-preservation, of undertaking seriously and earnestly to adopt means, not necessarily to shut off immigration, or even materially to diminish it, but at least to deal with it so that it may not continue to threaten our social and civil order."[56] The BI (ensconced within the US Department of Commerce and Labor for most of this period) worked closely with Congress, the executive branch, the mostly foreign-owned shipping lines and its overseas counterparties to weed out a very small minority of would-be migrants to the US who were deemed "undesirable" and to improve precautionary measures for the safe and orderly processing of the vast majority who were permitted entry.[57] This approach was designed to meet the concerns of immigration restriction advocates in America without acceding to their proposals for a major quantitative blockage of would-be entrants to the country. This lightly-regulated, open-border regime basically worked smoothly and consistently up to World War I.

Despite these mostly viable policies, promulgated through a sometimes overstretched but ultimately effective international network, agitation in

---

[55] One sizable exception, Russia's passport requirement, was largely honoured in the breach. See Arthur Salz, "Auswanderung und Schiffahrt mit besonderer Berücksichtigung der österreichischen Verhältnisse," *Archiv für Sozialwissenschaften und Sozialpolitik*, XLII (1916), 880-881; Nugent, *Crossings*, 42-43; Just, *Transitprobleme*, 29-30 and 106-107; and Thomas Pitkin, *The Keepers of the Gate: A History of Ellis Island* (New York, 1975), 25.

[56] BI, *Annual Report, 1901* (Washington, DC, 1902), 36.

[57] Space does not permit a discussion of the relationships with a range of more tangentially involved American agencies, such as the US Customs Service, marine health inspectors, local city officials and port authorities, state immigration and assimilation bodies, and the like.

America for much more serious barriers to immigration grew slightly over the period.[58] One recurring complaint of the "restrictionists" was that by engaging in fare wars and other ticket price reductions steamship lines made journeys to America's still relatively "pristine" shores possible for the "scum" of Europe who otherwise would not have been able to afford the passage. Here again, as with the inflated perceptions about the power of steamship agents, many contemporary observers and some later historical analysts have been a bit too quick to ascribe factual significance to politically-motivated exaggerations.

Costs of Migration

Falling transatlantic ticket prices cannot be an explanation for rising migration to America after 1900 because fares did not fall over the period, not even in real terms.[59] Mass transatlantic migration on steamships was generally positively correlated with passage prices for two reasons: first, because decisions to migrate depended much less on the fluctuations of cross-Atlantic ticket prices than on economic conditions in America and second, because North Atlantic steamship fare wars tended to erupt during recessionary drops in migrant traffic.[60] Both these reasons diminished in importance after 1900, although only slightly. The rising incidence of repeat and return migration produced a segment of experienced migrant passengers, based mainly in America, who were at times ready to make relatively opportunistic and discretionary interim moves back and forth across the Atlantic in response to travel bargains.[61] This occurred notably during the 1904-1905 fare war in the UK, the

---

[58]These included the aforementioned literacy test, which would have cut migration to the US by about one-third, a figure that was still much less severe than the ninety percent cutoff actually adopted in the 1920s.

[59]Average fares between Europe and the US rose about twenty-three percent between 1900 and 1913 (see appendix 5), whereas consumer prices in America went up by eighteen percent (calculated from Eh.net, "How Much is That"? [http://: eh.net/hmit/compare]). The outbreak of transatlantic steamship fare wars during recessionary slumps in US immigration in the late nineteenth and early twentieth centuries has been widely noted. See, for example, Otto Mathies, *Hamburgs Reederei 1814-1914* (Hamburg, 1924), 90-91; William Henry Flayhart III, *The American Line (1871-1902)* (New York, 2000), 103 and 165-169; Robin Bastin, "Cunard and the Liverpool Emigrant Traffic, 1860-1900" (Unpublished MA thesis, University of Liverpool, 1971), 79-83, 95 and 100; Himer, *Geschichte der Hamburg-Amerika Linie*, 33-34; and Murken, *Die großen transatlantischen Linienreederei-Verbände*, 335.

[60]Keeling, "Transportation Revolution," 42-43.

[61]Particularly of short term trips to northern Europe by migrants already established in America. See Keeling, "Business," 155 and 347.

most severe episode of price-slashing of the period. The stabilizing effect of market-sharing "conference" (cartel) mechanisms, eventually strengthened after that fare war, is apparent in the relatively slight fluctuation in fares during the 1908 recession, the most severe of the period (see appendix 5).[62] Overall, however, fundamental decisions to relocate across the Atlantic remained little affected by changes in oceanic fares. The fare data in appendices 5-7 show no major shift in average levels either seasonally or secularly across the fifteen-year period, and cyclical fare declines (in 1904, 1908 and 1911) were associated with lower, not higher, volumes of westward migration.[63]

---

[62]Second class fares were correlated with steerage fares, although they fluctuated less; see appendix 6. Eastbound fares were closely tied to westbound fares, but were generally a bit lower. Travel times (and costs) were also slightly lower eastbound than westbound, and the influence of cartel agreements covered eastward passenger flows less comprehensively than westward; see Murken, *Die großen transatlantischen Linienreederei-Verbände*, 45-46, 75-77 and 374.

[63]The higher level of fares from Rotterdam compared to Liverpool shown in appendix 6 is consistent with the general pattern of transatlantic fares being higher from Europe than from Britain throughout the nineteenth century. This was most probably due to stronger market-sharing conferences among the continental lines after the early 1890s, reinforcing a legacy of lower fares from British ports inherited from the mid-nineteenth century when a large percentage of continental emigrants went to North America via the UK; see Coleman, *Passage to America*, 23, 68, 73-74 and 135; Hansen, *Atlantic Migration*, 194; Cecil, *Albert Ballin*, 12-22 and 27-62; and Derek Aldcroft (ed.),*The Development of British Industry and Foreign Competition, 1875-1914* (London, 1968), 331-342. In other words, the lower fares from Liverpool can be seen as compensating for the additional costs of getting to Liverpool from continental ports and then crossing the Atlantic from there, versus going directly to America. There are other offsets which help explain how the fare difference could have persisted over time, because Cunard was roughly typical of other UK lines (such as White Star), and Holland America was similar in many respects to other North European lines (such as the two large German lines). Cunard's steerage fares from Liverpool were only about two-thirds to three-quarters as high as Holland America's from Rotterdam, but Holland America's ships were, overall (east and west) only about two-thirds as full as Cunard's vessels (round-trip capacity utilization in steerage was twenty-seven percent versus Cunard's forty percent). Cunard also had a higher rate of space usage in the first cabin, as well as much higher average prices there. Moreover, Cunard also had a considerably higher percentage of vessel space devoted to the upper-class customers, which effectively lowered the portion of its operating costs applicable to migrant carriage. Crew levels and rates of coal usage were two to three times higher on Cunard's vessels, largely to provide faster transit and more spacious accommodations for the benefit of those luxury tourist passengers. For example, Holland America's 12,600-gross ton *Potsdam* (1900) had room for twenty percent more passengers in all classes than Cunard's 12,900-ton *Campania* (1893) but burned only 140 tons of coal per day versus 485 for the Cunard liner, and had a total crew of 255 versus 415 on *Campania*. Crew wages averaged thirty percent higher on Cunard's vessels during 1900-1914, although

Fluctuations in Atlantic fares were more significant in shaping how people left Europe than in whether or not they would depart in the first place. The slashing of steerage rates by up to two-thirds in the fare war of 1904-1905, which mainly affected traffic between the UK and the US, diverted travellers from other routes, increased the incidence of short-term roundtrip visits home to Europe by migrants already in the US, and led residents of the British Isles to cross the ocean sooner than otherwise planned in order to benefit from the relative travel bargain. In other words, the cut-rate fares mainly affected the routing, timing and degree of circularity exhibited by those whose initial decision to leave Europe had already been made. To a lesser extent, an increase in the number of Europeans deciding to go to America for the first time is detectable as well during this fare war.[64] Such infrequent exceptions aside, the impact of "fence-sitting" potential migrants induced by fare reductions to decide to leave home pales in comparison to the much more powerful effects of a fluctuating job market in America accessed by extended kinship networks, whose operations were facilitated by the political and commercial coalitions that smoothed mass travel and kept border barriers to a minimum.[65]

There remains the theoretical possibility that the costs of migration other than outlays for the Atlantic traverse may have been salient factors in determining who left Europe and who did not. But here again a closer look at actual magnitudes and mechanisms undermines commonly-held assumptions. The breadth, diversity and longevity of mass migration to the US a century ago, and the relatively minimal legal restrictions placed upon it, makes it highly implausible that more than a small minority of Europeans by 1900 could

---

Holland America was disadvantaged by a longer route, requiring about a forty percent-longer transit time (an average of ten days to reach New York from Rotterdam versus seven from Liverpool, during which coal was burned and wages paid) and incurred a price per ton of coal about ten percent higher. Figures and estimates from appendix 6 and Keeling, "Capacity," appendices 3-8. See also Aldcroft (ed.), *Development*, 341; and Adam W. Kirkaldy, *British Shipping: Its History, Organisation and Importance* (London, 1919), 639.

[64]These effects are measured and described more fully in Keeling, "Business," 155-165 and 359-364.

[65]The widely observed and extreme sensitivity of transatlantic migration to the US business cycle was first comprehensively analyzed in Harry Jerome, *Migration and Business Cycles* (St. Albans, VT, 1926). The cyclicality of migration was also well-recognized by contemporaries. In testimony before Congress in 1899, proponents and opponents of mass immigration agreed that "the most important influence" behind it was "the degree of prosperity in this country;" see United States, Congress, House of Representatives, 57th Congress, 1st session, document no. 184, Industrial Commission on Immigration and Education, 1901, Reports, XXXIX-XL.

have been unaware of at least the general possibility of economic betterment in America. Despite such readily-apparent advantages, however, roughly eighty percent of those most prone to leave Europe stayed there instead, and moving costs are unlikely to have been the leading reason for such stay-at-home decisions.[66]

The notion that a great preponderance of potential European emigrants did not go abroad because they could not afford to is inconsistent with the repeated finding that their counterparts who did migrate came overwhelmingly from the lower-middle economic rungs of their societies, not from the upper-middle levels.[67] The relatively low significance of migration costs to migration decisions is underscored by a specific examination of such costs, the results of which are shown in appendices 8-10.

A transatlantic steamship ticket in 1900 represented about half of the total cost of migrating from Europe to the US. Other costs included the savings not accumulated during the period of being unemployed while migrating, the costs of overland travel and the costs of getting established in America (see appendix 8).[68] The widespread adoption of steamships and railroads as modes of travel by transatlantic migrants in the 1860s and 1870s lowered these costs, but from the 1880s to 1914 their overall level hardly changed at all (see appendix 9). Taking into account rising wages over the nineteenth century, the affordability of migrating did decline (see appendix 10), but by the 1860s the total costs of relocation could be recouped after less than six months work in the US. Most migrant passages were indeed financed, directly or indirectly, out of future earnings in America or by past earnings of relatives already there.[69] By 1900, however, an average European could save enough to finance

---

[66]Just under one-fifth of males between the ages of fifteen and forty-four living in the emigration-prone lands of south and east Europe in 1900 migrated to the Western Hemisphere during the subsequent fifteen years; Drew Keeling, "The Economics of Migratory Transport between Europe and the USA, 1900-14" (Unpublished working paper, University of California World History Workshop, April 2005), 2; and appendix 6. On the sharp decline in information barriers to transatlantic migration, see, for example, J.D. Gould, "European Inter-Continental Emigration, 1815-1914: Patterns and Causes," *Journal of European Economic History*, VIII (1979), 618.

[67]Bodnar, *Transplanted*, 13 and 23; Timothy J. Hatton and Jeffrey G. Williamson, *Global Migration and the World Economy: Two Centuries of Policy and Performance* (Cambridge, MA, 2005), 88-94.

[68]On the phenomenon of "working their passage" as crew on an oceanic steamer, see Lewis R. Fischer, "The Sea as Highway: Maritime Service as a Means of International Migration, 1863-1913," in Friedland (ed.), *Maritime Aspects of Migration*, 293-307.

[69]Taylor, *Distant Magnet*, 101.

a transatlantic move by working for a year in Europe first (even without any funding from relatives already in the US). A year is not a long period for a long-distance migrant. Migrants to America who later moved back to Europe in this period were typically in the host country for at least a few years.[70] Even today, long-distance migrants tend to be away from home for more than a year. Often, in fact, the one-year cutoff is used to define migrants in distinction to short-term visitors.[71]

The migration cost and affordability estimates for the late nineteenth and early twentieth centuries shown in appendices 8-10 are approximate and, because they aggregate across all of Europe, do not show variations such as those between migrants from northern and western Europe, on the one hand, and those from southern and eastern Europe on the other.[72] Nevertheless, it is difficult to see how the costs of migrating could possibly be a main explanation for why the overwhelming majority of Europeans did not pursue the widely-recognized and legally-accessible economic opportunities of relocating to North America after 1900. It is conceivable, for example, that the affordability of migrating to America from Russia may have improved between 1880 and 1910 slightly faster than it did from Germany over the same time span. This can hardly explain, however, why migration to the US in the 1880s was six times higher from Germany than from Russia, whereas during 1900 and 1910 the ratio was almost the reverse: the Russian flow was four and a half times that of the German.[73]

Of greater significance to this reversal were developments within Germany towards the end of the nineteenth century. The adoption of social security and social welfare measures, a relaxation of measures against Socialists, labour unions and Catholics and – not least – Germany's epochal industrial boom which turned it from a net exporter to an importer of labour combined to reduce the risks and consequences of unemployment there which correspondingly lowered the relative attractiveness of relocation to North Amer-

---

[70]A third of those recorded as leaving in 1910 had been in the US for over five years; see BI, *Annual Report, 1910* (Washington, DC, 1911), 68.

[71]United States, National Archives and Records Administration (NARA), Record Group (RG) 85, entry 9, 53420, circular 24 dated August 1, 1908; and *Economist*, 15 June 2002.

[72]Travel costs were higher from southern and eastern regions. Effective railroad connections, and concurrent declines in overland travel costs and time, came in the 1870s and 1880s, a generation later than in northern and western Europe.

[73]*Historical Statistics of the United States*, 105-106.

ica.[74] Contemporaneous trends in Russia were heading in a roughly opposite direction after 1880, at least for many Jews in the "Pale of Settlement" from whence roughly half of Russian migrants to America came between 1880 and 1914.[75]

In general, however, most people, most of the time, consider it riskier to leave home for a distant foreign land than to remain in familiar surroundings. Normal human aversion to risk is thus one reason why most people do not migrate.[76] To better understand the role of migration risks in European emigration decisions a century ago, however, and how important they were relative to costs and other factors in shaping migrant self-selection, those risks need to be considered more explicitly.

Risks Related to Migration

Risk, in the commonly understood general sense of a danger of a negative event, was a salient aspect of transatlantic migration, present in many forms. These risks varied in severity, probability, predictability and preventability, and in their geographic, demographic and temporal incidence. The three most important groups of networks involved in the processes of transatlantic relocation – migrants, shipping firms and governments – were both bearers and producers of these risks.[77]

---

[74]Gordon A. Craig, *Germany, 1866-1945* (Oxford, 1978), 77-78, 151 and 172-174; Klaus J. Bade, "German Migration to the United States and Continental Immigration to Germany in the Late Nineteenth and Early Twentieth Centuries," *Central European History*, XIII, No. 4 (1980), 348-350.

[75]BI, *Annual Reports*, various years; and Nugent, *Crossings*, 93-94.

[76]This is not meant to imply that persons migrating across long distances are any more or less "rational" than other humans but only that those contemplating such relocations have fears; that such fears are not without foundation; and that during 1900-1914, at least, such fears, and the risks which underlay them, were an important barrier to relocation across the North Atlantic.

[77]Migrants were subject to the risks – petty and grievous – of those who preyed upon them in port cities, as well as to mishandling by steamship crews or government officials. Migrants also faced risks from other migrants. Companies in the inherently trans-national North Atlantic shipping business had to cope not only with the challenges of industry competition and the double risk of adverse actions by both domestic and foreign governments but also with the numerous problems and uncertainties associated with shepherding "huddled masses" across their many-thousand-mile journeys. US politicians, to widely varying degrees, perceived a range of dangers associated with an essentially privately-determined mass population influx – from sanitation and disease to cultural or "racial" incompatibilities of the newcomers – and saw their

"What greater gamble is there than immigration?" asked Stephen Birmingham in the introduction to his 1984 account of Eastern European Jewish emigration. Other historians have tended to agree that to migrate across the Atlantic a century ago was, generally speaking, to trade a familiar if often unsatisfactory present for a more promising yet more uncertain future.[78] Risk was also an important consideration for the transport and public policy networks involved with that mass migration.[79]

The two most serious risks faced by early twentieth-century transatlantic migrants and shipping lines were an economic setback in America, which could eliminate the employment opportunities that prompted such migration in the first place, and the lurking if unlikely threat of severe legal restriction by the US government against the inflows of foreign labour. The risk of restriction was, in turn, based largely on the risks which mass in-migration posed (especially in the perceptions of politicians pressing for restriction) to the societal cohesion or "racial" composition of the US. Because a political shutdown was a relatively remote possibility, however, and neither migrants nor the shipping lines which carried them across the Atlantic had any significant direct influence over the formulation of such policies, both the transporters and the transported paid relatively greater attention to the risk of a general downswing in the US economy and the associated effects on labour markets.

Cyclical risks were endemic to nineteenth- and early twentieth-century *laissez-faire* capitalism in general, and to transatlantic labour migration in particular, and were an acute concern for those migrants and their transporters during that era. Because European migrants in early twentieth-century America worked disproportionately at temporary and marginal jobs and in cyclical industries, their employment prospects were highly cyclical. The marginal shift into employment associated with westward migration to the US was even more

---

transporters as potential instigators or augmenters of such threats. European governments had related concerns about mass departures and/or mass through-transits. Diverse risks might either offset or compound each other (as with *Titanic*). Avoiding, shifting, hedging or diversifying against risk was a key component of strategies by migrants, shipping lines and governments towards mass relocation before World War I. The greatest risks for all three groups (transporters, transportees and regulators) were also among the most difficult to foresee in advance: economic cyclicality and political upheaval. See the variation data presented in footnote 26; and Keeling, "Business," particularly 9-11, 41-64, 234-236, 302-306, 309-313, 322-335 and 343.

[78]Stephen Birmingham, *The Rest of Us: The Rise of America's Eastern European Jews* (Boston, 1984), xii. See also Taylor, *Distant Magnet*, 91; Wyman, *Round-Trip to America*, 83-88 and 193; and Julianna Puskás, "Hungarian Overseas Migration: A Microanalysis," in Vecoli and Sinke (eds.), *Century of European Migrations*, 227.

[79]See the immediately preceding footnote; and Keeling, "Economics," 8-17.

cyclical. High fixed costs in shipping meant that this cyclical variation was magnified still further in its impacts on the net income of transport lines.[80]

As a business, shipping is well known for its "hazards" and "great fluctuations." Transatlantic passenger steamship lines have been described as being engaged in a "huge gamble" in a commerce "as shifting and unstable as the sea" itself.[81] "There are few investments which represent more uncertainty of returns than the modern fast steamer," wrote one turn-of-the-century observer.[82] The combination of passenger flow swings that were much wider than those of gross national products, together with expensive, complex and mobile assets, and costs that barely budged at all with shifts in revenues, meant that early twentieth-century transatlantic migrant transport was "a business that is exposed to the very greatest fluctuations" and beset with "continual dangers."[83] A ten percent move up or down in ticket receipts from migrant passengers might be magnified into something like a fifty percent swing in bottom-line profits.[84] Bankruptcies of North Atlantic passenger lines between 1890 and 1914 have been attributed to the cyclical downturns in migrant traffic

---

[80]See Keeling, "Economics," 5-7 and 9-13.

[81]Martin Stopford, *Maritime Economics* (London, 1988; 2nd ed., London, 1997), 219; Earl A. Saliers, "Some Financial Aspects of the International Mercantile Marine Company," *Journal of Political Economy*, XXIII, No. 9 (November 1915), 910-925; Kirkaldy, *British Shipping*, 205-206; Ottmüller-Wetzel, "Auswanderung über Hamburg," 143; and Jean Strouse, *Morgan: American Financier* (New York, 1999), 476.

[82]George Walsh, "The Cost of Running a Modern Steamer," *Harper's Weekly*, 5 January 1901.

[83]Passenger swings were often exacerbated in their effect by the tendency of cutthroat price reductions to come during recessionary slumps. The early twentieth-century North Atlantic steamers cost anywhere from half a million dollars (Hellenic Line's 6000-ton *Themistocles* of 1907) to ten million dollars (Cunard's 46,000-ton *Aquitania* of 1914). See Vassilis Kardasis, "The International Trends and Greek Shipping: The Business Strategy of Demetrios Moraitis, 1893-1908," in David J. Starkey and Gelina Harlaftis (eds.), *Global Markets; The Internationalization of the Sea Transport Industries since 1850* (St John's, 1997), 296; J.B. Isherwood, "Steamers of the Past," *Sea Breezes*, XLVIII (1974), 73; and M.G. De Boer, *The Holland-America Line, 1873-1923* (Amsterdam, 1923), introduction.

[84]This is a rough estimate which takes into account the limited ability of shipping managers to cancel some voyages, and the roughly fifty percent of revenues that came, on average, from other, less cyclical business segments, principally tourist travellers, freight transport and mail carriage. As appendix 1 shows, however, fluctuations of more than ten percent in migrant traffic were all too common.

over that period, and the trend of overall profits of the major lines during 1900-1914 closely tracks the jagged curve of migration flows in those years.[85]

From a public policy perspective, the risks posed by immigrants to the US at the outset of the twentieth century fell into two general categories depending upon the viewpoint of the observer.[86] Pro-restriction perceptions with a nativist and Social Darwinist tinge were encapsulated in the remarks of Francis Walker in 1899:

> The entrance into our political, social, and industrial life of such vast masses of peasantry, degraded below our utmost conceptions, is a matter which no intelligent patriot can look upon without the gravest apprehension and alarm. These people...have none of the inherited instincts and tendencies which made it comparatively easy to deal with the immigration of the olden time. They are beaten men from beaten races; representing the worst failures in the struggle for existence...Have we the right to expose the republic to any increase of the dangers from this source which now so manifestly threaten our peace and safety? For it is never to be forgotten that self-defense is the first law of nature and of nations.[87]

From a quite – if not entirely – different perspective three years later, the risks stemming from an influx of foreigners were seen as limited and qualitative, rather than massive and quantitative:

> Our policy of excluding the diseased, the degenerate, and the incompetent has had excellent results, and may profitably be still further extended. But there is no occasion for a panic fear that the American republic will be washed away by the "scum of Europe."[88]

---

[85]This was true despite the fact that about half of those companies' revenues came from businesses other than migrant transport.

[86]Policy on *immigrants* is not the same thing as policy on *immigration*, but most perceptions and commentaries merge the two, including observations made concerning the risks of migration to America in the early twentieth century.

[87]Francis A. Walker, "The Restriction of Immigration," in Philip Davis (ed.), *Immigration and Americanization* (1899; reprint, Boston, 1920), 370-371.

[88]Samuel E. Moffett, "This Year's High Tide of Immigration," *American Monthly Review of Reviews*, XXVIII, No. 1 (July 1903), 57-58.

Federal politicians and immigration officials developed a formula to accommodate both proponents and opponents of immigration restriction. Their policies essentially treated the limited qualitative risks of a growing, but before the 1920s very small, selected minority of "undesirable" migrants, while adopting some of the rhetoric of the restrictionists by gradually increasing the number of reasons for exclusion and the ratio of arriving migrants debarred under them. US Commissioner of Immigration Frank Sargent put it this way in 1904: "There comes a class of very undesirable aliens against whom further restrictive legislation is needed...This can easily be accomplished and still leave a large immigration to which no such objections can be urged."[89] The main attention of the BI was directed towards coping with the practical risks of the large crowds resulting from the policy of allowing, *de facto*, over ninety percent of would-be immigrants to enter the US. To cope with those challenges, a cooperative network of foreign governments, port authorities and shipping lines was needed.

Nevertheless, the most important networks of migration were the webs of inter-linkages among groups of migrants themselves. The operations of these networks need to be examined more specifically to evaluate the relative important of migration costs and risks in both their extent and function.

Migrant Networks and Risk Management

Reliance upon extended kinship networks has been a widely-observed feature of long-distance migration in general and of transatlantic movement a century ago in particular. Family and community networks were essential to provide potential migrants with multiple destination and timing options and to spread the relocation process over multiple partners and stages.

"Chain migration," in which initial "pioneers" were followed by relatives "as if they were links in a chain," was the dominant means by which tens of millions of Europeans moved across the Atlantic.[90] Family, kinship and community networks largely shaped decisions of potential migrants regarding how, when and where to move:

> By and large, the effective units of migration were (and are)...sets of people linked by acquaintance, kinship, and work experience who somehow incorporated American destinations into the mobility alternatives they considered when

---

[89]Frank Sargent, "The Need of Closer Inspection and Greater Restriction of Immigrants," *Century Magazine*, LXVII (January 1904), 472.

[90]See Andrew Godley, *Jewish Immigrant Entrepreneurship in New York and London, 1880-1914: Enterprise and Culture* (New York, 2001), 71.

they reached critical decision points in their individual or collective lives.[91]

Because they helped identify, manage and diversify the risks of relocation, these networks were also vital to decisions about whether to migrate in the first place. The better developed the available chain migration network and the stronger its role in providing information, reducing costs and lowering uncertainties and risks, the more likely any European contemplating an overseas move would be to take the plunge and leave.[92]

Migration networks served both to narrow and broaden channels of transatlantic labour transfer. Usually, migration networks connected Europeans from one local home community to just one overseas destination country (e.g., the US), although there were certainly individual instances of migrants with multiple networks or "networks of networks:" Italians, for example, with relatives in both Buenos Aires and New York.[93] Over time, migrant networks also dispersed across multiple locations within the destination country.

Beyond their significance in narrowing or constraining long-distance transfers, migration networks also served to multiply, replicate and divide the movement process. Instead of individuals making one-time individual decisions to use their resources to implement single, once-and-for-all, and uni-directional moves, migration through networks involved group decisions which broke the process down into stages carried out by migration "partners" making multiple and two-way moves across the Atlantic.

One manifestation of network effects was in the financing of overseas moves.[94] This made eminent sense given the higher wages in America that

---

[91]See Tilly, "Transplanted Networks," 84.

[92]See Bodnar, *Transplanted*, 54-70; and Taylor, *Distant Magnet*, 210-238.

[93]Of countries sending large numbers of migrants to the turn-of-the-century US, Italy had the most also moving to another country (Argentina). See Nugent, *Crossings*, 46 and 95. Relatively few families, however, sent members to both the US and Argentina; see Dino Cinel, *The National Integration of Italian Return Migration, 1870–1929* (Cambridge, 1991), 110; and J.D. Gould, "European Inter-Continental Emigration, the Road Home: Return Migration from the USA," *Journal of European Economic History*, IX (1980), 593-679. Migrant networks of other European ethnic groups also specialized mostly in just one destination country; see, for example, Godley, *Jewish Immigrant Entrepreneurship*, 70-71.

[94]By the late nineteenth century, according to Taylor, *Distant Magnet*, 101, "remittances, in cash or in the form of prepaid tickets, undoubtedly became the mainstay of all but pioneer migration."

were the main attraction for most migrants in the first place.[95] Between 1900 and 1914, a quarter of US immigrants were recorded as being dependents without occupations, and an overlapping, but non-identical, quarter to half travelled on tickets prepaid by relatives already in America (see appendix 11).

A growing return rate to Europe is also attributable in no small degree to the accumulating impact of migration "chains."[96] Two-way migration reinforced these networks. Migrants returned to Europe to bring labour, savings and expertise back to their origin communities, for short-term visits to renew ties and connections to family members in Europe and to help additional relatives relocate to North America. Family networks, on both sides of the Atlantic, provided a safety net for migrants against the risk of being debarred from entry to America or of cyclical unemployment or other hazards encountered in the New World.[97]

Migrant networks thus helped to raise both the overall volume of people migrating across the North Atlantic and the number of crossings per migrant. These accomplishments came because the networks lowered the costs and brought down or made more manageable the risks of migrating. Which of these two effects, the decrease in costs or the enhanced capability for coping with risks, was most important?[98]

At first glance, the question may seem tangential to an understanding of the fundamental processes of migration. Risks and costs of migration are, after all, intertwined to the extent that one may often be seen as a subset of the other. In an implicit "cost-benefit" comparison, for example, the potential migrant may regard migration risk as a premium to be added to more tangible costs in assessing the overall "hurdle" to relocation.[99] Alternatively, the upfront expenses of moving may be identified as part of the total investment in the migration "gamble." Changes to costs and risks are often bundled together. Growing legal barriers to the international movement of labour in the twentieth

---

[95]How many migrants could not have afforded to travel to America without funding from relatives is a separate question addressed below.

[96]In the 1870s, eastward crossings of migrants were twenty-one percent as numerous as westward. Between 1900 and 1914 this ratio was twice as high (forty-two percent). This is based on Keeling, "Repeat Migration," table 1.

[97]See Wyman, *Round-Trip to America*, 190-209.

[98]Ways in which migration networks affected decisions to migrate, other than those involving relocation costs and risks, such as their function as communication channels and transferors of information, were more important earlier in the nineteenth century, when migration to (and return migration from) America was much less commonplace across Europe.

[99]See Godley, *Jewish Immigrant Entrepreneurship*, 71.

century, for example, have tended to make illegal migration more likely, thus simultaneously raising both the average risks and average costs of cross-border relocation.

Risks and costs are not the same, however. Migration costs are more predictable and can be overcome, at least potentially, with money, time or ingenuity. Migration risks, by contrast, are generally more uncertain, variable and difficult to undo, and thus are more often managed or endured instead by pooling, diversification, hedging and flexibility. Some risks can be readily transformed into costs, but others cannot be.[100] There was, for example, no way for American immigrants in 1910 to "buy insurance" against the risk of becoming unemployed due to a cyclical recession.

If costs were the most important criteria for potential European emigrants and their networks, then historical explanations of the shifting incidence and patterns of transatlantic migrant self-selection would need to concentrate on factors such as trends in travel times, financing mechanisms and real wage differences between countries. But if risks played the larger role in shaping who migrated and who did not, then fluctuations in unemployment rates in migrant-origin regions of Europe versus immigrant sectors of the US economy, and the relative availability of collective safety nets against unemployment, on-the-job injury and so forth, deserve the greater focus.

Both risks and costs clearly were significant limiting factors on European emigration. Large segments of European society would not have wanted to move to the Americas at any cost: they had too much at stake at home to think seriously about leaving. The relatively higher risks associated with fashioning new careers overseas were the operative constraint keeping them in their regions of origin. On the other hand, compared to labour movements within Europe, a relatively low fraction of transatlantic migrants made seasonal sojourns of only a few months. Migration costs thus inhibited many – probably millions – of short-term moves between Europe and North America.[101]

Migration networks lowered the constraining effects of both the costs and risks associated with establishing new domiciles across the Atlantic. By providing a conduit to financing from America, for example, networks reduced the time needed to save funds for the journey, thus increasing migration by

---

[100]Examples of such transformation can be found in US government policies which lowered the risk of imported disease by a system of inspections imposed on shipping companies and carried out by government inspection stations, such as that on Ellis Island, largely funded by the fines imposed on non-complying shipping lines and the head tax indirectly paid by migrants as part of their fare.

[101]See Klaus J. Bade, *Europa in Bewegung: Migration von späten 18. Jahrhundert bis zur Gegenwart* (Munich, 2002), 86, 90, 91, 94, 98 and 106-108.

cutting the interval during which intervening circumstances might arise to hinder the envisaged relocation. Having a family in America, or one to go back to in Europe, however, also made it easier to manage the risks of becoming jobless in the US and thus to contemplate exposing oneself to such risks in the first place.

Comprehensively considered, the basic trends and dynamics of transatlantic migration during 1900-1914 strongly suggest that risks were a more important constraint than costs. This, in turn, makes it highly likely that the more critical effects of migration networks in helping shape the magnitude, intensity and incidence of the transatlantic flows lay in risk management rather than cost reduction. This conclusion is based on three separate observations.

First, although there were few legal encumbrances upon migrating to America between 1900 and 1914, and while the advantages of doing so were widely and accurately appreciated across Europe, most Europeans did not try to move overseas. The costs of moving were not high enough to constitute a significant barrier for most potential migrants, but there were considerable risks associated with being a stranger in a land where wages and job prospects were attractive but highly fluctuating, and only minimal social safety nets were available in case of unemployment or other mishap.[102]

Second, migration from the principal origin regions in southern and eastern Europe grew rapidly after the 1880s. Travel costs from these countries, including journey times, did not change much. On the other hand, the risks of remaining in Sicily or the Jewish Pale of Settlement, for example, were high, if not growing, while the contemporaneous risks of relocating to America diminished (mainly due to the proliferation and expansion of migration networks available to help contain the impact of those risks).

Contemporary anecdotal evidence from migrants and others constitutes a third observation that reinforces the first two. Among reasons given for not moving to America, risks outweighed costs. A Slovenian village in 1908 was horrified at residents returning from America with incurable diseases or "without an arm or minus a leg." One such returnee read a copy of Upton Sinclair's *The Jungle*, the 1906 muck-raking novel of immigrant woes in America, to fellow-villagers. Among contemporary returnees to Italy, America was known as the "land of the dollar and of sorrow." The misfortunes of the small minority of would-be migrants who were rejected by European or US inspectors sometimes had magnified effects when word reached their home communities. An investigator in 1906 found that "one immigrant who is sent

---

[102]Keeling, "Economics," 25.

back to his native town can frighten three hundred neighbours away from the steamship ticket offices."[103]

There are, however, few accounts of people wanting to migrate but being unable to do so due to costs. Even then, their remarks typically concern having to wait for funds after deciding to leave; that is, this affects the timing, not the ability, to move.[104] "The poverty of the immigrant is no matter for worry if he is able-bodied. He usually borrows the money to come here," wrote the same observer in 1905.[105]

The correspondence, remittances and prepaid tickets flowing back to Europe from America, and the relative-fetching trips to the home country, used by migration networks were, in turn, dependent upon reliable regular steamship connections across the North Atlantic. This was part of a series of risk-management synergies between migrants and their transporters.[106]

In addition to "self-insuring" against cyclical busts by building up financial reserves during boom periods, steamship lines also used networks to "pool" their migrant traffic and thereby share the pain of steep migration slumps during US recessions. Shipping companies' market-sharing passenger conferences, or cartels, grew in effectiveness over the period. These "pools" raised average fares slightly, which had only minimal effects on migrant volumes, but their principal purpose and impact were to help mitigate the transport lines' vulnerability to the cyclical slumps in migrant traffic.[107] The use of

---

[103]Louis Adamic, *Laughing in the Jungle: The Autobiography of an Immigrant in America* (New York, 1932), 7-38; Wyman, *Round-Trip to America*, 85; and Broughton Brandenburg, "The Tragedy of the Rejected Immigrant," *Outlook*, 13 October 1906.

[104]Of course, a source bias applies here in that there are no "non-immigrant historical associations" collecting diaries or autobiographies of those who decided not to leave their homelands. Any such evidence would, however, undoubtedly reveal a range of motives, financial and non-financial. Cost also does not loom large in accounts of how families decided which members should migrate and when.

[105]Broughton Brandenburg, "The Stranger within the Gates," *Harper's Weekly*, 17 June 1905.

[106]In coping with the risks of the US business cycle by relying on kinship networks and returns to Europe during recessions, migrants reduced the cyclicality of passenger revenues for shipping lines. In protecting their reputations by maintaining regular schedules even during cyclical slowdowns shipping companies enabled migrants to escape back to Europe during recessions. Migrants and shipping lines were, so to speak, in the same cyclical "boat," and their respective risk-management strategies were more complementary than contradictory. See Keeling, "Economics," 17-19.

[107]Puskás, "Hungarian Overseas Migration," 225.

these cartels as a defence against "cutthroat competition" and fare wars has not been well appreciated by migrant historians and warrants brief additional scrutiny.

Cyclicality and Shipping Industry Networks

Historians of migration and shipping, as well as contemporaries, are in widespread agreement that late nineteenth- and early twentieth-century migration across the North Atlantic closely tracked the cyclical patterns of the US economy.[108] They also agree, though, that it did so in magnified amplitude and that these fluctuations were the primary reason why passenger shipping in those years was such an unusually variable and uncertain business.[109] Rather than making futile efforts to vary their long-term, fixed-cost assets to match these short-term revenue variations, successful shipping companies built up reserves both on and off their balance sheets during good times to achieve both the appearance and reality of being able to cover losses during bad years.[110] Though most thus survived cyclical contractions, mainly by being able to outlast them, they could do little to predict general economic recessions and nothing to prevent their occurrence.[111] A related set of risks was more directly addressable, however.

Throughout the nineteenth century, shipping depressions were associated with overcapacity and a tendency for firms to seek partial amelioration by cutting fares to attract larger slices of cyclically-shrunken markets. These often desperate ploys rarely worked, but firms on the brink of bankruptcy had little to lose, while other firms, in less dire straits, sometimes seized the opportunity – not to gain immediate market share but to knock out a weaker rival. Both motives were evident in the price wars accompanying cyclical slumps in the

---

[108]Between 1900 and 1913, three cyclical recessions in the US qualified as moderate or severe and lasted about a year: in 1904, 1907-1908 and 1911; see Jerome, *Migration and Business Cycles*, 95-116.

[109]See Michael J. Piore, *Birds of Passage: Migrant Labour and Industrial Societies* (Cambridge, 1979), 43; Karl Thiess, *Deutsche Schiffahrt und Schiffahrtspolitik der Gegenwart* (Leipzig, 1907), 67; Hyde, *Cunard and the North Atlantic*, 130; Stopford, *Maritime Economics*, 219; De Boer, *Holland-America Line*, introduction; *The Chautauquan* (October 1900), 5-6; *Harper's Weekly*, 5 January 1901; and HAPAG, *Annual Report, 1908*, 3.

[110]See Thiess, *Deutsche Schiffahrt*, 142-143. On "open" and "secret" balance sheet reserves, see Boyce, *Information, Mediation, and Institutional Development*, 225-226.

[111]Edward S. Meade, "The Capitalization of the International Mercantile Marine," in W. Ripley, *Trusts, Pools, and Corporations* (Boston, 1905), 110-111.

mid-1870s, mid-1880s and mid-1890s. However a fare war began, once it was well underway all firms along the affected route tended to participate, at least partially, in order to prevent already cyclically-reduced flows of passengers from drifting away towards bargain ticket prices on other lines. Fare wars thus tended to exacerbate the cyclicality of overall passenger shipping industry earnings.[112]

Agreements to limit price reductions were difficult to enforce during cyclical slumps, but in 1891 the Nordatlantischer Dampfschiff Linien Verband (NDLV) was established for this purpose. NDLV was the first long-lived mul-tinational passenger cartel (or "conference"), and its success was due in part to its passenger volume shares (semi-public and easily monitored) rather than being based on a more readily-evadable agreement fixing minimum fares. Any NDLV company exceeding its agreed-upon quota of steerage passengers had to pay into a "pool" which was used to reimburse those participating firms with actual passenger levels correspondingly below the fixed percentage specified by the agreement. The reimbursement rate, typically around $20 per excess passenger, acted as a "floor price" because a cartel-abiding carrier luring cus-tomers in excess of its quota by cutting fares below that $20 level would lose money on each such passenger.[113] The pool arrangement of the NDLV was extended to, or replicated in, parallel agreements with other firms in 1898, 1903, 1908 and 1909. Although, over time, these cartel pools reinforced un-derlying tendencies towards competition through quality improvements, the agreements continued to fulfil their fundamental purpose of inhibiting the out-break of industry-wide price wars, especially for steerage traffic where the risks of cutthroat price competition were greatest due to the cyclicality of mi-gration.[114] The cartels were not, however, able to raise general fares to mo-

---

[112]Flayhart, *American Line*, 165-166, Murken, *Die großen transatlantischen Linienreederei-Verbände*, 57-58; and Hyde, *Cunard and the North Atlantic*, 95-96 and 103. Even in the 1904-1905 fare war (see above), the additional passenger volume gen-erated on the UK routes was not sufficient to compensate for the sharply lower fares charged. See *New York Times*, 4 April 1905; and Murken, *Die großen transatlantischen Linienreederei-Verbände*, 278-281.

[113]More precisely, a hypothetical conference-adhering but fare-cutting line would incur not only the $20 due the pool for each excess passenger but also the mar-ginal costs of transporting the passenger; these, however, especially in slack periods, were close to zero, thus effectively making the "floor price" imposed by the cartel equal to the compensation rate under the pool. Robert Schachner, *Das Tarifwesen in der Personenbeförderung der transozeanischen Dampfschiffahrt* (Karlsruhe, 1904), 121-122. A detailed history of the NDLV can be found in Murken, *Die großen transatlan-tischen Linienreederei-Verbände*, especially 11-77.

[114]The obvious loophole – booking would-be steerage passengers in second class as second class passengers (e.g., outside of steerage quotas) but at steerage rates

nopolistic "revenue maximizing" levels because of the general tendency of companies to compete by building new capacity (at high fixed costs but with low marginal costs of usage) and because the cartels had only limited ability to block the formation of new competing lines.[115] By 1910, the extension and replication of NDLV and similar arrangements covered nearly all European migrant carriers.[116]

---

was expressly forbidden under NDLV and other cartel rules. Because there were no volume agreements and generally only loosely monitored minimum fares for second class, evasions of universal (but rather difficult to enforce) cartel provisions specifying a minimum excess of second class fares over steerage fares might have seriously eviscerated the efficacy of the steerage pools, except that plenty of migrants were willing to opt to travel second class at normal second class fares. In other words, most of the time, shipping lines wanting to attract "up-scale" migrants in order to book more than were allowed under the steerage pool, but without thereby falling into an excess position, could do so without undercutting the agreed-upon differential of second class over steerage fares. In such instances, cartels inhibited competition by price, and companies competed on quality instead. On the second-class loophole, see Murken, *Die großen transatlantischen Linienreederei-Verbände*, 37, 66, 637, 645, 663 and 681; on the issue of quality, see Aldcroft (ed.), *Development*, 355; and Thiess, *Deutsche Schiffahrt*, 77.

[115]See Schachner, *Das Tarifwesen*, 62; and Thiess, *Deutsche Schiffahrt*, 73.

[116]The most authoritative and comprehensive account is Murken, *Die großen transatlantischen Linienreederei-Verbände*, especially 325-411 and 633-689. See also United States, Congress, House of Representatives, 63rd Congress, 2nd session, 1914, document no. 805 (*Alexander Report*); and Keeling, "Transatlantic Shipping Cartels." The essentially defensive purpose of the cartels is also shown by the lack of mechanisms to coordinate fare increases; see Murken, *Die großen transatlantischen Linienreederei-Verbände*, 636-689. Sustained fare-raising, in or out of cartels, was inhibited by the risk of provoking price cuts by new upstart lines not under the cartels' jurisdiction. See Andrew Gibson and Arthur Donovan, *The Abandoned Ocean: A History of United States Maritime Policy* (Columbia, SC, 2000), 97-98; and Industrial Commission, 109. On an episodic, monthly or voyage basis, fare changes were used within cartels to help adjust actual market shares towards the proportions specified in the agreements. Members whose actual market shares exceeded their cartel quotas were expected to raise their fares temporarily to encourage passengers to travel instead with under-quota members. See Zosa Szajkowski, "Sufferings of Jewish Emigrants to America in Transit Through Germany," *Jewish Social Studies*, XXXIX (Winter-Spring 1977), 105-106; Great Britain, National Archives, Public Record Office (TNA, PRO), Foreign Office (FO) 881/93111, "Report on Activity of the Hamburg-American Packet Company" (1908), 17. Less frequently, coordinated price cuts within cartels were also used to defend overall cartel market share against incursions by non-cartel rivals. So-called "conference" or "fighting" ships were sent by cartel members on a rotating and subsidized basis on routes identical to those of outsiders at very low fares. In the 1911-1915 anti-trust case, US justices deemed the tactic temporary, defensive and non-detrimental to the fare-paying public's long-term interests and found the conferences

The conferences were complicated to administer and consumed large amounts of management time for monitoring, adaptation and defence against outsiders. They were subject to incessant renegotiation and not infrequently broke down, though usually not entirely. One of their chief architects, master negotiator Albert Ballin, also instigated fare wars on several notable occasions to pressure reluctant competitors to accept more binding conference arrangements or to secure better terms for his company, HAPAG. Nevertheless, the information, coordination and networking which led to more solid market-carving cartels for migrant traffic were indispensable and more effective at achieving their goals than were cartels in other industries. One reason for their success was that each major shipping line was at least to some degree protected by regulatory authorities in its home port and country. Integrated coordination and cooperation between shipping lines and governments were at least as important to the physical processes of migration as were cooperative networked arrangements among the transport firms themselves.[117]

Networks of Policy-Making and Processing

Early twentieth-century mass migration across the North Atlantic was legally and practically possible because of a prevailing regime of open borders which, in turn, depended upon intricate and flexible coalitions of policy-making and crowd-processing networks. The political formulation of migration policy in the US played an especially crucial role in this regard.

Despite periodic public debates in America during the first fifteen years of the twentieth century over whether immigration should be significantly curtailed, the predominant view remained that US government inspectors, transatlantic transport lines and overseas organizations should be encouraged or required to work together for quality control rather than quantity limitation. Proposals for a "literacy test" requirement, which would have cut deeply into the flow of Europeans (especially from the less "desirable" southern and eastern regions) to the US, were tabled, blocked or vetoed a half

---

overall not in violation of US anti-trust laws; see Hyde, *Cunard and the North Atlantic*, 117.

[117]Boyce, *Information, Mediation, and Institutional Development*, 3-4, 7, 121-122, 159-174 and 194-195; Cecil, *Albert Ballin*, 18-20; Himer, *Geschichte der Hamburg-Amerika Linie*, 10-13; Broeze, "Albert Ballin," 9-14, 16-19 and 27-32; and William Sjostrom, "The Stability of Ocean Shipping Cartels," in Peter Z. Grossman (ed.), *How Cartels Endure and How They Fail: Studies of Industrial Collusion* (Cheltenham, 2004), 82-110.

dozen times between 1897 and 1913.[118] In the years prior to the First World War, immigrants benefited from political configurations which helped contain the risks of the erection of significant legal barriers to their entry into the US.

The most vocal and persistent advocates for significant quantitative curtailment of European immigration during these years were politicians from the dominant political party, the Republicans. A leading spokesman was Senator Henry Cabot Lodge of Massachusetts, who was also the closest political ally of Theodore Roosevelt, the American president from late 1901 through early 1909. The Republican Party was, however, also very dependent on the votes of naturalized ("first generation") immigrants and their descendents, particularly in national elections.[119] The curious juxtaposition of pro- and anti-immigration efforts coexisting within the most successful national political body led to a set of compromises which protected immigrants against the risk of significant border controls while indirectly lowering some other risks and uncertainties and making it generally easier for migrant networks to function.

At the turn of the twentieth century, over eighty percent of America's foreign-born population resided in just sixteen major states in the Midwest and Northeast. These were populous states containing over half of all electoral votes, and the Republican Party won all sixteen in every presidential election from 1900 to 1908.[120] The Party's electoral success in these immigrant-rich states was based to a considerable degree on the ability of its leaders to compromise with (and out-manoeuvre) restrictionists so that foreign-born voters would not be antagonized. The Republicans had sizeable majorities in both houses of Congress throughout this period as well. Democrats gained a majority in the House of Representatives in the 1910 mid-term elections and won the presidency in 1912, but prior to World War I this had no appreciable effect on

---

[118]BI, *Annual Report, 1911* (Washington, DC, 1912), 215; *New York Times*, 7 May 1906; and Edward Hutchinson, *Legislative History of American Immigration Policy, 1798-1965* (Philadelphia, 1981), 120-121, 124-125, 130, 140 and 154.

[119]Higham, *Strangers in the Land*, 98, 101-104, 107, 126-129 and 163.

[120]See appendix 12. In the 1896-1908 presidential elections, the correlation with Republican electoral success is slightly less strong if the states are ranked by percentage of foreign-born rather than by the absolute number of foreign residents. In 1912, the Democrat Woodrow Wilson won most of these immigrant states, but his popular vote in all sixteen was behind the combined total of his two presidential predecessors, Roosevelt ("Bull Moose") and Taft (Republican), who split the Republican vote. For census data, see http://fisher.lib.Virginia.edu/cgilocal/censusbin/census/cen.pl. For votes, see http://www.archives.gov/federal_register/electoral_college/votes_index.html#state.

the national immigration policy the Republicans had established over the prior decade and a half.[121]

As early as 1896, "alert conservatives" had noted that without the "overwhelming support" of foreign-born voters, Republican William McKinley "might well have lost" the presidential race to populist Democrat William Jennings Bryan. From 1898 on, midwestern Republicans "from immigrant districts" were especially attentive to growing agitation among ethnic societies and the foreign-language press, particularly German groups, against immigration restriction. In the 1904 election campaign, Senator Lodge agreed to have the "immigration plank" dropped from the Republican Party platform. In 1906, the Republican "machine" in the House of Representatives managed a last-minute replacement of a literacy test clause in that year's immigration bill by a section establishing an investigative panel (later to be known as the "Dillingham Commission").[122] In 1908, Theodore Roosevelt attended the Broadway premiere of Israel Zangwil's ode to immigration, "The Melting Pot," which was dedicated to the outgoing president. Republican bosses funnelled over $100,000 to the foreign-language press in 1912 to promote the presidential campaign of Roosevelt's successor, William Howard Taft, who promised if re-elected to veto the literacy test recommended by the Dillingham Commission. Taft lost the election but vetoed the last pre-World War I literacy test immigration bill anyway before leaving office in 1913.[123]

A nexus of the foreign language-press in the US, the steamship companies whose agents who advertised in it and whose lobbyists helped fund po-

---

[121]John Milton Cooper, Jr., *Pivotal Decades: The United States 1900-1920* (New York, 1990), 25. Democrats also counted foreign-born or "ethnic" voters among their supporters, notably urban Irish-Americans, but their party's position shifted rather more markedly towards immigration restriction than did the Republicans after 1900. See Jones, *American Immigration*, 224; and Daniel J. Tichenor, *The Politics of Immigration Control in America* (Princeton, 2002), 199-120. On immigration politics and policies after 1914, see Higham, *Strangers in the Land*, 194-206 and 300-330.

[122]This was the last and most sweeping of a series of periodic special governmental panels which, at frequent intervals from the 1880s to 1914, researched immigration questions. In addition to the valuable tangible information and data generated by such commissions, voting to establish them also gave nervous politicians opportunities to placate immigration restrictionists by demonstrating a concern over the issue while offering an excuse to postpone any consideration of major legislation which might arouse discontent among foreign-born voters.

[123]Higham, *Strangers in the Land*, 104-107, 113, 124-128 and 189-191; *New York Times*, 26 June 1906; Tichenor, *Politics of Immigration Control*, 124-128; and Walter Zimmerman, *The First Great Triumph: How Five Americans Made Their Country a World Power* (New York, 2002), 462.

litical campaigns, the naturalized and second-generation immigrant readers of those newspapers and the politicians for whom those foreign-born citizens voted, in coalition with immigrant employers and other advocates of open borders, warded off attempts by nativists and trade unions to restrict immigration quantitatively before 1914.[124] A favourite slogan of policy-makers, designed to appeal to both restrictionists and their opponents, was that "we cannot have too much of the right kind of immigration" or "too little of the wrong kind."[125] What this ambivalence meant in practice was a gradual extension of reasons for immigrant exclusion applicable to a minute fraction of potential migrants.

Increased "quality control" over immigration to block the few "bad apples" had two principal effects. The first was a rise in the percentage of would-be immigrants refused entry at US ports. The debarment rate rose from one percent in 1900 to two percent in 1914.[126] The second and more important result was an intensified focus by government officials in America and Europe on the practical risks and challenges associated with the relocation and processing of large crowds of migrants. There were several dimensions to these local and international crowd control measures which warrant closer scrutiny.

To monitor and supervise growing flows of transatlantic migrants smoothly and effectively became the joint objective of networks of immigration officials in the US, American officers stationed in European ports, public authorities in Europe, port officials, railroad executives and the managers of North Atlantic passenger steamship lines after 1900. (Representatives of migrant organizations were generally supportive as well because better organization and control of mass movements often helped protect migrants against risks encountered *en route*). The extensive resources and technical expertise of shipping companies made them indispensable to the implementation of these transnational "crowd control" measures. In this era of small government and big business, the annual budget of the BI between 1900 and 1914 averaged less than ten percent of the revenue earned in those years by Cunard and CGT (the fourth and sixth largest carriers of migrants between Europe and the US during these years; see appendix 13).

---

[124]Higham, *Strangers in the Land*, 186-188.

[125]William Williams, Roosevelt's commissioner at Ellis Island, quoted in *New York Times*, 11 March 1905.

[126]A somewhat larger, but still small, fraction of would-be immigrants were blocked at European ports during inspections or deterred from even attempting the move. Over ninety percent of those debarred were blocked for medical unfitness or because they were "likely to become a public charge" in America, but the typical young, healthy and ambitious immigrant had little reason to fear rejection. See Keeling, "Economics," 5-7 and 16-17; and Keeling, "Business," 199-202.

International and inter-organizational networks of information and operational coordination were and are inherently vital to maritime enterprise.[127] North Atlantic shipping lines, for instance, had close links with railroad freight transporters and governments which provided them subsidies, competitive protection and port infrastructure. In return, governments received mail carriage, travel service for diplomats and dedicated troop-carrying vessels in wartime. The various marine and overland entities involved in migrant travel also had shared interests in reducing the risks of congestion and overcrowding.

Uncontrolled throngs of migrants were understandably viewed as both sources and victims of multiple hazards. Governments in early twentieth-century European "transit" countries, notably Britain and Germany, feared "undesirable" migrants lingering rather than passing through, or bringing dangerous diseases with them, as apparently occurred with the cholera epidemic that shut down Hamburg's migrant traffic for six months in 1892-1893.[128] Railroads in Europe needed orderly scheduled and organized migrant flows to protect sanitation, their other transport segments and their overall reputations. Migrants backed up in ports awaiting ships threatened the reputations of the steamship lines and represented a costly mismatch of carrying capacity and passengers. Without adequate facilities and procedures, inspectors at US entry ports could not properly protect arriving migrants and the American public from each other. Without systematic precautions and monitoring, migrants were notably vulnerable to abuse and exploitation at the hands of thieves, con artists and corrupt officials, particularly while in the port cities.

A series of US regulations, increasingly backed by fines, forced steamship lines to implement governmental monitoring and screening measures. These complemented the "crowd processing" measures already being developed by the lines in voluntary cooperation with networks of government, private and migrant groups. Steamship companies and their agents provided migrant networks with travel bookings, remittance delivery and pre-paid passage services. They also coordinated with railroads to offer combination rail-and-steamer tickets and to schedule emigrant-only train connections.[129] In conjunction with European and US officials, shipping lines after 1900 increasingly organized standardized lodging and carried out health inspections at transit

---

[127]For a definitive treatment of early twentieth-century shipping from the perspective of corporate strategy, see Boyce, *Information, Mediation, and Institutional Development*.

[128]Murken, *Die großen transatlantischen Linienreederei-Verbände*, 55-57.

[129]For example, one-quarter of passengers on the 3 May 1900 departure of the Holland America steamer *Maasdam* from Rotterdam travelled on combination tickets covering both rail travel and transatlantic steamer passage.

stations and embarkation ports. The long tenure of key steamship representatives, particularly in New York, was a source of experience that government immigration officials willingly tapped. Steamship executives meanwhile recognized the value of remaining on good terms with public authorities.[130]

Detailed passenger lists, required under US immigration regulations and filled out by shipping lines, were central to the control, inspection and statistics-gathering functions of the BI.[131] Organizing passengers into groups of up to thirty (the number of lines on one BI passenger list page) also made it easier for shipping companies to load them onto ships and to assign berths to keep "friends and acquaintances" together and have the "various nationalities quartered near together as much as possible." Having passengers speaking the same language in adjacent berths was a benefit both to those passengers and to the translators among the crew, while having passengers landed and inspected according to the same groupings also helped make inspection in America smoother and more efficient.[132]

A somewhat overstated boast by the *Liverpool Daily Mercury* in 1900 that the "embarkation or debarkation of passengers proceeds with the smoothness and regularity of well-oiled machinery" nevertheless exemplifies a general goal of migration-processing networks operating from origin through destination.[133] In effect, the risks of quantitative restriction were defused by increasingly integrated measures to alleviate the more tangible qualitative risks presented by hundreds or thousands of migrants departing from European embarkation ports and arriving at US ports of entry each day during this time.

Conclusions and Some Possible Implications

Migration networks are typically credited with shaping the direction, timing and spatial incidence of international migration. A closer look at the physical

---

[130]Cordial relations between steamship lines and the BI can be seen in Catholic University of America Archives, Powderly Papers, Correspondence, 1896-1902, box 122, A.S. Anderson, Manager, Passenger Department, International Navigation Company to Commissioner-General Powderly, 27 June 1902; and NARA, RG 85, entry 9, 52,420 and 51,758, correspondence between Ellis Island and the Trans-Atlantic Passenger conferences.

[131]*Dillingham Report*, XXXIX, 101-103. On fines for incorrect manifests, see Pitkin, *Keepers of the Gate*, 37 and 92-93. The fines, $10 for each passenger not properly recorded, were authorized under section 15 of the 1903 Immigration Act (*Dillingham Report*, XXXIX, 105).

[132]*Dillingham Report*, XXXVII, 24; Stephen Graham, *With Poor Immigrants to America* (London, 1914), 11; and *Lloyd Nachrichten* (1904), 463.

[133]*Liverpool Daily Mercury*, 22 September 1900.

processes of the "Great Migration" between Europe and the US on the eve of the "Great War" indicates that family and community networks also influenced decisions to migrate and thus levels of migration.

The ubiquity of networks in transatlantic migration shows their indispensability, but their components and how they functioned are difficult to evaluate across millions of individual relocations. A comprehensive assessment of how migration networks shaped the selection of those who moved to the US thus lies outside the scope of this examination.[134] Nevertheless, the bulk of the available historical evidence – quantitative, qualitative and circumstantial – from the peak years of 1900-1914 points to two significant conclusions: that costs were not as important as risks in limiting the magnitude of the overall relocation to America and that the role of networks had more to do with risk management than with cost reduction.

Scholarship on migration, which has nearly always focused more on effects than causes, often tends to assume implicitly that the causes can be routinely underemphasized, if not ignored, because they are basically exogenous, that is, determined outside of the migratory processes, or are too complex to be assessed, or too geographically, ethnically or temporally contingent, to be capable of systematic evaluation and definitive generalization anyway. The causes underlying the inherently risky processes of transatlantic migration during the early twentieth century were, however, more tangible than has been hitherto appreciated. Risk considerations had a greater impact than costs or wage differentials in effecting migration decisions in the period, and "chain migration" networks acting to mitigate those risks helped to determine not just how people migrated overseas but also who made long-distance moves.

To better understand how such risk management measures helped shape migration movements it is also important to consider the risk concerns, strategies and interactions within networks not just of migrants but also of their transporters, regulators and agents. In many instances, these interactive strategies for coping with the migration risks were congruent and self-reinforcing. No similar "positive feedback" appears to apply to transatlantic travel cost

---

[134]A full consideration would have to take into account the factors determining the movement of early "pioneer" migrants who acted without the benefit or constraint of networks (in many cases well before 1900), the historical paths by which the movements of such "pioneers" evolved into or otherwise influenced the migration networks operable during 1900-1914, and the various other ways in which migration networks to the US evolved out of, or competed against, networks oriented towards moving to other overseas locations, moving within Europe or remaining within the immediate home regions. The conclusions here are also essentially limited to the 1900-1914 period. It is believed that migration costs were more important than risk before 1800, that risks became more important to migrant self-selection in the middle third of the nineteenth century and that the transatlantic fare alone ceased to be the main limitation on movement in the seventeenth century. See Keeling, "Business," 3-4.

trends in the period, and to the extent that the migration was fundamentally motivated by large wage gaps, mass movements of labour from low-wage to high-wage regions can hardly be expected on their own to have further widened the differentials. Migration decisions based on risk, and self-replicating and positively-reinforcing risk mitigation by networks involved with that migration, are consistent with the accelerating post-1900 transatlantic flows.

Further attention to the underlying causes of international migration, the processes by which decisions to migrate are reached, the associated risks and strategies for their mitigation and the role of migration networks would seem an excellent approach to better understand the fundamental nature of this basic human phenomenon. Two examples can illustrate the possibilities.

The all-time apex of transatlantic migration relative to source and destination populations occurred between Ireland and North America during the potato famine of 1846-1855. Were travel costs at an all-time low then as well? Possibly, given that foregone "opportunity" costs almost surely were at rock bottom. On the other hand, the general trend of out-of-pocket costs was gradually downwards over the nineteenth and early twentieth centuries; thus, overall travel expenses during the hunger years were probably not hugely lower than before or after. The risks of migrating relative to the risks of staying home, however, were quite possibly significantly lower for potential Irish overseas emigrants in this period. Perhaps the famine migration of 1846-1855 from Ireland was less unique than is commonly believed and would be more accurately viewed as an extreme instance of a more general phenomenon: that perceptions of the relative risks of remaining at home versus moving abroad play a significant role in shaping migrant self-selection.

Contemporary movement from Mexico to the US is another example where a more thorough attention to migration risks might be warranted. Are wage differentials a principal factor in the selection of those seeking to enter the US, legally or clandestinely, across its southern border in the early twenty-first century? Or might tolerance for risk play a greater role in determining which potential border-crossers chose to go north and which decided to stay in Mexico? The viability of policies, such as the deregulation of businesses and international trade, ostensibly intended to help lower the North-South gap in economic opportunity but which are also thought to increase economic disruption and uncertainty, may be due for re-evaluation as a result.

Potential migrants across the North Atlantic a century ago faced neither the dauntingly high costs of prior periods nor the severe legal barriers of later times. Atlantic crossings then also represented the culmination of a long-lasting, widespread, legal, diverse and well-documented relocation. This makes the period and place somewhat atypical, but it also means that the fundamental processes of voluntary mass migration during this epoch are more clearly traceable. The interacting strategies of risk-mitigating networks in that episode of large-scale, long-distance migration offer insights applicable to other times and places, including the early twenty-first century, when evolving strategies for coping with the risks of globalization seem likely to continue to command serious societal attention.

Appendix 1

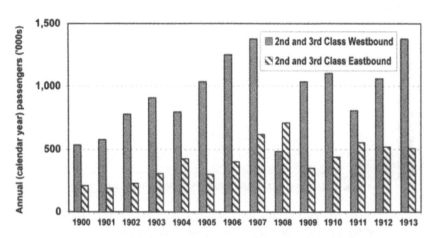

Note: The data depicted here on second and third class passenger movements between all European ports and New York, Boston, Philadelphia and Baltimore overstate the number of migrant crossings on these routes by about four percent (mostly by including the minority of second class passengers who were actually tourists rather than migrants). This overcount coincidentally is almost exactly equal to the undercount resulting from not including here westbound migrants to the US arriving at a port other than one of these four (see the first footnote in the text and appendix 4 below). A rather more traditional measurement of migration – the US Bureau of Immigration (BI) time series for "immigrants" – undercounts migrants by more than ten percent. The difference between these two measures is partly semantic, since the BI (at least after 1906) wanted to track net additions to the US population (although the inconsistent application of that goal means that the BI's figures over the period are actually an inconsistent mixture of gross and net flows). The measurement in this figure, by contrast, is based on consistently considering migration as a repeatable process, not a once-and-for-all transformation, and therefore counts gross flows. Roughly one-fifth of the westbound crossings shown here were repeat traverses made by migrants who had already crossed westward earlier in this period (see, again, the first text footnote). The BI data suffer from further inconsistencies over the period and count "emigrants" (eastbound return migrants) to Europe only starting in 1908 and with severe inconsistencies and inaccuracies. See Keeling, "Business," 345-346; and Keeling "Repeat," 10-13.

Source: Transatlantic Passenger Conference reports.

Drew Keeling

Appendix 2

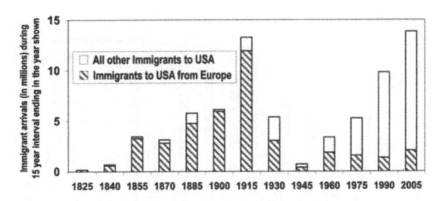

Sources: 1811-1819: Grabbe, *Vor der goßen Flut,* 93; 1820-1970: *Historical Statistics of the US, 1970-2005,* estimated based on (USCIS tables); and US Citizenship and Immigration Service files from http://uscis.gov/graphics/.

Appendix 3

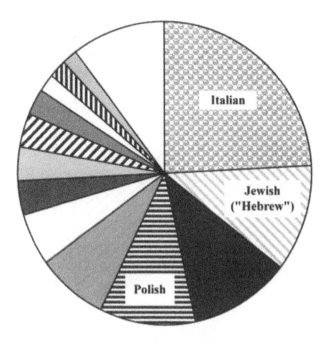

Italian	Hebrew
■ English, Scotch, Welsh, Irish	☰ Polish
▨ German	☐ Scandinavian
■ Slovak	▨ Croatian & Slovenian
▨ Magyar	■ Greek
☐ Ruthenian	Ⅲ Lithuanian
▨ Russian	☐ 17 others

Note: The figure shows the relative proportions of total US immigration, 1900-1914, broken down by "race."

Source: BI, *Annual Report 1914*, 101-102.

Appendix 4

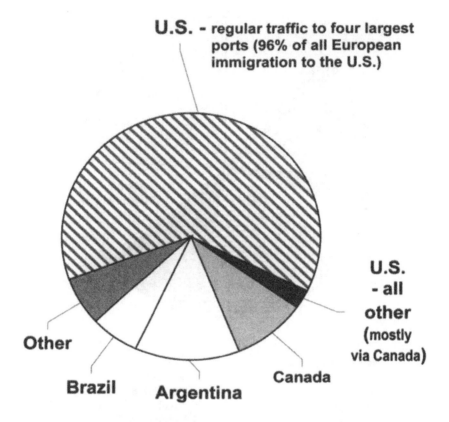

U.S. - regular traffic to four largest ports (96% of all European immigration to the U.S.)

U.S. - all other (mostly via Canada)

Other

Brazil   Argentina   Canada

Note: Total westbound transatlantic migration, 1900-1914, was about 22.5 million. The figure shows this migration broken down by destination.

Sources: Keeling, "Business," 333-334; and Walter F. Willcox and Imre Ferenczi, *International Migrations* (2 vols., New York, 1931), I, 364-365 and 501-573. "U.S.-all other" estimated for 1900-1905 based on BI figures of Immigrants "entering Canada on to their way to the US" (BI, *Annual Report 1904*, 78 and *Annual Report 1905*, 63) and for 1906-1914 based on BI, table 1 ("Immigrant Aliens Admitted through Canada") less (from tables 5 and 8), immigrants whose "last permanent residence" was in Canada.

Appendix 5

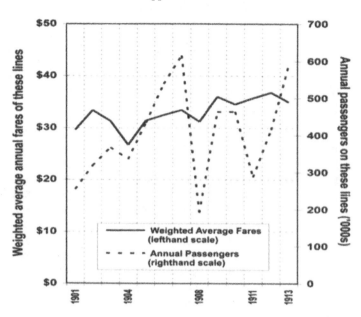

Notes: Shipping Lines and Ports: The figure shows steerage passengers and weighted average steerage fares westbound to the United States for the following steamship lines and routes: Cunard (Liverpool, Fiume), Anchor (Glasgow), migrants to US from Kristiania (Oslo) on various lines, Holland America (Rotterdam), Italian lines (Italian ports), HAPAG (Hamburg) and NDL (Bremen). US ports: New York, Boston, Philadelphia and Baltimore. The lines and routes shown carried half of all steerage passengers from Europe to the US in this period (based on data in the Transatlantic Passenger Conference reports). Correlations of fares with passengers (major lines): Cunard, six percent; Holland America, twenty-two percent; Italian lines, forty-five percent; and German lines, thirty-seven percent. Recession years in the US: 1904, 1908, 1911 and 1913 (Jerome, *Migration and Business Cycles,* 100-119).

Sources: Fares from Cunard Voyage Accounts (CVA), Glasgow Business History Centre Archive, UGD 255/1/2/7; Riksarkviet Oslo, Kristiania Emigranten Protokollen; Gemeentearchief Rotterdam, Holland America Passagegelden; *Bollettino d' Emigrazione* (Rome, 1915), 60-77; Hamburg Staatsarchiv, *Zeitschrift der HAPAG,* Kludas, *Deutschen Passagierschiffahrt,* III, 331-332; Murken, *Linienreederei-Verbände,* 76-77, 352, 355, 569 and 579; and Steamship line brochures. The fares are adjusted for differences in the lengths of the routes and weighted by the number of passengers carried. Route lengths are from US Commissioner of Navigation, *Annual Report for 1900* (Washington, DC, 1901), 312-327. Passengers are from appendix 1.

Appendix 6
Fares: Quarterly Westbound Comparison

		CUNARD Liverpool-New York			HOLLAND AMERICA Rotterdam-New York		
		TRAVEL CLASS:			TRAVEL CLASS:		
YEAR	QTR	1st	2nd	3rd	1st	2nd	3rd
1903	I	$78	$39	$19	$57	$43	$29
	II	$91	$39	$21	$67	$43	$31
	III	$107	$42	$20	$78	$45	$33
	IV	$110	$40	$21	$73	$45	$32
1904	I	$73	$38	$18	$58	$43	$32
	II	$91	$39	$18	$67	$43	$29
	III	$107	$42	$8	$79	$46	$25
	IV	$101	$41	$9	$70	$44	$24
1905	I	$75	$38	$11	$57	$43	$30
	II	$97	$41	$21	$68	$45	$32
	III	$108	$44	$22	$78	$46	$33
	IV	$115	$43	$21	$78	$46	$32
1906	I	$91	$42	$20	$66	$45	$34
	II	$104	$42	$21	$81	$45	$35
	III	$117	$43	$21	$84	$47	$36
	IV	$114	$42	$19	$78	$47	$37
1907	I	$90	$41	$19	$61	$45	$28
	II	$104	$42	$23	$85	$47	$30
	III	$117	$43	$22	$72	$46	$31
	IV	$111	$43	$21	$79	$46	$32
1908	I	$93	$37	$16	$46	$40	$28
	II	$122	$46	$16	$86	$45	$30
	III	$137	$51	$19	$104	$49	$31
	IV	$132	$48	$26	$101	$48	$31
1909	I	$124	$48	$26	$78	$46	$38
	II	$139	$48	$27	$93	$47	$40
	III	$156	$53	$28	$109	$49	$40
	IV	$144	$50	$28	$103	$48	$40
1910	I	$129	$50	$26	$78	$48	$40
	II	$155	$50	$27	$96	$49	$38
	III	$160	$55	$28	$112	$50	$38
	IV	$150	$52	$27	$113	$51	$41
1911	I	$133	$51	$26	$83	$50	$41
	II	$148	$50	$28	$97	$50	$42
	III	$155	$54	$28	$112	$53	$40
	IV	$152	$53	$28	$123	$54	$37

		CUNARD Liverpool-New York			HOLLAND AMERICA Rotterdam-New York		
		TRAVEL CLASS:			TRAVEL CLASS:		
YEAR	QTR	1st	2nd	3rd	1st	2nd	3rd
1912	I	$124	$51	$27	$88	$52	$40
	II	$146	$52	$28	$101	$53	$43
	III	$163	$56	$29	$116	$55	$42
	IV	$154	$54	$26	$118	$54	$43
1913	I	$125	$51	$25	$89	$53	$40
	II	$142	$51	$27	$99	$53	$35
	III	$162	$56	$25	$116	$54	$40
	IV	$153	$54	$25	$116	$54	$41
1914	I	$128	$52	$22	$85	$52	$33
	II	$143	$53	$20	$102	$53	$30
Average 1903-13:							
	I	$103	$44	$21	$69	$46	$35
	II	$122	$46	$23	$86	$47	$35
	III	$135	$49	$23	$96	$49	$35
	IV	$131	$47	$23	$96	$49	$36
	Annual	$123	$47	$23	$87	$48	$35
Cunard fares as percentage of Holland America fares:							
	I				143%	97%	64%
	II				142%	97%	64%
	III				143%	97%	64%
	IV				143%	97%	64%
	Annual				143%	97%	64%

Notes: The Holland America fares were measured by dividing actual receipts from passengers by the number of (adult equivalent) passengers. The Cunard fares were derived by dividing passenger revenues in the summarized accounting record by the adult equivalent passenger figures. It can be presumed that the Cunard revenue figures were net of the US head tax imposed on each entering foreigner because head taxes were not listed in the cost columns of those accounts. According to the report of the 1901 US Industrial Commission, 18 and 105, however, the head tax was added to the ticket price paid by westbound foreign passengers. Thus, the head tax presumably was included in Holland America's compilations. The head tax was raised in 1903 and 1907. The precise effect of the head tax on average fare levels depended on the number of foreigner in each travel class, but based on the general frequency of migrants by class (see Keeling, "Business," 345-346), it can be assumed to have resulted in about an extra $3 being levied on westbound migrants. The average $12 difference between the steerage fares of Cunard ($23) and Holland America ($35) shown here was thus actually only about $9.

Sources: Cunard Voyage Accounts (CVA); and Holland America Passagegelden.

Appendix 7
Passengers: Quarterly Westbound Comparison

		CUNARD Liverpool-New York TRAVEL CLASS:			HOLLAND AMERICA Rotterdam-New York TRAVEL CLASS:		
YEAR	QTR	1st	2nd	3rd	1st	2nd	3rd
1903	I	1036	1647	5273	169	692	6055
	II	1035	2609	12,844	428	1540	17,263
	III	3033	4579	9445	1665	1951	8810
	IV	1474	3028	6219	767	1254	4635
1904	I	774	1563	5903	184	891	4019
	II	1198	2782	8500	468	1428	7721
	III	2762	5492	14,207	1645	1731	7171
	IV	1214	2360	10,319	730	1091	6719
1905	I	899	1564	8743	181	1023	9641
	II	1276	2296	11,337	364	1870	15,546
	III	4264	4459	10,829	1719	1964	9414
	IV	1774	2609	7153	1003	1800	7543
1906	I	1181	1922	8441	183	1615	10,232
	II	1859	3865	22,956	524	2889	18,518
	III	4005	4746	16,152	1881	3112	10,170
	IV	2059	3366	14,749	1280	2599	4068
1907	I	1195	2382	8740	268	1538	8301
	II	1768	4503	22,530	579	3340	24,385
	III	4310	5775	15,501	1920	3622	8370
	IV	3684	4960	14,973	1375	2704	5662
1908	I	2083	3349	6327	246	1181	3537
	II	2619	3910	9986	649	1493	2437
	III	5580	6546	9354	2184	2782	2229
	IV	2611	3845	6729	1025	1567	3233
1909	I	1872	2486	7429	227	1757	8474
	II	3078	3861	15,972	629	3112	9585
	III	5912	6073	12,676	2327	4198	6485
	IV	3492	3702	6653	1274	3490	5868
1910	I	2164	2836	9356	220	2545	5314
	II	3291	4749	18,238	682	3762	13,155
	III	6380	6217	15,532	2724	4356	11,800
	IV	3822	4138	9287	1696	3380	5545
1911	I	2862	3562	7861	275	2573	3241
	II	3042	4716	12,037	789	3555	5947
	III	5470	6051	9946	2652	3987	5914
	IV	3299	3280	6600	1636	2785	7642

YEAR	QTR	CUNARD Liverpool-New York TRAVEL CLASS:			HOLLAND AMERICA Rotterdam-New York TRAVEL CLASS:		
		1st	2nd	3rd	1st	2nd	3rd
1912	I	2332	3681	7291	341	2408	5251
	II	2891	3962	11,886	905	3209	8573
	III	5103	5354	10,574	2817	4357	11,134
	IV	3449	4128	10,474	1512	3064	8900
1913	I	2193	3239	7370	392	2945	6324
	II	2894	4391	15,338	958	4098	19,150
	III	4444	5208	13,541	2526	4979	15,884
	IV	3463	4338	11,840	1448	3203	7800
1914	I	2195	3027	5576	335	2092	4425
	II	3005	3444	8911	1681	2361	8922
Average 1903-13:							
	I	4660	5500	12,523	2187	3367	8853
	II	2758	3614	9545	1250	2449	6147
	III	1795	2692	7549	259	1870	6251
	IV	2447	3862	14,336	748	2829	12,176
	Annual	2834	3839	10,904	1076	2563	8500

Source: Transatlantic Passenger Conference reports.

Appendix 8
Estimated Costs of Migrating between Europe and the US, 1900-1914

Foregone European Savings	$7	10%
Living Costs while Finding Work in America	$4	6%
All Other Travel-related Costs (except steamship fare)	$23	34%
Transatlantic Steamship Fare	$35	50%
Total	$69	100%

Notes: Wages, travel tickets and travel times are averaged over the various European source countries, transatlantic routes and US inland destinations, weighted by migrant passenger volumes. The figure for "Foregone European Savings" is based on an estimated weekly wage rate of $4.40 times an average employment rate of ninety percent, from which weekly living costs of $2.25 are subtracted, yielding estimated monthly savings of $1.71. This is then multiplied by an average total migration time of four weeks to produce the $7 figure ($1.71*4). The four-week migration time is based on five days preparation before departure, three days travel to the European port, two days waiting in that port, eleven days to cross the Atlantic, one day travel within the US and five days to find work there. The figure for "Other Travel-related Costs" is the sum of travel from source to European port, $6; food *en route*, $3; travel from US port to US destination, $5; lodging *en route*, $2; other, $4; and evasion costs for illegal migrants, $3. Some "Other Travel-related" costs were at times part of the oceanic fare. The fare here is net of the estimated effects of such bundling. Included with the price of the oceanic ticket, not deducted here, were US head taxes ($1-4) and food during the oceanic crossing.

Sources: Travel time within Europe: *Dillingham Report*, XXXVII, 29-31; Taylor, *Distant Magnet*, 146-148; and Broughton Brandenburg, *Imported Americans* (New York, 1904), 130-150. Travel time within US: Taylor, *Distant Magnet*, 166; and *Dillingham Report*, III, 288. Time waiting in ports: Taylor, *Distant Magnet*, 145-150 and 165; and Brandenburg, *Imported Americans*, 130-131. Travel time transatlantic: Keeling, "Business;" and voyage database. Time to prepare for departure, look for work: Brandenburg, *Imported Americans*, 113-130 and 228-245; Ivan Molek, *Two Worlds* (New York, 1978), 17-37; and Michael La Sorte, *La Merica: Images of Italian Greenhorn Experience* (Philadelphia, 1985), 68-109. European wages: Hatton and Williamson, *Age of Mass Migration*, 35; *Dillingham Report*, IV, 164; Andrew F. Rolle, *The American Italians* (Belmont, CA, 1972), 3, 4 and 7, Michael C. Le May, *From Dutch Door to Open Door* (New York, 1987), 42; Hvidt, "Emigration Agents," 94; and Cinel, *Italian Return Migration*, 160. US wages: Hourwich, *Immigration and Labor*, 403, 441 and 525; Whitney Coombs, *The Wages of Unskilled Labor in Manufacturing Industries in the United States, 1890-1924* (New York, 1926), 51 and 136-137; and Rolle, *American Italians*, 3 and 7. US living costs while finding work: Brandenburg, *Imported Americans*, 240; Cinel, *Italian Return Migration*, 159-160; Taylor, *Distant Magnet*, 175 and 203; and *Dillingham Report*, VI, 555. Transatlantic passage costs: see appendix 5 (Overland Travel, Food, Lodging, etc.); Taylor, *Distant Magnet*, 95-96, 146 and 165; Brandenburg, *Imported Americans*, 143; Salz, "Auswanderung," 864; Just, *Transitproblem*, 67-68; Holland America Passagegelden; and *Dillingham Report*, XXXVII, 13, 30-31 and 40.

Appendix 9

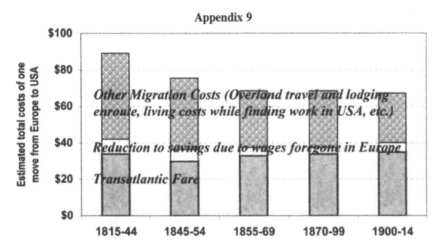

Note: Measures shown are estimated period averages for migration from Europe
to the US.

Sources: For definitions and for the 1900-1914 period, see appendix 8. For prior
periods, European wages, living costs and foregone savings, see B.R.
Mitchell, *International Historical Statistics* (5th ed., London, 2003),
"Europe" volume, 186-195; Dudley Baines, *Migration in a Mature Economy: Emigration and Internal Migration in England and Wales, 1861-1900*
(Cambridge, 1985), 85-86 and 332-333; Grabbe, *Vor der großen Flut,* 153-
179; Hatton and Willliamson, *Age of Mass Migration,* 35; and Hvidt, "Emigration Agents," 194. US wage and living costs: eh.net, "How Much is
that?" Travel times: Albion, *Square-Riggers on Schedule,* 276-287; Coleman, *Passage to America,* 111; Hermann Wätjen, *Aus der Frühzeit des
Nordatlantikverkehrs* (Leipzig, 1932), 103; Hansen, *Atlantic Migration,*
183, 187-188 and 194; and Grabbe, *Vor der großen Flut,* 316. Steamship
arrivals, 1906: Ellis Island Archive, STLI-23741. Other travel-related costs:
Coleman, *Passage to America,* 75-55 and 163-164; Taylor, *Distant Magnet,*
95-96 and 135; Gordon Read, "Indirect Passage: Jewish Emigrant Experiences on the East Coast-Liverpool Route," in Aubrey Newman and Stephen
W. Massi (eds.), *Patterns of Migration, 1850-1914* (London, 1996), 269;
Cecil Woodham-Smith, *The Great Hunger* (New York, 1962), 259-262;
and Wätjen, *Aus der Frühzeit des Nordatlantikverkehrs,* 114-115 and 121-
130. Transatlantic passage fares: Keeling "Transportation Revolution," 42-
43 and 64-65; *New York Tribune,* 9 January 1878; *New York Commercial
Advertiser,* 10 June 1887; *New York Times,* 9 April 1892; Rolle, *American
Italians,* 3; Hyde, *Cunard and the North Atlantic,* 60-64; Hansen, *Atlantic
Migration,* 83 and 181; Agnes Bretting and Hartmut Bickelmann, *Auswan-
derungsagenturen und Auswanderungsvereine im 19. und 20. Jahrhundert*
(Stuttgart, 1991), 70; Bonsor, *North Atlantic Seaway,* II, 510, 541, 737,
810 and 830; Taylor, *Distant Magnet,* 94; and Cohn, "Transition from Sail
to Steam," 483.

Appendix 10

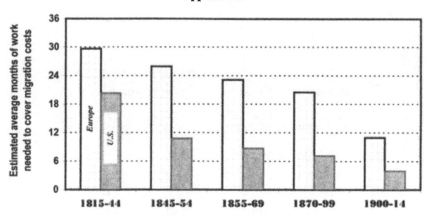

Note: Measures shown are estimated average months of working in Europe or in
           the US to cover (through accumulated savings) migration costs from Europe
           to the US. Calculations include the assumption that the average European
           migrant working in the US was unemployed during 1815-1870 ten percent
           of the time; 1870-1900, 12.5%; and 1900-1913, fifteen percent. If working
           in Europe (to save for migration in advance), the estimate is that the average
           migrant was unemployed ten percent of the time for all periods.

Sources: See appendix 9.

Appendix 11
Dependant Migrants

	Dependants as Percentage of all Migrants West-bound to the US				Steerage Prepaids as Percentage of all Steerage Revenues	
	Under 14 yrs	Over 44 yrs	No Occu-pation	Passage Paid by Relative	Holland Amer-ica	North-ern Europe Lines
1899			35%			
1900	12%	5%	30%			
1901	13%	6%	30%			
1902	11%	5%	24%			
1903	12%	5%	23%			
1904	13%	6%	26%			
1905	11%	5%	23%			
1906	12%	5%	26%			
1907	11%	4%	24%			
1908	14%	5%	31%	35%		26%
1909	12%	5%	30%	29%	41%	22%
1910	12%	5%	25%	26%	50%	
1911	13%	5%	28%	32%	59%	
1912	14%	5%	28%	35%	53%	
1913	12%	5%	25%	31%	57%	
1914	13%	6%	26%	36%		
Recession Years:	13%	5%	29%	34%	59%	26%
Expansion Years:	12%	5%	26%	31%	50%	22%

Notes: "Dependant" here means a migrant whose relocation costs were borne directly or indirectly by someone else (usually a relative). Recession years in the US were 1904, 1908, 1911 and 1913 (see appendix 5).

Sources: *Dillingham Report*, III, 88-91, 178 and 360; BI, *Annual Reports*, 1899-1914; Holland-America Passagegelden; Hastings Law School Library microfilm collection, US v. HAPAG, *et al.* (239 US 387), reel 27, frame 2454 (Petitioner's Exhibit 727).

Appendix 12
Foreign-Born Population in the United States and Electoral
Votes in Presidential Elections, by State, 1900-1908

	1900 Census Population Figures ('000s)		1910 Census		Presidential Elections Electoral Votes for the Winning Republican Candidate		
	For- eign Born Whites	Total Popu- lation	For- eign Born Whites	Total Popu- lation	*McKin- ley* 1900	*Roose- velt* 1904	*Taft* 1908
NY	1890	7269	2729	9114	36	39	39
PA	983	6302	1439	7665	32	34	34
IL	965	4822	1203	5639	24	27	27
MA	840	2805	1051	3366	15	16	16
MI	540	2421	596	2810	14	14	14
WI	516	2069	513	2334	12	13	13
MIN	505	1751	543	2076	9	11	11
OH	458	4158	597	4767	23	23	23
NJ	430	1884	658	2537	10	12	12
IO	306	2232	273	2225	13	13	13
CT	237	908	329	1115	6	7	7
IN	142	2516	159	2701	15	15	15
RI	134	429	178	543	4	4	4
ME	93	694	110	742	6	6	6
NH.	88	412	97	431	4	4	4
VT	45	344	50	356	4	4	4
Totals These States	8170	41,016	10,524	48,420	227	242	242
All States	10,138	74,607	13,321	91,641	447	476	483
These States/All States	81%	55%	79%	53%	51%	51%	50%

Total Votes of Presidential Election Winner:	292	336	321
Total Votes as % of All Electoral Votes:	65%	71%	66%

Sources: http://fisher.lib.virginia.edu/cgi-local/censusbin/census/cen.pl; and http://www.archives.gov/federal_register/electoral_college/votes_index.html#state.

Appendix 13
Shipping Company Revenue versus BI Spending, 1900-1914
(All Figures in $ '000 or Equivalent Except as Indicated)

| | Voyage Revenues | | BI |
	Cunard	CGT	Annual Spending
1900	5217	10,152	1103
1901	4828	9047	905
1902	4718	9475	1024
1903	5791	10,228	826
1904	5961	9731	1297
1905	7333	10,835	1509
1906	9668	12,904	1571
1907	10,637	13,660	1646
1908	10,062	12,842	2658
1909	11,582	13,573	3238
1910	12,623	14,835	2760
1911	12,282	15,534	2841
1912	13,766	16,748	2927
1913	13,773	19,010	2899
1914	11,922	14,813	
1900-1913	127,944	178,576	27,204
1900-1913 Average BI / (Cunard + CGT) =			8.9%

Notes: Cunard voyage revenues on Liverpool-New York, Liverpool-Boston and Mediterranean-New York routes; CGT voyage revenues on Le Havre-New York route.

Sources: BI *Annual Report 1913*, 32; University of Liverpool Archive, Cunard annual reports; CVA, CGT Archive; and CGT annual reports.

Conclusion

Michael B. Miller

Oddly enough, migration historians and maritime historians have often written about transoceanic crossings like two ships passing in the night. In November 2005, historians from the two fields met in Florence to discuss what each could learn from the other and how, together, they could advance our understanding of the great cross-Atlantic migrations of the long nineteenth century. Such is the provenance of the articles in this volume. Not surprisingly, a number of the articles still bear the imprint of their author's first identification. Jelle van Lottum and Annemarie Steidl have written about patterns of migration over time and space. Others have concentrated on port cities and shipping companies, but have framed these within the history of the emigration trades. In either case, however, there are recurrent themes and questions that show how entangled, and thus mutually informative, the histories of peoples and seas can be.

Debates over causal factors force us to think about some of these. We know that several tens of millions of Europeans left farms, villages or towns and sailed across an ocean to a foreign land between 1820 and 1914. But what determined why they went and where they ended up? And more important, in the context of the bringing together of maritime and migration scholars, what role did maritime institutions – shipping companies, ports, and commercial agents – play in this decision-making process? At one end of the spectrum, the answer is not necessarily much at all, except to facilitate or prosper from a passage already pre-determined. Van Lottum, whose insightful comparison across centuries concerns primarily early modern times but is not unconnected to nineteenth-century migration, stresses push-and-pull factors, mostly of a demographic and economic nature. Steidl's refined analysis of patterns of departures from the Austrian half of the Habsburg Empire after 1870 lays out the classic migrationist case. Emigration occurred through a chain migration predicated on information and support networks provided by family and friends. These migrants clearly did not walk across the Atlantic, but otherwise neither ships nor shipping companies need be brought into the picture. Drew Keeling writes a great deal about shipping companies, but his judgements are, with modifications, comparably restrictive. Without regular steamship services there would have been no massive emigration. As Keeling has written elsewhere, steamships altered fundamentally the conditions of transoceanic travel and hence removed the risks and, to some degree, the disincentives, to ocean

175

passage.[1] His wide-ranging work points to a variety of ways in which steamship companies were central to the migration process, but chiefly as facilitators. Keeling is unequivocal when it comes to causation: chain migration, as a mitigator of risk, was far and away the key factor. Steamships may have lowered costs, but at least for the final decade and a half before the First World War, when over eleven million Europeans came to America, lower fares could only affect the timing of departure, not the reasons for picking up and going. On the question of recruitment agents employed in droves by steamship companies, Keeling is still more dismissive. They were, at best, travel agents, operations men (and hence, again, mere facilitators). There is, he asserts, no evidence to demonstrate that large numbers of Europeans were persuaded by the siren calls of agents to gamble on new lives abroad. Comparative standings of shipping companies and ports may well have been affected by the deployment of agents, forcing a replication of initiatives and presumably eventual impasse. Yet the sheer number of migrants was relatively unaffected by such strategies.

Torsten Feys, at the other end of the spectrum, argues for a more decisive maritime role. Whereas Keeling questions the role of agents, and Steidl does not consider them, Feys questions chain-migration methodology and asserts that ports, companies and agents, including consular representatives, brought the New World a lot closer in the mental map of many Europeans, thereby becoming central actors in stimulating emigration flows. Feys may still fall into the Keeling trap, since he suggests more than proves the operative influence of agents in individual decisions to cross the seas. Yet his critique of chain-migration theory opens space for other avenues of causation, while he also channels Keeling's stress on information flows back through the circuits of state and commercial representatives.

Somewhere between these two poles can be situated the contributions of Nicholas Evans, Nicholas Manitakis and Golapan Balachandran. Of these three, only Balachandran would argue for the overriding importance of transport in the migration patterns he confronts, but only, as he would be the first to acknowledge, because sailors went where their ships took them. For Balachandran, considerably more important in conditioning the locational fate of his Asian seamen were such factors as history (in the form of global conflicts), legal and state measures, and national or cultural inputs. Evans and Manitakis concentrate directly upon ports and companies, although causation for them concerns access to the emigrant trade rather than why emigrants departed in the first place. In Evans' analysis, company agents were absolutely decisive for a time, but only in assuring British shipping companies and the port of Liverpool a sizeable share of emigration streams once their principal prove-

---

[1]Drew Keeling, "The Transportation Revolution and Transatlantic Migration, 1850-1914," *Research in Economic History*, XIX (1999), 39-74.

nance was the continent rather than the British Isles. His is a zero-sum preoccupation: who got the business and where it went. Either Scandinavian, German and Russian emigrants left from Hamburg, Bremen and other continental ports or company initiatives and transportation infrastructures (in this case the trans-Pennine rail route) diverted these flows through Liverpool. The success of the latter shows how companies made a difference in the facts of emigration, but primarily in regard to routing. Manitakis provides essentially the same perspective on emigration from Greece. Those companies that offered superior services or minimized risks and uncertainties, including playing to cultural preferences, came to dominate the transport of Greek migrants to America.

In this regard, neither Evans nor Manitakis are very far from Keeling's focus on maritime companies as facilitators. Evans says as much when he confesses that "it is difficult to ascertain comprehensively whether such 'agents' served as a push factor in augmenting rates of emigration." Neither author's judgement, however, can be left simply at that. Evans's migrants may have had other transport choices, but the activities of agents and recruiters in assuring steady volumes of business allowed companies to run more regular services, which in turn were likely to have induced steadier streams of people willing to make the voyage. The power of steamships to intensify transatlantic migration in the second half of the nineteenth century cannot be separated from the liner services that came in their wake. Consequently, causation of a different sort may still have been at play. One would equally be tempted to investigate whether the establishment of direct trans-oceanic service from Greek ports, as Manitakis has described, truly had little effect upon the numbers of Greeks who decided to migrate.

Perhaps more important, Evans and Manitakis, as well as Balachandran, show how integrally connected were the histories of migrants, shipping companies and ports, regardless of the reason for departure. Thus, together, they underscore the degree to which debates over causation may have displaced attention from the more rewarding inter-relationships that can be drawn between the fields of migration and maritime history. Here both Keeling and Feys would agree. Keeling's impressive study on how and why millions of Europeans crossed to the United States between 1900 and 1914 works because he writes about migrants and transport in equal doses. Feys, like Evans and Manitakis, is full of ideas stemming from the basic facts of migration. If migration historians would do well to move beyond chain-migration theory, so too, he implies, would maritime historians do well to ask how ports and companies adapted strategies to the chain migration that did occur. The history of ports, he shows, was often far from independent of the history of migration; even services which seemingly had little or nothing to do with migration may have had their origins in the wooing of migration trades. The term "facilitator" carries with it the stigma of a second order of analysis, somewhat like barons or squires, powerful men in their own domains but ill at ease at the courts of counts and dukes. Yet no one crossed the Atlantic without ships or purchased prepaid tickets without shipping company services, so that whether one is talking about causal or facilitating factors, the history of migration was intimately caught up in, abetted by and made possible through the history of shipping.

The impact of the state is also important to many of these contributors. Feys describes how once regular shipping services were established between Rotterdam and Antwerp and North America, the shipping company agent came to supplant the consular representative as the key intermediary in foreign lands. Yet Feys' article is all about the triangular relationship between states (and port cities), shipping companies and immigrants. He begins with consuls, either honorary or career civil servants, as important sources of information and lobbyists for port interests in migration matters. These were advance men in more ways than one. Shipping companies later hired lobbyists to prevent interference with their emigration trades, a testimony not only to the controlling influence states could always exercise over who left and who came in, but also, again, to the role of shipping companies and their agents in shaping just how migration occurred. In one set of particularly interesting observations, Feys remarks upon the differences that could exist between state policies and their impacts. Belgium actively promoted emigration, while the Dutch did not. Dutch access to southeast Asian colonial trades and Belgian ruptures with these provided different incentives for actively pursuing cross-Atlantic shipping services. Dutch organization of its East Indies trades slowed the transition to steam, and with it the force that would propel ever more emigrants across the Atlantic. In several ways, therefore, state priorities intersected with maritime and migration progressions in each of these two countries.

Balachandran, Keeling, Evans and Steidl, like Feys, all note the impact of state intervention. Balachandran's Asian seamen were nothing if not the objects of state concerns and regulations. The right to enter territories, to disembark ships, to travel to regions north of certain lines or to seek wider labour opportunities were all determined by overlapping or conflicting interests influencing the formulation of state policy. These men may have been employed by private shipping companies, but they were, no less, the wards of governments. States could impede but could also facilitate this form of migration, either through indifference or by cynically encouraging desertion among Chinese crews in order to fill labour shortages in wartime. Keeling discusses the state's power to restrict immigration, and the limitations on carrying this through, in the heyday of the flows from Europe. In a still more suggestive passage, he calls our attention to how the US recruited shipping companies and port officials to monitor and control population flows across its borders. States set health and safety policies and sought information on who was coming in, but they relied on shipping companies to implement controls and inspections and to collect statistics. Evans remarks upon the impact of state management of immigration flows after the First World War. Restrictive laws in 1921 and then again in 1923 severely cut the number of immigrants allowed into America. Yet, as Evans argues in a particularly perceptive passage, no less effective in curtailing transatlantic migration was the insistence of immigration officials in the US that the numbers transported under permissible quotas be spread out over several months. This measure struck not only at numbers but also at the business dynamics that had underpinned the trade throughout its most buoyant days: the regularity of scheduled services. How shipping companies worked as complex business organizations has too often been left out of the equation between emigrants, steamships and the transport of massive numbers across the ocean. Evans brings it back in, ironically, at the very moment that the state was taking it out. Steidl's article, meanwhile, is itself an outcome of state intervention. Here the history of migration comes, in effect, full circle. Historians identify how the state affected immigration patterns, but that very process in turn influences how historians subsequently identify and write about migration. With the data collected by US immigration officials, Steidl is able to reconstruct the networks of family and kin that drive her analysis. There is a further catch. By demanding specific responses of incoming Europeans, the state almost certainly structured the information it gathered. Immigrants told officials what they wanted to hear about contact persons, whether this had any bearing or not upon the reality of their case. Steidl is not insensitive to this problem, and rightly concludes that we must work with what information we have. Still, she and others who have used these materials are, like Balachandran's seamen, to a degree wards of the state.

Taken together, such reflections upon the state imply that alongside chain migration there was also chain reaction. We can think of it this way. Shipping companies made possible higher volumes of migration flows. High volume flows in turn set in motion state concerns over the body politic. These concerns then forced shipping companies and port representatives to defend the quality of the emigrants passing through their harbours or on board their ships (although Richard Evans in his *Death in Hamburg* has raised serious questions as to how readily they construed the danger).[2] By concentrating migration flows through a limited number of home ports, big shipping companies nonetheless facilitated the implementation of state-initiated health controls.[3] In turn, again, shipping companies found themselves incorporated into surveillance projects. Moreover, to lure emigrants through their harbours and on to their boats, but also to protect the reputation of their migration passengers in host

---

[2]Richard Evans, *Death in Hamburg: Society and Politics in the Cholera Years 1830-1910* (Oxford, 1987).

[3]Adam McKeown, "The Impact of Maritime and Migration Networks on Transatlantic Labour Migration, 18th-20th Centuries" (Unpublished paper, Florence, 18 November 2005).

and receiving countries, shipping companies began to erect substantial facilities to lodge and inspect the men, women and children they were going to embark upon their ships. Migrants, meanwhile, conformed to circumstances and used these as best they could to their advantage. Thus, lines of force, initiative and response ricocheted back and forth between the three constitutive elements: migrants, companies and states. None was a completely autonomous actor, and, as these authors have seen, none can be written about independently of the other.

All the contributors to this volume have placed networks at the centre of their presentations. Van Lottum's reconstruction of migration volumes in the North Sea region between 1550 and 1800 points to the networks of trade and shipping that created common ties between Dutch, Belgians, Germans, Scots, English and Scandinavians and that prefigured the mobility of peoples from one part of the sea to another. After 1550, he implies, migration itself functioned as the network that held the region together. Balachandran writes about an Asian maritime "migration" network that linked Asia and the US through Europe. He suggests that boarding houses and cafés set up for Sylheti seamen served as an initial network for the far larger Sylheti migration in the post-World War II years. He explains that Chinese seamen gravitated to Chinese communities in New York during the Second World War in search of an alternative network for homeland contact, once their own connections had been severed in the course of the war. Steidl's history of Austrian chain migration is, of course, equally a history of networks. As she points out, however, not all networks were equal. If most functioned as sources of information and support, then those predicated on weak ties expanded the range of geographical and economic mobility. Networks therefore may have been critical to migration, but their benefits varied by class and ethnicity because close family-and-friend ties were not always the decisive variable. Rather, those populations where urban skills or professional experience were more widely distributed, and those with a longer history of social mobility, enjoyed access to wider networks overseas. Put slightly differently, Czech, German and Jewish networks were, in terms of opportunity, superior to Polish or Ruthenian networks.

The maritime historians are no less fixated on networks. Manitakis writes about shipping company networks in the geographical sense of the term: routes and points of service determined passages and trades. Evans describes the deployment of agent networks, some of them vast, in the steering of migration to British harbours and ships. Keeling and Feys could not be more in agreement on the importance of information flows through networks. Keeling, in fact, organizes his rich discussion around what he identifies as four sets of networks: chain migration; steamship agents; shipping company intra- and inter-firm networks; and regulatory networks combining states and private entities, including shipping companies. He emphasizes that networks were more about reducing risks than reducing costs, but his key observation is that the "ubiquity" of networks in transatlantic migration shows their indispensability. Feys likewise writes about a variety of maritime networks: information networks, agency networks, networks that formed from the proximity of company offices, or Van Toorn's New York Dutch networks that he was capable of mobilizing to neutralize attacks against him and to establish himself in New York business circles. Yet, paradoxically, despite the unanimous agreement that networks mattered, this centring of networks by all participants points to the problems with which this project began and that, evidently, have not altogether abated. With the exception of Keeling and Feys, the authors are still discussing two separate sets of networks – migratory and maritime.

Whether these differences can ever fully be bridged is questionable. After all, migration historians are interested in far more than how immigrants crossed seas, while maritime historians will perhaps always cleave closer to the two histories for the simple reason that shipping companies and ports thrived (and in some instances grew up) on the great transatlantic movement of peoples; yet they too have other fish to fry. Future research will continue to wrestle with this possibly intractable problem. Still, the articles in this collection also point the way towards some resolution through the three thematic concentrations that join them. First, as all the authors would agree, neither migration nor maritime history can be pursued apart from a study of networks, and it is thus essential that we look more deeply into where and how these networks entangled. Second, neither the history of the seas nor the history of migrations, as these articles attest, can proceed without taking into account the state, yet to write about the state requires factoring in migrants, shipping companies, harbours and consular officials because the state did not act without support or reaction from each. As attention increasingly is focused on the state, it is likely that historians of both fields will perceive the intersections and crossovers. Third, if there is no consensus on causation, it is nonetheless clear from the majority of these essays that transatlantic migration in the tens of millions entailed far more than boarding a ship at one end and getting off at the other. If, however, we shift from asking why to asking how – how did it occur? how could it occur? how did maritime networks and structures facilitate its occurrence? – we will force a more meaningful collaboration.

The question therefore becomes "which networks" and "which structures." The authors in this volume have rightly identified routes, agents and the operations of shipping companies in the business of transporting immigrants as a starting point. Yet why stop here? Migration, from the maritime perspective, was never more than one facet of larger structures, procedures, operations, accumulated expertise and contacts already in place which funnelled large numbers of emigrants through specific ports or enabled steamship companies to build and run a successful migration trade. The maritime history of migration begins therefore not with the transport of migrants but with the infrastructures – ports and steamship companies – through which it occurred.

Take, for instance, ports. These were more than a collection of interests desirous of attracting migration traffic. The relationship between ports and migrants was always far more complex. It was based, to begin with, on pre-existing port services and infrastructures which provided docks, quays, pilots, dredged fairways, bunkers, chandlers, customs houses, shipyards, agents, stevedores and insurers, everything that enabled ports to function as major conduits, whether it be people or goods that passed through them. Without these composite facilities and services, it was uncertain how emigrants would ever make it on board ships, let alone sail out of the harbour. Moreover, while networks of recruiters focused emigrants upon specific ports, these networks were enveloped within still larger networks – transportation lines, merchant connections, spheres of influence and local contacts – that ports had built up over time. Hinterland networks can be reconstructed for all the major migration ports. Very likely then, certain path dependencies grew out of the interplay between three different kinds of networks: chain migration networks, recruitment networks and the larger hinterland networks that drained inwards via rail lines, waterways and older trading relationships. Yet even these broader connections are not altogether insufficient because a fourth – overseas – set of networks must also be considered. Simply put, such networks consisted of shipping company and trading company connections. We know, for example, that German shipping companies with major passenger and freight business to South America sponsored German migration to these very lands. Here again we directly confront the role of maritime business firms as initiators of migration. Other, less explicit yet potentially more widespread, ties between shipping, trade and migration are also possible to configure. For example, it would be interesting to see just how far German networks throughout the continent – German *finca* owners and coffee traders in Guatemala or Mexico or German trading networks in Brazil, Argentina and Chile, all of which were integrated with German shipping services – intertwined with German migration or with migration recruited and transported to Latin America by Bremen and Hamburg shipping companies. The point is that the relationship between ports and migration could transpire across a full array of port functions and connections.

The same approach to ports applies to steamship companies. Major carriers like White Star, Cunard, Norddeutscher Lloyd, HAPAG, Compagnie Générale Transatlantique or Holland Amerika functioned through large networked organizations that established the facilities, methods and connections for moving all goods across the seas, whether these were people or freight. The dynamic with migration thus cut both ways. On the one hand, the liner business and the trans-Atlantic passenger (read emigrant) business grew up together. We cannot neglect the degree to which emigration shaped shipping company organizations. This has been a matter primarily left to maritime historians, although historians of migration might consider that if business was necessary for migration to occur, then those who know the history of migration inside and out might equally have something valuable to contribute regarding how that business side grew. Comprehensive perspectives do not simply apply to one side of the continuum. On the other hand, a comprehensive maritime history of migration starts with the shipping industry as a whole and how it worked. Passenger and freight divisions were never completely divisible into separate spheres. The smooth running of each depended on the full range of company resources. There were central scheduling decisions. Nautical divisions oversaw ship maintenance and technical harbour information. Shipping agents dealt with both passengers and freight when a ship arrived in port. Networks engaged in recruiting and transporting immigrants to the Americas formed part of a far more expansive networking system that extended to port authorities, customs houses, railroad companies, brokers and dealers, chambers of commerce, markets and exchanges, and anyone in a position to supply shipping companies with traffic. Since assembling, sustaining and extending networks is what shipping companies did, any study of the transport networks central to the carriage of migrants must take into account the methods, experiences and contacts developed over a larger and longer history of shipping.

The role of shipping agents, who formed the nodal points in these networks, was perhaps no less vital, and we need to know more about their overlap with emigration agents. As I have described elsewhere, nothing moved without the intercession of agents.[4] They were the point men in ports who turned around ships, a multi-tasked operation encompassing wide familiarity with port authorities, port businesses and medical officials. This, however, was just a start. Agents were selected for their local connections with shippers, consuls, port operators and colleagues – anyone in a position to do them a favour. Their job was no less to attract and build new business and to serve as listening posts for any information critical to running a shipping company extending across thousands of miles of ocean. Often they managed a shipping company's business in a port or territory. In the East, recruitment and processing of emigrants or pilgrims fell within the larger purview of agent activities and functioned well because of these. What is necessary to contemplate is whether, at the level of day-to-day practice, agents in the West acted accordingly.

Marrying maritime history to migration history is therefore full of promise, but only if each school begins to think more comprehensively about the grander preoccupations of the other. For maritime historians, this means understanding how migration patterns and motivations may have entered into

---

[4]Michael B. Miller, "Ship Agents in the Twentieth Century," in Gordon Boyce and Richard Gorski (eds.), *Resources and Infrastructures in the Maritime Economy, 1500-2000* (St. John's, 2002), 5-22.

port and steamship company strategies. The growing interest in the intersection between migration and states is also open to investigation since ports and companies were often third or fourth parties to these "negotiations." For migration historians, more attention to the business of migration would be a good departure point, but an even better one would be to grasp how ports and shipping companies worked to transport anything on a daily basis. One useful exercise would be to fold migration-specific networks into the compass of shipping networks as a whole, and then to fold these in turn into the gamut of port networks and connections. Maritime historians could benefit from doing the exercise in reverse. When completed from both ends, we will probably know a good deal more than we ever did about shipping, ports and the movements of people, and how all three were often bound into the same historical narrative.

Printed and bound by CPI Group (UK) Ltd, Croydon, CR0 4YY

14/06/2023

03227122-0005